OYA

Also by Judith Gleason

Leaf and Bone: African Praise-Poems

Santería, Bronx

A Recitation of Ifa, Oracle of the Yoruba

Orisha, The Gods of Yorubaland

Agotime, Her Legend

This Africa: A Study of West African Novels
in French and English

OYA

In Praise of an African Goddess

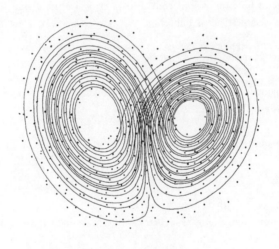

Judith Gleason

HarperSanFrancisco

A Division of HarperCollins*Publishers*

FIRST HARPERCOLLINS EDITION

Originally published by Shambhala Publications, Inc., in 1987 with the subtitle: In Praise of The Goddess

Diagrams and Drawings by Susan DiMirjian. Photos by the author.

Library of Congress Cataloging-in-Publication Data

Gleason, Judith Illsley.
    Oya : in praise of an African goddess / Judith Gleason. — 1st HarperCollins ed.
        p.   cm.
    Originally published: Boston : Shambhala, 1987. With new introd.
    Includes bibliographical references.
    1. Oya (Yoruba deity)   2. Yoruba (African people) — Religion.
    I. Title.
    BL2480.Y6G57   1992
    299'.63 — dc20   91-58917
    ISBN 0–06–250461–4   CIP

92 93 94 95 96 HAD 10 9 8 7 6 5 4 3 2 1

This edition is printed on acid-free paper that meets the American National Standards Institute Z39.48 Standard.

Table of Contents

Acknowledgments

I would like to acknowledge the financial assistance provided by the Joint Committee on Africa of the Social Science Research Council and the American Council of Learned Societies for research done along the Niger River in 1976–1977. A summer stipend from the National Endowment for the Humanities in 1980 enabled me to work on the Buffalo-woman/hunters theme in Mali. A fellowship in creative writing from the National Endowment for the Arts in 1983 permitted me to revisit Salvador, Bahia, and to return to Nigeria during the spring semester of 1983. For all of this aid I am grateful. I could not have done the work without it.

During the course of my travels I have been hosted, helped, and inspired by many people. Here I would like especially to thank the following people. In Nigeria: the late Chief Fagbemi Ajanaku, the Alagba of Lagos; Adunni Awolola, Iya Agan of Lagos; Chief Joseph Bolariwa, Alapinni of Oyo; Prince Robert Ola Awujola of Iwo; Joseph Ologbin, Onirá of Oyo; Adepate Elegun, Morenike Agbeke, and Oya Kupola of Oyo; Laide Soyinka of Ibadan; Suzanne Wenger of Oshogbo. In Mali: Baru Doumbiya of Maghanbougou; Thiemoko Diakité of Bougouni; the late Herta and Heinz Macher of Bamako. In Brazil: Babalorixa Balbino of Ile Ase Aganju, Yvone (Oloia), Mariá (Oloia) and Cici (Oloxala) of Aganju *terreiro*; Nancy Bernabô and Carybé, Pierre Fatumbi Verger of Afonja *terreiro*. In Paris: Germaine Dieterlen, Solange de Ganay, the late Dominique Zahan, and Youssef Tata Cissé (also of Mali). In the United

States, in the earlier stages, James Fernandez, Robert Farris Thompson, Edward Christopher Whitmont, and my Madrina, the late Ascención "Sunta" Serrano, were all in their ways supportive and helpful. I have continuously appreciated the sterling examples of my colleagues Karen Brown (anthropology), Herbert Leibowitz (literary criticism), and Donald Kalshed (analytical psychology). In the Santería community I would like to give especial thanks to John Turpin and Yrmino "Chiqui" Valdes Garriz for their encouragement. In later stages of research, John Amira has proved unfailingly helpful and generous with his time; I would also like to thank Orlando "Puntilla" Rios, Emilio Barreto, Xiomara Rodriguez, Richard Gonzales, Jerry Shilgi, Louis Bauzo, José Manuel Guinart, the Egbe Omo Oya, Dr. Afolabi Epega, Susan DiMirjian, Joan Burroughs, Francisco Rivela, and Bubette McLeod; and to Esther Gleason and Timothy McKeown gratitude and devotion! Many thanks to those who discovered an important part of themselves in *Oya* and wrote to me about it. Some, like Pat Hall-Smith, Karen Brown, Christine Downing, Elinor Gadon, and Betty Meador, went on to champion the book. For their loyal efforts I'm extremely grateful, and I hope that this second edition doesn't disappoint them, nor those at Harper San Francisco who took it on and edited and designed it. Special thanks to Barbara Moulton and Barbara Archer.

I would like to continue to dedicate this work back in time to that great-great-grandmother Maria, whose history will never be known, and to the future as embodied in my little granddaughters Elizabeth Anne Holley and Magdelena Sanchez-Gleason. Because Robert (Bobby) Holley has recently arrived in the world, I want to dedicate it to him also, and this time, because I realize how much not only I but all of us working toward the sources owe to that infinite resource: Pierre Fatumbi Verger, I would like to add his name here in fond dedication.

OYA

Bareback on the Horse of the Wind

The goddess Oya, Orisha Oya, of African origin, manifests herself in various natural forms: wind, which can be playful and refreshing, but especially strong wind, escalating into tornadoes; fire both generative and all-enveloping, but especially quick, nervy, directional lightning; the river Niger, especially that part of it that runs around the island of Jebba, Oya's island in Nupe, a place of transit on the way out of the Yoruba world, this world, and on to the next. She also takes the form of an African buffalo, which appreciates muddy wallows; but except for horns seen on her altars, because her species is missing in the New World, few have seen her this way over here. That figures; for Oya has the habit of becoming invisible, only to reappear somewhere else where you least expect her.

Oya is also associated with certain cultural phenomena among the Yoruba people, who were the first to serve her as an Orisha.* In Nigeria she has given birth to an extraordinary clan of ancestral apparitions clothed in bulky, billowing cloth who perform at festivals for the dead. But whether or not Egungun masquerades come out in miraculous display, Oya plays an essential role at traditional funerals, and wherever and however the link with those who have gone before is established, there you will find Oya; but you may not recognize her unless you're privy to those secrets. To the leader of the market women in Yoruba communities she offers special

---

*See Glossary for pronunciations and definitions of African names and terms.

protection and encouragement in negotiation with civil authorities and arbitration of disputes among peers. Thus, one may speak of Oya as patron of feminine leadership, of intelligent persuasive charm reinforced by àjẹ́, an efficacious faculty, usually translated "witchcraft" (by those who have reason to fear it). Oya speaks her mind. Always a purifying element, in social situations, especially tense ones, she clears the atmosphere of bad faith and mystification. Although she is associated with pointed speech, most of what she's up to is obscure until it happens. More abstractly, Oya is the goddess of edges, of the dynamic interplay between surfaces, of transformation from one state of being to another.

To describe and elaborate upon Oya's various manifestations is inevitably to present an idea not commonly thought of when the word *goddess* is mentioned. The idea of sculpting her into one fixed image and putting her on a pedestal would blow her away, scattering tools and materials to the four directions. But of her followers she does exact homage, in words both playful and serious, preferably sung out loud, with backup chorus and accompanied by *bàtá* drumming. Furthermore, Oya's patterns, persisting through many media—from air to the human psyche—suggest something like a unified field theory of a certain type of energy that our culture certainly does not think of as feminine. But even where it is identified as feminine, great effort is expended in controlling its unmitigated expression, in rounding its contours and putting the lid on it. Where, as in Africa, the feminine remains primary to the imagination, womankind beyond the limits of the motherly—always deeply venerated—is regarded with suspicion. What is especially interesting about Oya in Yoruba cultural context is her refusal to stay out of the enclaves of ideology and social control long, long ago preempted by men.

To speak of Oya between the covers of a book and with an audacity befitting her own, it has been necessary to attempt to combine two ways of thinking: African and European. Years ago at the museum of the Villa Giulia in Rome I saw for the first time a type of drinking cup (kantharos) that exactly portrays the juxtapostion I have in mind here. Between bowl and stem are two carefully modeled heads, back to back. One is the portrait of a black woman, the other of a woman with a pointed nose and light skin. Their hair has been arranged in parallel loops; indeed, one braid seems to be flowing into the other, and back and forth. Only their faces, looking out in opposite directions, are different. Inside that antique cup continues to brim liberation.

Unlike the goddesses of antiquity, Oya continues in recognition, placation, and celebration, not only in Africa but in Brazil and right here among growing communities of those who practice the Yoruba religion. This does not mean we ought perversely to congratulate the slave-shippers of yore. Even recent boat lifts of Cuban refugees who practice and make music for Santería cannot be praised for the conditions that launched them. The Cuban way of worshiping the Orisha represents remarkable retentions and ingenious adaptations. Yet lively though it may be, and however intrinsically worthy of interest, no one version of a religion can comprise the whole story of its itinerant divinities. I am not alone in persistently returning to the sources, but I should clarify my need to do so.

As I see it, the genius of the worldview that gave rise to the religion is embedded in the culture of

Attic kantharos, fifth century, B.C., Casteliani Collection, Museum of the Villa Giulia, Rome, Italy.

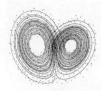

the Yoruba-speaking peoples and their neighbors to the west and upriver. (Each Orisha was originally a local spirit, which in the course of time merged with others of its ilk and eventually became more widely worshiped.) Oya, whose geographical origin is always said to be "Tapa" (Nupe), was integrated into the state religion of the Oyo branch of the Yoruba. Even the idea of dedicating oneself entirely to the understanding of a single Orisha is more an African than a Caribbean affair, even though the minimal African ancestry that some might say has been compelling me all along can never be traced beyond St. Croix in the Virgin Islands.

How does one fall into the worship of a phenomenon like Oya? Yoruba sages say that when a person is born he or she "chooses a head," thereby becoming endowed with a portion of cosmic essence. Such primal substances of which our various heads are made can be experienced in their natural manifestations as water, wind, fire, tree, and so on. These environing forces are not worshiped as such but rather as loci of beings the Yoruba call òrìṣà. The word *orisha* literally means "head-calabash." Calabashes, gourds that grow on trees in tropical climates, are used as containers—of water, of food, of anything that can be put into them, magical substances as well as humdrum items. Our "inner" heads, like calabashes, contain a modicum of sacred substance, shared with Orisha, whose portions are plenitude. The Orisha with whom we have prenatally chosen to be consubstantial is called "owner of the head."

How can one know of what stuff one's soul is made? Apart from family tradition, from which it is possible to diverge, intuition can't be discounted, nor dreams, nor a sudden identification by a seer or someone in trance; but the only way to be sure is by consultation of the oracle in the form of cowrie shells or, preferably, according to a bias widely shared, Ifa—far more elaborate and philosophical than the shells. Each of the 256 configurations of the Ifa oracle contains sacred oral texts, memorized by the diviner-healer-priest known as *babaláwo* ("father of secrets"). Certain configurations of the oracle speak of certain Orisha, or it might be said in reverse that the Orisha speak through certain channels of Ifa. Among the secrets the diviner knows are what foods the Orisha is fond of and what its prohibitions are. These the client is advised personally to respect. Such avoidances help define the person not only individually but communally. Orisha are shared legacies. One's reincarnated guardian spirit doesn't fight with the Orisha that rules one's head. Another way Yoruba sages describe the organic affiliation between ourselves and the great gods is by topological analogue. Linking the bulge at the back of the head to a hilltop and the occipital cavity at the nape of the neck to a pool of water, they say that one's destiny exists in whatever source one was tapped from.[1]

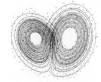

Not all Yoruba are Orisha worshipers today. Christianity and Islam, following two centuries of heavy proselytizing and jihad, are now considered more compatible with modernism. Yet lineage affiliations remain powerful enough to balance the disintegrative effects of individualism, European style. In times of stress, illness, reversal of fortune, nominal Christians will consult Ifa, whether or not in the end they will actually make the necessary sacrifices to the appropriate divinities or placations to the negative forces deemed responsible for their sufferings.

In Yoruba-speaking Nigeria, certain households have always maintained shrines for tutelary Orisha. And this tradition persists, especially up-country. Not everyone is involved, but only the person whose calling it is to be so. When the keeper of a shrine dies, the Orisha itself will claim a successor. Once every market week and upon the yearly festival time of the Orisha, those who tend its family shrines will gather together as an ẹgbẹ́ ("society" or "group of affiliates"). In the New World, such lineage continuities were ruptured. Individuals drawn to the reconstituted African religions of the Caribbean formed and still form new spiritual families— "houses" (terreiros in Brazil, casas in Cuba) presided over by the ruling Orisha of the founder's head but including all the others. In recent years, here in New York and perhaps elsewhere as well, ẹgbẹ́ have been formed whose membership consists of those with a common head-ruling Orisha. This trend might be considered an Africanism, were there not historical precedents for such societies dating back to the patron saints of clandestine African religious practice while slavery was still operative in the Caribbean.

Returning to the sources of a religious conception inevitably leads one back to the expressive language in which it is articulated. Oya is a verb form conveying her passage as an event with apparently disastrous consequences. Ọ-ya means "she tore" in Yoruba. And what happened? A big tree was uprooted, literally and figuratively: the head of the household, the one in whose shade we felt secure, suddenly perished. She tore, and a river overflowed its banks. Whole cloth was ripped into shreds. Barriers were broken down. Tumultuous feeling abruptly destroyed one's peace of mind. Ēèepàà! one exclaims by way of homage. Ēèpàà Heyi! She is also known as Yansan, which means "mother of nine." These progeny to which she gave birth in the light of day are the nine (a rough count and allegorical number of) estuaries through which her river empties into the sea. Behind the curtain of death she gave birth to nine anomalous beings, the youngest of whom is Egungun, ancestor who returns in masquerade form. Nine indeed is Oya's number, an arithmetical wonder that, when multiplied by any other, always returns in the added digits of the product.

But her name, Oya, and its attributive, Yansan, are only the beginning of her cultural apprehension and definition. Generally speaking, all African beings have praise-epithets attached to them, and these may be concatenated into litanies of character, metaphorically portrayed, and recited upon significant occasions, usually by professionals, in order to inspirit the person and encourage him or her to validate ancestral precedents and noteworthy personal virtues in social performance. (Hunters, as we shall see, have developed repertoires of animal praises with which to charm their prey.) These epithetical encomia may be expanded in order tersely to tell or at least to allude to stories about the praisee. In Yoruba, praise-names and sequences thereof are known as *oríkì* ("greetings to the head"). All Orisha have theirs, some universal and canonical, others varying from region to region. In actual performance by the Orisha's *egbe*, these praises include refrains so that no matter who for the moment is taking the lead, all assembled may join the chorus. Here follow, without further ado, three sets of traditional praises for Oya, first in Yoruba, then in English translation.

I. Praises of Oya collected by Fela Ṣowande and Fagbemi Ajanaku in the 1960s

1 Ọya Òpéré Làlàóyàn,	1 Complete Oya, strolling along with full confidence and importance
2 A gbé agbọ̀n obì siwaju ọkọ	2 She takes a basket of kola to place before her husband
3 O-ni-ìlọ́ṣìn	3 Owner of the place of worship
4 Ọya rúmú bi ẹní gbẹ́ ike	4 Oya, deep in thought, carving out concepts
5 Ọya òpèré, 'Wá gbà jẹ, kò dé inú.	5 Complete Oya, come receive your offering without offense
6 Ọya l'o L'Ọ́sin,	6 Owner of the place of worship
7 Ki Olónje ńaa há onjẹ rè	7 May those who have prepared food begin to serve it
8 Ọya péré bi ewé bọ́!	8 Oya who causes the leaves to flutter

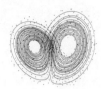

9 Ọya fùfù lẹ̀lẹ̀ bí iná là l'okè!

10 Ọya má mà dá igi l'ẹ́kùlé mi

11 Ọya a ri iná bo ara bí aṣọ!

12 Bi ẹ ba nwá Ọya, bi e kò bá rí Ọya,

13 Ki ẹ wá Ọya dé ìsọ̀ obì,

14 Nibi ti Ọya gbé ńdá kéwú sí ẹnu.

15 Ki ẹ wa Ọya dé ìsọ̀ kọ̀lá,

16 Nibi ti Ọya gbé ndá kéwú sí ẹnu.

17 Ki ẹ wa Ọya dé ìsọ̀ osùn,

18 Nibi ti Ọya gbé ńfọ́ búkẹ́ si ara.

19 Kẹ́ ẹ wá Ọya dé ìsọ̀ bàtá,

20 Nibi ti Ọya gbé nla ijó mọ́ra.

21 Ìyá, iyá, mo ní ng ó mà jẹ ìgbẹ́ Ọya,

22 Nwọn ní kí n'má ṣe jẹ ìgbẹ́ Ọya.

23 Baba, Baba, mo ní ng ó mà jẹ ìgbẹ́ Ọya,

24 Nwọn ní kí n'mà ṣe jẹ ìgbẹ́ Ọya.

25 Mo ní kíni kí n'wa ṣe?

26 Nwọn ní kí n'sare ṣẹ́ṣẹ́ ki n'fún Ọya L'aṣọ

27 Kí n'fi àtàmpàràkò la obì n'Iyàn.

28 Ọya nwọn funẹ ni idà o kò pa ẹran,

29 Ìyà sãn nwọn fun ẹ ni idà o kò pa ẹnia.

30 Nwọn fun ẹ ni idà o kò bẹ́ rí.

31 O ní kini o yio fi idàkídà ṣe!

32 Ọya a-r'íná bora bí aṣọ,

33 Efùfù lẹ̀lẹ̀ ti ńdá igi lókèlokè.

34 Ọ̀jẹ̀lónìkẹ́ a-ní-iyì L'ójẹ̀.

35 Iya mi pòrò bí ọmú ṣẹ́ l'aíyà.

9 Oya, strong wind who gave birth to fire while traversing the mountain

10 Oya, please don't fell the tree in my backyard

11 Oya, we have seen fire covering your body like cloth

12 If you are looking for Oya and can't find Oya

13 Maybe you'll meet her at the kola nut stall

14 Where Oya enjoys throwing little pieces into her mouth

15 Maybe you'll meet her at the bitter kola nut stall

16 Where Oya enjoys throwing little pieces into her mouth

17 Maybe you'll meet her at the camwood stall

18 Where Oya enjoys rubbing red salve onto her body

19 Maybe you'll meet her at the batá drum stall

20 Where Oya moves her body in an enormous dance

21 Mother, mother, I will always respond to Oya's call

22 They warned me not to respond to her call

23 Father, father, I will always respond to Oya's call

24 They warned me not to respond to her call

25 Where can I go, what can I do?

26 They said I should offer little pieces of cloth to Oya

27 They said I should offer kola nut and pounded yam to Egungun

28 They give a sword to Oya but she doesn't use it to kill an animal

29 To Mother they should present a sword but not for killing any animal

30 They give her a sword but not for beheading people

31 She said, "What can I do with my sword?"

32 Oya saw fire as a body covering, like cloth

33 Strong wind who knocks down trees everywhere in the wilds

34 Egungun deserves pampering and respect from cult members

35 Mother, pour into me as from your breasts, world-mother

36 Òjè l'ó ni òketè

37 Ṣe Oya l'ó ni Eégun.

38 Aṣẹ!

36 Egungun worshiper, owner of bush rat

37 Oya, owner of Egungun

38 Ashe! (vitality, authority, so be it!)

II. Praises sung on Oya's day in Ogbomosho, February 15, 1977

1 Iya o Oya o

2 K'o ṣoni òla la gbomu

3 (Chorus) Ìyá o Oya o

4   Olodi mà mà gba

5 A dele àjẹ lẹrẹ l'ẹgba

6 (Chorus) Ìyá o Oya o

7   Olodi mà mà gba

8 Egun ẹlẹgbà baba . . .

9 (Chorus) Ìyá o Oya o

10   Olodi mà mà gba

11 Kangba kangba oriṣa ad'agba mọ yẹwu

12 A f(i) õtọ nu deru ika bale

13 (Chorus) Ìyá o Oya o

14   Olodi mà mà gba

15 Onibode bi ero

16 Abo l'omode pinum me gbe gbeojọ

17 (Chorus) Ìyá o Oya o

18   Onibode bi ero

19 Iyawo Ogun agbelu afa ilùya

20 Ode l'abe òdan a fòdan ya

21 (Chorus) Ìyá o Oya o

22   A danu gbogbo ohun

23 Agbe ina nle agbe wa ja

24 A rọgba ka de Olodumare

25 Kò ṣe ba ni ile

26 (Chorus) Oluwa mi o

1 O mother, Oya o

2 It's not from today that she is honorable (but from long ago)

3   *O mother, Oya o*

4   *May you not be received rudely*

5 The one who enters witch's house dragging muddy feet

6   *O mother, Oya o*

7   *May you not be received impolitely*

8 Ancestor, owner of the whip, elder Egun

9   *O mother, Oya o*

10   *May you not be received improperly*

11 Mighty, mighty Orisha who dares confine the elder to his room

12 Authority in the house who uses truth to terrify the wicked person

13   *O mother, Oya o*

14   *May you not be received disrespectfully*

15 Customs officer in charge of the life-death frontier

16 She reaches an agreement with the parent of a child and never breaks it

17   *O mother, Oya o*

18   *Customs officer at the frontier*

19 Wife of Ogun picked up the drum and played it on her vast chest

20 She slipped under the Odan tree and the Odan tree got uprooted

21   *O mother, Oya o*

22   *When she's got her eye on something she never changes her intention*

23 Person who causes lightning to rip through the house

24 She patrols the compound around, around waiting for Olodumare to show up

25 If he arrives, he won't find the culprit inside

26   *O my lady of power*

27	A danu oju bi ye	27	*When she's got her eye on something she never changes her intention*
28	Oya ò n'ile kò l'ona	28	Oya has no home, no special road
29	Eni ro òko	29	The person who thinks about her isn't likely to encounter her
30	(*Chorus*) Oluwa mi o	30	*O my lady of power*
31	A danu oju bi ye	31	*When she's got her eye on something she never changes her intention*
32	Aba ni ja, mà jebi eni	32	When she fights with you it's never her fault
33	Aba ni ja kò l'ominu	33	When she fights with you it's without remorse
34	Gbogbo iṣe a ṣe gbe ni	34	Everything she does she gets away with
35	(*Chorus*) Oluwa mi o	35	*O my lady of power*
36	A danu oju bi ye	36	*When she's got her eye on something she never changes her intention*
37	B'o ṣe lẹgbẹ, B'o ṣe bembẹ	37	If her group is performing If bembe drums are playing
38	O jo bembẹ, O jo ṣẹkẹrẹ	38	She dances bembé, dances shekere
39	(*Chorus*) Oluwa mi jo	39	*O my lady dances*
40	Tani le jo bàtá?	40	Who's dancing to the batá drums?
41	(*Chorus*) Oluwa mi jo	41	*O my lady dances*
42	Iyawo Ogun. . . .	42	Wife of Ogun . . .
43	O ti nṣe ẽgun ojọ pẹ	43	She's been performing Egungun a long, long time
44	Ọya ni yi ti o pada o d'òrìṣà	44	Oya turned around and became Orisha
45	O dọna ṣe aiye o dọna ṣe orun	45	She guards the road into the world and guards the road to heaven.

Ēèpàà! Heyi!

Ēèpàà! Heyi!

III. Praises of Oya sung by Oya Kupola at Irá, Oyo city, February 17, 1983

1	Òbò mèjá	1	Vagina is highly intelligent
2	Oṣó ó gùn	2	Wizard's penis is long
3	Ọmọ rùkú	3	Child who carried the corpse
4	Ọya bopéjà	4	Oya, the complete fighter
5	Iyawórun pá pá	5	Massive woman up in the sky: *pow, pow*
6	Afàro f'araba	6	She frowned, whirling the huge tree
7	owó tiri tidi	7	which collapsed reluctantly
8	Ma gbá bi ọlà	8	May she sweep riches
9	òla oṣe bikan	9	tomorrow into the same place
10	Afefe lẹlẹ	10	Strong breeze
11	Afufu lẹlẹ	11	Purifying wind
12	aja lọsa	12	fought the surface of lagoon

13	ti fun l'oke	13	assaulted hilltop from above
14	Olotọti ti'mbe l'orun	14	Mysterious, commendable force
15	oloto ti orun	15	from the heavens, sky-sent power
16	Efufu Osa	16	Wind over the lake
17	ti fo l'oke	17	lept freely across the wilderness
18	Bi obinrin Ṣango	18	Wife of Shango
19	Ogun l'ogbọyọ, iya ọmọ wẹwẹ	19	She has the powers of Ogun of Oyo
20	Ologbọyọ alagba	20	Mother of children, with Ogun's powers
21	Efufu esa	21	Wind over lagoon
22	ti fun l'oke l'oke	22	leaping from mountain to mountain
23	Bolá ti l'ori Yansan	23	Honor be upon the head of Yansan
24	Oya kayin ti mokò	24	I praise the force of Oya
25	emi mokò	25	which I have encountered
26	Ti mo gbé Oya kayin	26	Uplifted, I now lift up
27	Oya kayin	27	praise-worthy Oya
28	lokun mi gbé.	28	whose uplifting strengthens me.

Behind each of these selections lies a tale or two. The first set may be found in a slim paperback book (of the sort assigned for student use) compiled by the musicologist and composer Fela Ṣowande in collaboration with Fagbemi Ajanaku, the Araba, or chief Ifa diviner of Lagos.[2] Both men, deeply dedicated to the preservation and propagation of Yoruba poetry and music, during the years immediately following independence (1960) notably used radio broadcasting as a way of familiarizing a colonized generation of young people with their own traditions. The Araba, who among other activities established a clinic for the practice of herbal medicine and traditional healing, was extremely hospitable to researchers and pilgrims on the way to the sources from the States. When I last saw him, in 1983, he had suffered a debilitating stroke, but nonetheless eagerly carried on conversation with notebook and ballpoint pen. At that time I copied out the oriki for Oya and those having to do with Egungun by hand, because the local bookstores were out of the book. Only a couple of weeks ago, my friend John Fagbemi Turpin from Oakland, California, sent a meticulously typed copy of these very praises as a good luck message. In the last chapter, there is another version of lines 12–20 in the course of a story collected by a very old friend, Pierre Verger, whose Ifa-name is also Fagbemi.

The main difficulty in working with the two sets of "live" performances following the printed one is the establishment of a text. Because of the colloquially elided, allusive (comprehensible only to an in-group), and pun-studded nature of chanted Yoruba, it's a good idea to hang around a town long enough to have the transcription made and checked with the performer(s) *in situ.* Alas, in the case of the second (Ogbomosho, 1977) I didn't do this, but naively relied upon my then collaborator, John Ogundipe (who lived in New York), upon my eventual return to perform what

turned out, given the age and toothlessness of the lead singer, and not the Ogun- rather than Oya-saturated nature of his own upbringing, to be so difficult that I felt I could publish only a rather knowledgable, but partly by-guess-and-by-gosh English version. For this edition of the book, though, I was determined to establish a workable text, and with the help of Dr. Afolabi Epega, I hope it's here. Up in his little "Ifa room" in the Bronx on a bright Sunday morning in August, we worked intently on fine points of the translation. "Oya is really *something!*" Afolabi repeatedly said. He was particularly impressed with the little scene (lines 23–25) in which the divine

Oya Kupola, singer of the praises of Oya, seated in Ologbin compound, March 1983.

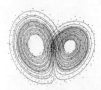

pyromaniac takes charge of post-lightning-strike operations by cordoning off the entire compound with her own circuitous presence. Being an Orisha, Oya doesn't wait for the local authorities to appear but rather for the high god (Olodumare), who, notoriously reluctant to intervene in mundane affairs, probably won't show up. And of course if he does, being Oya, and behaving like any common felon under the circumstances, she will have disappeared.

The Ogbomosho praises, as intimated, were sung by a small but sturdy group of old women, clothed for the occasion in red and purple. It was Oya's day of the week (ọjọ ọṣẹ ọya) and they had gathered to do her homage in the compound of the town's senior Oya priest. *Bàtá* drums, played by men, accompanied their singing and eventual dancing. The senior priest, also a man, took nominal charge of the event, which effectively the women ran in collaboration.

Two special performances linger on in memory. Midway through the singing, a youngish woman dressed like a beggar in burlap appeared at the entrance to the compound. She entered shyly, then gallivanted crazily about for a bit. Her face was smeared with gray ashes. She was not mad; she was fulfilling an obligation. Long barren, this woman had begged Oya for a child. (See line 16.) Oya spoke through the cowries and said that her wish would be granted but that she must promise for a year after the birth to perform like this every fourth day at the praise session: a fool for the goddess! The second haunting image was that of a very old, blind woman who had seated herself out of sight in the shadows of an adobe veranda that encircled the interior of the compound. As the praising broke into dancing, she got up from her stool and danced privately. She wore a frayed wrap and no blouse, her feet bare. The expression on her face was indescribable. She was the senior custodian of Oya in Ogbomosho. The young man in charge was her grandson.

The third set of praises was sung to me privately by Oya Kupola, a young priestess of Oya, as we sat in the empty parlor in Ologbin compound. Across the yard sits the little building housing Oya's principal shrine. This is Irá—Rome or Mecca to the Oya-worshiper. The first three lines of this sequence, a sort of introduction, mention three supernatural powers to whose magical medicines the chief of the compound, who is also the chief priest of Oya in Oyo town, has direct access: witch, wizard, and Egungun (reputedly the first ever performed in public). Since it was not Oya's but Ogun's day of the week, mention of her possession of his powers

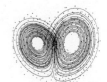

(lines 19 and 20) is appropriate. Eventually the reader will cross the yard and enter that special Oya-Egungun shrine, thereby gaining further insight into the relation between Oya and both her husbands, Ogun first and then Shango.

I had been staying in the compound for a month—deep immersion—and was feeling more confident in the spoken language than I ever have. Remarkably, I didn't have a tape recorder with me, and it seemed perfectly natural to write the praise-phrases down line by line, asking her to repeat if necessary. It was 1983. I should have learned by then to seek out somebody literate in Yoruba in order to establish Oya Kupola's text, tonal markings and all. But it never occurred to me to do this. Instead, what struck me was the intimacy of the exchange, the relative ease with which at long last the language was flowing back and forth, speaking of our common mother. Thanks again to Afolabi, who not only deftly corrected the rough and highly elided Yoruba but also gave me an insight into the aesthetic unity of Oya Kupola's recitation. "Up, on top of," he would emphasize, "she's fighting the lake (or the mountain) from above." It was only last night that I realized the connection between this perspective and the way Oya Kupola concludes with a series of changes rung on the process of "uplifting."

Now that Oya's contours have become a bit familiar through her oriki, we are ready to go on to the body of the book, during the course of which more traditional praises of Oya will be heard, mostly in the context of Ifa divination stories about her. Each section to follow presents one of these sacred oracular texts in translation with commentary. So however widely the argument may range—from continent to continent, touching upon various fields of discourse and frames of experience—these "likely stories" from the source may serve as philosophical fulcrum. Indeed, for stylistic reasons I surmise that parts of the Sowande-Ajanaku text are attributable to the latter's remarkable memory of Ifa verses, which incorporate traditional materials from authentic popular sources to parts of which may be lent a rhythm and a moral emphasis that is Ifa's own. Diviners who in the course of consultations recite such praises are concerned not only with getting people who ought to be worshiping a certain Orisha to do so properly but with attempting to keep Oya and her putative colleagues in line as well. For Ifa would seem to have arrived on the scene in order to foster a balance of forces in the universe, society, and the human soul. By contrast, the worshipers of a particular Orisha, those who

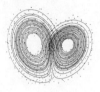

depend on her (or him), hope in the utterance of magical words to render her (or his) powers—no matter how violent in nature and to others— benevolent to themselves. Unlike the temperate babalawo, such enthusiastic praisers shamelessly extol such powers. They would, if they could, seduce the world to their own, their god's own brand of madness.

Oya is not the only goddess of her type loose in the world. With Nyalé, a Malinké-Bambara divinity of the upper Niger, who also appears in many guises, Oya has much in common. Though Nyalé has been severely repressed by Islamic attitudes and ideology, still traces of her may be found, and some of these I have been at pains to track down. Certain paths were open to me in Mali that would not have been so in Nigeria, and so I took them—always with a unified field theory of the goddess in mind. (It would be possible to compare Oya's role in the Egungun masquerade cult with that of a comparable feminine presence in the Dogon funereal masquerading complex, but for reasons of space and lack of participatory field experience, I have not done so here).

Greek parallels may occur to some readers. Artemis-Hecate is perhaps closest. And yes, in the language of Jung and as more rapturously voiced by followers of James Hillman's new polytheism,[3] one could certainly say that Oya and the other Orisha, introspectively understood, are numinous archetypal forces, wounds that heal us, sanctifying madnesses. What is missing, however, from most intuitive affiliations with classical soul-mates, even in their reconstructed pre-Homeric forms, is the essential mediating community of worshipers, the *thiasos*, which collectively transmits sacred technology and knowledge. Carol Christ's touching auto-initiation into a personally revived cult of Aphrodite is a case in point.[4] Other readers may be reminded of the Hindu goddess Durga, "the inaccessible," dancing in tantrum upon inertia and ruin. But generally speaking this book does not venture cross-cultural comparisons, except within Oya's extended territory. As it is, there is more than enough to be done within African and Caribbean parameters. Even how she's shaping up in other parts of this country is beyond consideration here. Comment from whatever realm of vicarious research or provocative discourse that has been added can be blamed on an attempt along with Oya Kupola to raise her up.

In preparing this new edition I have first of all cast a cold eye on the book that was. Without doing violence to what's signed and sealed, I've done what editing I could. Also, with the idea of making the material

more "reader friendly," a few bridges have been constructed across Oya's rapids (disaster to Mungo Park and perilous to other explorers). These bridges, commissioned by the present editors, but willingly executed by the author, explain what the reader will be in for section by section, and occasionally chapter by chapter. In the meantime, since I have moved my research on Oya into a (to me) fascinating and frustratingly unfamiliar territory, preliminary results of which are included in section four, I can sympathize with the bafflement of readers unused to Oya's behavior in other contexts, including the discursive, where she loves to break frame/ shift direction. But though dynamic fluid systems are not subjected to moment-by-moment prediction, beneath the chaos for those so inclined will begin to loom paradigmatic order.

Were I to begin the Oya project all over again with a renewed twenty-year lease on the middle years of my life, I would do it differently, I imagine, but then, many of those who helped me find my way would no longer be alive; and this would be a tremendous loss. And I think that I would be more apt to write up results in the rough, sketchy manner of the new *Moving Oya* chapter instead of in what my youngest daughter calls "your classical style." But this change I can make: At the conclusion of the original introduction I told how one of the cowrie shell oracle's prescriptions to me was to buy a bit to put on Oya's shrine. I figured that attempting to contain her within the covers of a book was in effect to make such a long-neglected purchase. Now I say there's no reason anymore to rein Oya in. On the contrary, now's the time to loosen up, grip the mane, and learn to ride her bareback.

New York, August 27, 1991

Notes

1. See *Eji Ogbe*, the Ifa verses published by Juana Elbein dos Santos and Deoscoredes dos Santos in *La Notion de Personne en Afrique noire* (Paris: CNRS, 1973), pp. 48–53.
2. Fela Ṣowande and Fagbemi Ajanaku, *Orúkọ Àmútọ̀runwá* (Ibadan: Oxford Univ. Press, 1964).
3. James Hillman, *Re-Visioning Psychology* (New York: Harper Colophon, 1977). Hillman is at pains to make clear that "polytheistic psychology" is not a religion (prologue to section 4).
4. Carol P. Christ, "Laughter of Aphrodite," in *Laughter of Aphrodite* (San Francisco: Harper & Row, 1987).

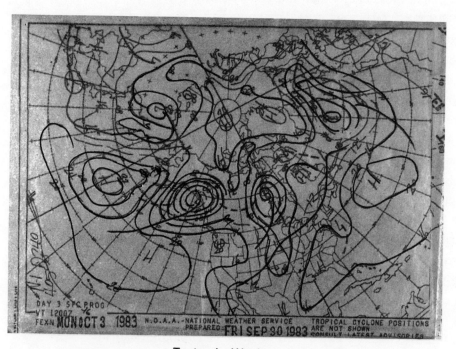

Tracing the Weather

part one

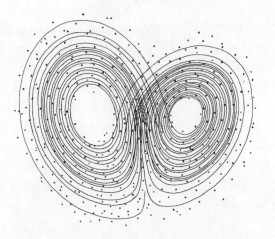

recalling the elements

Du kommst und gehest.
—Rilke

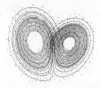

Orisha are forces of nature that certain individuals long ago were able to intuit magical means of tempering, placating, and rendering beneficial. Although it was the untrammeled power that was initially negotiated with, only the controllable aspect was "seated" in a shrine and ritually served. Originally these alliances between natural forces and people were private affairs, of benefit only to the priest's immediate family or community.[1]

Among the Yoruba divinities Oya is unusual in being manifest in various natural phenomena. Although wind is her primary vehicle, Oya is perforce a fiery element as well, for hers is a stormy weather whose turbulent airflows spiral into tropical tornadoes. Convective process is not Oya's only fiery aspect. She is also intricately involved in the generation of lightning.

All rivers in that part of Africa where Oya came to be worshiped are feminine spirits. Oya's own river shows up in European geographies as the Niger. Whether the entire river is meant by the name Oya or only that part which is of historical importance to the Yoruba is open to question. In order to understand the appropriateness of Oya's ownership of at least that segment which flows about Jebba Island, it is useful to establish verbal contact with the geological history of the entire riverbed, thence to consider the metaphysical dimensions of its unique double flood.

What sort of verbal contact? In Western theological discourse, speaker, speech, and listener form a systemic social unity that the non-human environment seldom, if ever, enters directly.[2] The following presentation of Oya's various meteorological and hydrologic theophanies aims to reverse this depersonalizing trend. One hopes, by responding imaginatively to Oya's power, one may coax her natural turbulence to enter the text as directly as possible!

Any resemblance between the patterns displayed by windstorms, river runs, and patterns of human thought or speech may be purely coincidental. However, since poets for millennia have assumed a putative fit between their rhythms and those forces inspiring and compelling them to

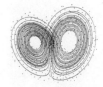

"clap hands and sing," we will begin by listening to poets, especially to bards from Oya's home continent.

In attempting thereafter to characterize Oya's natural patterns in prose, her advocate will inevitably show little patience with conventional boundaries set up between human disciplines and their characteristic modes of discourse, but rather move jaggedly between elementary scientific explanation, the figurative language of myth, and the sort of commentary myth generates, including reminiscences of lived experience.

Since ideological unity has always (until very recent times) been masculinist, its rupture here will bring not only aspects of the "nonhuman environment" to the fore but also a repressed feminine consciousness. There is nothing mystical about this consciousness. It is, rather, a socially constructed, culturally transmitted, and existentially accepted way of Being for which we are improvising a style based on its own interruptions. Just as women's lives are lived in layers and clusters of commitments and chores, in such a manner might our discourse air itself, especially with regard to multivarious goddesses, without undue sacrifice of situational precision.

The Goddess as Fire and Wind

As a whirlwind
swoops on an oak
Love shakes my heart.
—Sappho[3]

Per cognosciere meglio i venti

To know better the direction of the winds.
—Leonardo da Vinci[4]

dry tornado

Tornadoes rip out everything around me
And tornadoes tear from me leaves and futile words
Whirlwinds of passion hiss in silence
And blessings upon dry windswirl, upon the flight of rains.

You Wind, ardent Wind, pure Wind of my good season,
        Burn every flower, every vain thought
When sand falls again on the dunes of the heart.
Servant, suspend your antique gesture, and you, children,
        Suspend your games and your ivory laughter.
And You, may the wind consume your voice along with your body
        May it dry the perfume of your flesh
That flame, which illuminates my night as though it were a column
        As though it were a palm.

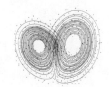

Set my lips ablaze with blood! Spirit, blow upon the strings of this kora
That my song may rise pure as the gold of Galam.
—Léopold Sédar Senghor[5]

Oya at her most awesome, untrammeled Oya, is a weather goddess. This is how she appeared before there was "world" as we know it and how she continues to manifest herself beyond the reach of meddlesome technological devices sent up to simulate, alter, and pluck the heart out of the mystery of her storms.[6] Caught in her updrafts, the religious imagination without apparatus seeks, though threatened with annihilation, to meet the weather goddess halfway, where sensuous experience remains possible. By reconnecting ourselves to the elements through which her urgent temperament expresses itself in patterns recognizable in our own swirls, inundations, and disjunctive ardors, we come upon a common language with which to invoke and reflect her power.

The sacramental language of the elements is not superseded by scientific formulae accounting for the smaller and smaller units to which the world's substances have been noetically reduced, nor does it suffer from translation. Vedic fire consumes shea butter in Bambara lamp basins of wrought iron. "Water" will always be the miracle flowing into Helen Keller's sightless hands as Annie Sullivan names it. For millennia wind, fire, and water have been chanted as primary constituents of an inhabited cosmos. Everywhere on earth they have been symbolically oriented about the magical circle drawn to encompass that space within which we seek to find ourselves. Therefore, by inheritance we cling to them still. As middle terms between energy systems of obscure purpose and our human desire to shape experience, the elements present themselves as matter already expressively organized, matter whose modes are reflected in and by our own moods—basal axes of our poetries. It is a language that the poet Sappho was the first, so far as we know, to make personal. Her elemental seizures were so deftly intimate as to exclude commentary. They happened as spoken. Soul-wind shook Sappho, and she became an oak in a gale. The catalyst she called Aphrodite. In another time and place she would have sacrificed to Oya.

All elemental discourse thereafter will seem clumsy, overcomplicated. But silence is no remedy. That which has been muted, misunderstood, banished from consideration, or as yet undiscovered cries for articulation. To seek adequate words with which to trace her elemental patterns is an act of homage to the goddess of tropical weathers in hopes that her compassion may reciprocally illuminate inner equivalents with which we have struggled in private darkness. It has been a struggle intensified by patriarchal discountenance of powerful emotion—its problematic relegated to women "in need of help." In being coached by compliant mothers to stifle rather than outride our storms, to dam and conceal our floods, to bank our fires and give tinder over to future husbands, the Oya in ourselves froze in its tracks. Yet such ice particles, negatively charged, at the heart of the mounting storm are the mysterious, generative sources of Oya's lightning.[7] Thus, in other ways obstructed, Oya strikes us— quirking here, cramping there. Done with our brains, the indefatigable goddess goes jaggedly to work upon our bodies, cutting off circulation, opening sluices, instilling victims who could be votaries with a variety of "female complaints," catching them up in mindless swirls of activity, throwing them down into incapacitating vortices, playing havoc with appetite. Stop, Oya, we beg you! We will sound your praises along all rivers from Hudson to Niger. We will hang prayer flags to flutter like laundry stretching from fire escape to fire escape, continent to continent. We will strive to know your winds the better to reclaim our part of fire.

I

Leonardo's playful weathervane, composite fork and spoon, suggests that as the wind lists, so swivels hunger. Ceaseless as the wind is appetite's fickle inclination, now pronged, now hollow, toward something unseen that can never be of substance. The wind may catch the bowl of the spoon like a sail and spin it around. The tines of the fork may penetrate and divide without pronging the slightest morsel. All of which is true of our weather goddess. Yet to know her winds, were this our only instrument, would be to remain in a state of torture, from which the African poet fortunately relieves us by invoking the most ardent of them as purifactory scourge of fleshly appetite. From the ashes of attachment will arise pure song.

Senghor's making of the poem is an imaginative act of fusion not only between two poetic traditions but between two elemental arts: that of metalsmith and that of bard. Far from the village life of his childhood, writing in a European language, Senghor pulls the two cultures (spoken

Serer, written French) back to a common vanishing point of origin. Pindar's poetry, from which Senghor's ode partially derives, in turn is rooted in a poetic praxis that seems magical nowadays. Words thus conceived are active agents, transformative of the situations they describe; and poets, composing these words in a cognitive state of passion, are similarly inspired. To the ancient Greeks a surge of energy, felt as a dark frenzy of the blood and a panting of the lungs, was considered generally to be the work of a daemon; and this heightened heart-breath could be the genesis, variously, of an act of valor, of falling in love, of a brilliant thought, or of a work of art.[8] Theirs was a physiology of consciousness whose bronchial tubes, like bellows on the hearth, lay open to the gusts of gods.

> On a sign from my father, the apprentices would start working the two pairs of sheep-skin bellows which were placed on the ground at each side of the forge and linked to it by earthen pipes. . . . For a whole hour they would both be working the levers of the bellows until the fire in the forge leapt into flame, becoming a living thing, a lively and merciless spirit.[9]

Thus in a famous passage from his novel *The African Child,* Camara Laye evokes the smelting process of that "gold of Galam" to whose purity Senghor's poem invoking the dry tornado aspires. But words accompany the metalworker, too, words intoned by a professional praise-singer, hired by the client to inspire the goldsmith to ancestral heights of competence, and words soundlessly uttered at the sacred moment of fusion in a silent forge by the master himself. These secret words were intended to placate and arouse

> the spirts of fire and gold, of fire and air, air breathed through the earthen pipes, of fire born of air, of gold married with fire . . . for they are the most elemental of all spirits, and their presence is essential at the smelting of gold.[10]

Senghor assumes the double role of smith and bard. In Africa these "technicians of the sacred" belong to special castes, which are considered impure by the majority of the population, who till the soil without pretense to special converse with volatile spirits. The spirits are dangerous and demanding. Legends speak of blood sacrifice, usually of close kin, required by powers of wind and fire. "Set my lips ablaze with blood," prays Senghor. The sacrificial process undergone by the poet of "Dry Tornado" is partly fictive, partly real—a self-discipline. He doesn't magically murder his mistress, of course; it is his desire for her that consumes itself in a fury of illumination. But the evocation of that desiccating wind thus to suck sap from flower and flesh pointedly recalls the sorcerous component of inspired craftsmanship.

Bards, who craft verbal praises rather than golden ornaments, are elementally affiliated with water. Though he wrote his poem in French, with the resonance of the classical tradition solemnifying his mode of address, Senghor thought of its being sung to a Sudanese musical instrument called the kora—a harp with a calabash resonator whose twenty-one strings, rapidly plucked, sound like water rushing over stones. It is an instrument considered consubstantial with the river. In Mali they say the great river Niger, locally called Djoliba, itself is a bard, harboring memories of heroic achievements and ritual secrets.[11] The kora player tunes his instrument to these liquid whisperings.[12] Water's voice is temperate, like the flow of Senghor's poetry. Wind lends it passionate expression. Water bathes the singer's soul with immemorial rhythms. Wind sings the impulse of the moment. And within wind, where the kora is played, inevitably hisses the sorcerous voice of fire.

Fire and wind, burning wind, are considered feminine elements in that part of Africa evoked by the poetry of Senghor, the prose of Camara Laye, and the music of the kora. The Bambara of the upper Niger River Valley, though overwhelmingly Islamized, retain memories of an elemental cosmology whose feminine components are personified by the goddess Nyalé. Her story is a tragic one, consonant with the adversative climatic role played by hot, dry winds from the Sahara and with the imposition of patriarchal values upon the population. Having energetically begun the creation of the Bambara world, Nyalé became a power to be curtailed. Banished from the ideal scheme of things, she went underground, demoted from goddess to sorceress—a diminutive "little old woman with white hair," by whose power women today in out-of-the-way villages perform magical transformations. The following account of Nyalé's role in the creation of cosmic life was told to me by a Frenchwoman who knew her story well. More than a generation ago Madame Solange de Ganay as a young woman participated in the famous Griaule expeditions to the upper Niger valley. I had written her a note appreciative of some work she had done then, and so we became friends by correspondence.

Paris, May 23, 1976. I call and invite Madame de Ganay to lunch. It is Sunday. She accepts immediately. I am grateful. It is somehow crucial that we talk. I know that Nyalé and Oya are sisters. That bond makes formalities fall away. All the same, it is kind of her to free herself on such short notice.

Our neglectfully unreserved table is placed so far out on the sidewalk that fumes of the Boulevard St. Germain traffic invade and disguise the *amaro* of our apéritifs. I am embarrassed, she gracious. But this awkwardness doesn't last for long. All noise vanishes in the intensity of our conversation. Her brown eyes, like those of a childhood friend, like those of a helpful animal in a fairy tale, like those of someone under a spell who is trying to convey the sorrow of her imprisonment, hold mine in steady gaze as first her hands, then a low, urgent voice, begin to speak. She is telling me a myth. Having pressed her palms together, with great effort now she pulls them apart. Creation has occurred. Consciousness has been dramatically severed from itself. Now there are two parts of it. From a secret recess—a self-containing sphere—suddenly god thought. And that "suddenly," said the countess, was the earliest instance of what later became known as Nyalé.

Pure impulse.

Now came the explanation: to accomplish thought, the perfect sphere had to divide slightly so that one part could reflect upon the other. Seeing himself as double meant that within the narrow separation between the hemispheres of god were simultaneously created light, distance, and time. And god heard upon this instant his own inner voice in the form of a vibration, which will subsequently animate the entirety of what is beginning to be created.

Implicit in this initial act are all four elements, she explained. Wind, together with fire, subtly initiates the process. Water reflects and therefore verbalizes Act into Being. Earth provides resistance (as witness the tension in her hands as she tried to pull them slightly apart). Earth is the halt preventing diffusion of spirit and ensuring that what is said will be heard, will endure. It is the implicit element of earth that engraves water's sinuous memories upon the brains of evolving creatures.

Alone, the countess continued, Nyalé dispersed creation's word throughout space. Touching all four directions into existence, she traveled as a whirlwind. Alone, born of herself by her own impetuosity, Nyalé carried on this self-appointed task. So air, striking against air, ignites fire, further accelerating air's displacement.

However, Nyalé was not as alone as she thought.

As one speaks, from the mouth issues a mist. So Faro, the great (androgynous) water spirit, was concealed within the vibration of that creative word Nyalé was spreading through space. Eventually feeling the

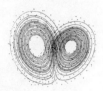

drag of this moisture, which threatened to deprive her of such exhilarating exclusivity, Nyalé sped up, becoming ever more ardent, more violent, effectively evaporating all the moisture enveloping the word. The moisture shriveled into a scum, like the dry foam found where the waters of a pond have receded. Thus, wishing to destroy Faro (water), she inadvertently caused Ndomadyiri (earth) to appear. For that scum solidified itself, acquired bulk, and became the second and final obstacle to her power.

The countess paused in her narration. We had hit the bottom and stayed there wordlessly, stayed with it—that streak of uncontrolled energy, that primary illusion of omnipotence by which impulsive women have been just as suddenly mortified as we were then, staring at the gleaming tablecloth with all its clutter. No more space than that divided us. Feminine shame in the wake of exaggeration gave masculine force the opportunity to move in. With the creator's help, Water and Earth conspired to banish Fire-Wind from the ostensible scheme of things. When we meet Nyalé next in Bambara myth she will have been diminished to Mousso Koroni, "The little old woman with white hair," who haunts the granary while the threshing of "red" millet takes place in the fields. Through the midwife's hands this secretive old crone works to expel a reluctant fetus. She intervenes where she can. She presides over the secret society of "red-eyed" women.

Addlebrained in the daylight, Nyalé appears occasionally in human form. I saw her thus once in the small, disorderly town of Avi on the shores of Lake Debo in Mali six months after my conversation with the countess. The ribald, cynical townspeople literally shoved her into my presence, as if to say, "Write *this* in your notebook." Sparse white hair clung like the scum of myth to her aged scalp. Her eyes swept distractedly through the crowd. But when they turned toward the visitors, there was sorrow and humiliation in their look. "I used to live in the water," the crazed woman apologized through an interpreter, "but now I live on land, most of the time." It was a terrible occasion. One felt the town, not the woman, to be crazed.

"Addlebrained." She sent that phrase now, as from her banishment beyond ego's reach. From that darkness Nyalé sends up countless fulgurations of consciousness, often without reassurance of moist matrix or containing clay. On impulse, I look the word up. There engraved in the heavy dictionary, *addle* means "mire"—specifically that produced by cow's urine. *Addle* is also applied to the lees of wine and to putrefaction discovered in an egg that can produce no chicken. Such decay is her bail-

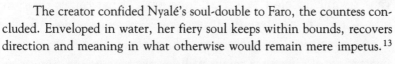

iwick in Bambara thinking. This bitter taste in the mouth—her almost-extinguished fire. Blow on it! What seems to have been most drastically lost is her wind.

> The creator confided Nyalé's soul-double to Faro, the countess concluded. Enveloped in water, her fiery soul keeps within bounds, recovers direction and meaning in what otherwise would remain mere impetus.[13]

I thought of the harmonious mind of her companion of all these years. In him a diffuse energy had found a sympathetic, shaping conduit. In her had he first found impetus? So one comes to live the appropriate myths, wherever in the world one is drawn to find them. That evening I called upon him. We spoke of sorcery. "Everything we do rebounds upon us," he said. "It is only necessary to search for the screen upon which the deed is reflected back again. It is that understanding of sorcery which will eventually make of us moral beings." It is water's intelligence speaking through him.

II

Turning now to the weather meteorologically mapped and depicted, it is possible to imagine the tornado goddesses Nyalé and Oya as phases of a single process occurring in different geographical contexts, which in turn have conditioned their mythologies. Along the latitudes of which Senghor sings and Madame de Ganay speaks, the rainy season—uninterrupted, relatively short, and recently unstable—is ushered in and out by cyclonic activity, often "dry" because of the highly evaporative texture of the atmosphere, for which Nyalé is "blamed" in Bambara cosmological thinking—an onus surely redounding upon the cosmologues. Farther south, along the Guinea coast and into Yoruba territory, the rainy season is double, and the tornadoes announcing it entail rainy squalls. Oya participates in this more southerly pluviometric situation. She arrives wet and she arrives twice, as a tumultuous event desired for its aftermath.

Together these two types of cyclonic activity are geared into a systemic pattern that meteorologists call the intertropical front. Thus, ferocious though Nyalé and Oya may appear locally, their appearances are periodic, subject to certain requirements over which they have no control, thus calling a halt to desire for infinite prerogative that is the perverse side of any great energy complex. So the ancient Greek furies were subject to

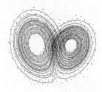

lot.[14] They were bound and so could be persuasively tamed, which, as we shall see, is also the case with tornado-Oya.

The intertropical front is a shifting encounter of winds. But what causes winds to blow in varied directions? What causes them to blow at all? Winds are the results of differences in temperature, to which air is acutely sensitive. Thermoscopy is a kind of thinking that air does. Indeed, perception of difference might well be regarded as the genesis of thought in all things. Such perception incites the restive air to move. Its thinking acts out. Contrasting thermal environments, slightly less than warm or more than tepid temperatures, which human skin would scarcely notice, to touchy air are provocation of a sheer shove across boundaries from one quality space to another. Some children are airlike in their perception of infinitesimal shifts in emotional climate. They learn to veer, to expand and contract themselves. They became shaky in their expectations.

But weathers of the world's soul set dangerous precedents for people. The greater the contrast between adjacent environments, the more vigorous air's impulse to overcome whatever marginal resistance there is; and in order to get where it is going, air must mount farther and farther from the ground, faster and faster, moving toward vertigo at the exponential speed of spirals. Ah, what the rising wind so avidly seeks is attained at last in con-

Patterns of "ideal" (i.e., stormless) atmospheric circulation. Source: William L. Donn, *Meteorology with Marine Applications* (New York: McGraw-Hill, 1951), p. 287.

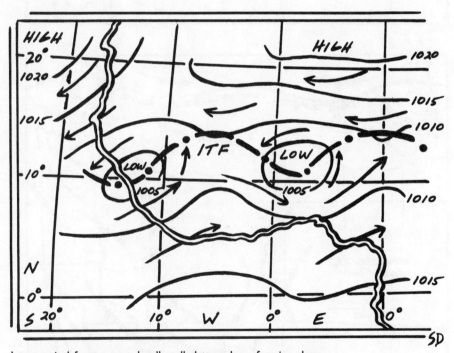

densation, where it ceases to be what it was. Droplets of moisture form. High up, the droplets freeze. Lightning storms develop. Over the tropics it rains. Below the mounting cloud column, cold flows sweep down to extenuate themselves with relief upon southern beaches—until the heady urge assails them, too, until again they begin to notice and respond to differences. Can a true child of air ever pause to reconcile? Or must she be forever stimulated by discrepancy?

Although locally these periodic aspirations and descents appear vertical, from an overall perspective their grander migrations move from pole to equator and back again. These horizontal flows are compromised by the magisterial rotation of the globe, which keeps bands of wind with a diagonal inclination flowing in opposite directions.[15] Where these slightly slanted, latitudinal flows in search of the less-warm, of the less-cold, converge at the tropics of Capricorn and Cancer, high-pressure atmospheric cells, like solenoidal batteries, keep the zonal circulation systems going, whipping discrepant impulses into line. But where north-easterly and southeasterly trade winds obliquely meet, they find themselves participating in a ride they didn't reckon on. For the encountering edge, roughly toward the equator, is itself unstable and in continuous longitudinal motion. This is the intertropical front, the context in which tornadoes occur—Nyalé and Oya's bizarre apportionment.

The grander rhythm determining the temperamental variations of the front is tied to the apparent

Intertropical front waves, locally called tornadoes, forming along the line of contact between the underrunning monsoon and the overriding harmattan over West Africa during late spring. Source: Maurice Garbell, *Tropical and Equatorial Meteorology* (New York: Pittman, 1947), p. 212.

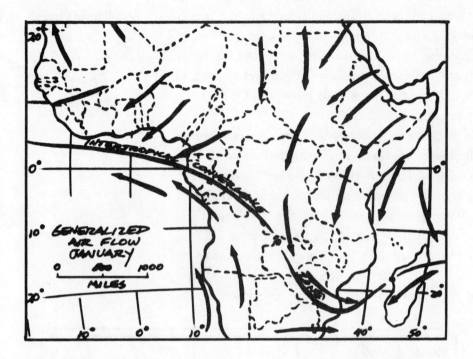

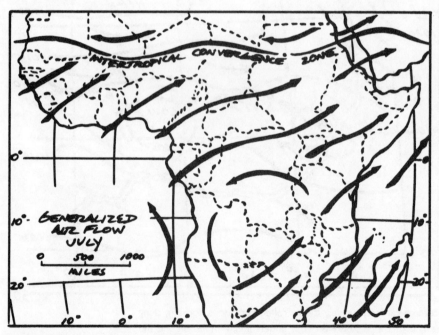

Pendular swings of the intertropical front shown at its nadir and at its apogee.
Source: George H. T. Kimble, *Tropical Africa*, vol. 1 (New York: Twentieth Century Fund, 1960), p. 41, after diagrams by Garbell.

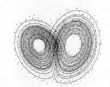

shifting of the sun from one hemisphere of the globe to its opposite. As the globe tilts toward solstice, equinox, opposite solstice, the depth of the front's swing varies, but on the Atlantic side of the African continent (upon which our work is focused), the latitudinal sweep it encompasses is roughly between 2°N and 18°N, its oscillations being experienced most intensely along the Guinea coast—far-off homeland to generations of displaced souls whose ritual songs continue to evoke it. Sometimes there are doldrums along the intertropical front, but the usual mood is turbulence caused by marked discrepancies between temperature and moisture contents of winds colliding along its competence. For these winds have blown across dramatically different surface environments—dry savanna and ocean.

As the front moves north from the southern apogee of its swing (2°N), a wide band of moist air from the sea follows. Six months later, as it moves south, desert winds pursue. This is the fundamental rhythm responsible for alternating rainy and dry seasons in West Africa. The movement of the front toward its northern apogee (18°N) is jittery. In May it skids to a temporary halt owing to seasonal activities of the anticyclone cell above the Sahara and the resulting surge of dry winds. Sometime in June the front struggles northward again, heralded by its characteristic turbulence, intensified by the contrast—now maximal—between encountering air masses.

Now storms along the seam, at their most violent (Nyalé, Senghor's "Dry Tornado"), drifting southwest over the Atlantic with ever-increasing amplitude, suddenly strike the Caribbean. Thus, by grace of atmospheric forces beyond human control, the tornadoes of West Africa, following the slave-trade routes along which those who first named them were hauled to the hurricane-prone islands of their diaspora, achieve in the New World their apotheosis. "*Kabiesi!*" ("Hail to the King"), the people greet the thunderstorms resulting from all that cyclonic activity. Destructive though these winds may be, they contain majesty, African power triumphant, which the descendants of the Yoruba people call Shango, Oya's rain-bearing consort. Moisture now lining her furious swirls, Nyalé, the banished, has reappeared on the weather maps homologous with Oya.

Storms, intrinsic to radical shifts of being, also mark the passage of life into death as the soul prepares to return to Guinea or to "Oya's

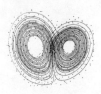

Island" in the midst of the Niger River. The following is a segment of an *ètùtù* (atonement) ceremony, first phase of a Yoruba funeral.

Sunday, February 6, 1982. The familiar sunlit apartment in the Bronx had been transformed into the stark site of coming demolition. Before an audience seated on straight chairs, the *soperas* (covered ceramic pots) from which the Orisha had already flown back to Africa were smashed with an ax. Each blow shuddered the spine. A black cloth was marked in white chalk with a spiral. Upon this cloth an upturned calabash, sprinkled with ash, was set to catch the broken beads of the departed *madrina's* necklaces. Standing above this container, four women, under instructions from the diviner, pulled necklace after necklace apart. The violence so minutely done was irreparable. . . . In Africa, when an important person dies, people sometimes pull the house in which he is buried down over the remains. Figuratively, this morning the house was thus demolished. Those to whom it had become a second home will never so congregate again.

As the intertropical front swings north these days, condensation does not occur, and Nyalé's homeland lies under threat of death. What has interfered with that fundamental rhythm? Why did the usual torrential rains in the Guinea highlands fail to appear in late March (1985)? United Nations experts blame deforestation. Local philosophers attribute lack of rain variously to increased individualism, contention, greed, failure to propitiate the ancient spirits, and Western technological tampering with the atmosphere. A community organizer in Mali, a person whose belief system might be described as socialist-animist, blames Islamization. "Allah is a desert god," he says. "Well, look, they got what they asked for." "It's Libya's fault," quipped a sorcerer from the Republic of Niger. "Qaddafi has sent up another high-pressure cell over the Sahara!" But aridity, within or without, is a mystery not simply to be willed away. Radical transformations in the weather signal the need for radical transformations in human thinking and feeling. A person working in the library of an office in Bamako, Mali, for an international agency allocating urgent aid to local development projects, has a dream:

Tues, June 25, 1985. Kader Coulibaly said: Day after day I pore over reports having to do with this terrible drought. Then one night I found myself dreaming of going to consult this famous sage. The old man (I had never seen him before) appears and says he will help me. But I must return to my house, he says. In the dream I did what he said. As I entered my house, everywhere I touched water began to spout forth.

From each familiar thing—doorpost, wall, chair. I went out into the backyard, and again, from this stone, that tree, water came. So I began running around, joyous as a child, touching everything in sight; and from everything fresh water was gushing at my touch. What is the meaning?

It is a dream that I think the earth is asking of all of us—a getting in touch with where we live.

As Kader Coulibaly compassionately reclaims the part of water, I would like to wrest woman's fire back from Promethean culture-bearers of the Western tradition who categorize the elements as active, creative, and masculine—fire and wind—as opposed to passive, submissive, and feminine—earth and water. Jung accepted the alchemical gendering of these energies uncritically.[16] Such identifications are culturally rather than phenomenologically determined and can lead to brainwashing in therapeutic situations that promise reclamation of the feminine.

Throughout the scintillating pages of Gaston Bachelard's *Psychoanalysis of Fire*, feminine "clients" are conspicuously missing. Empedocles leaps into the volcano while Joan of Arc prepares for the stake in somebody else's waiting room. While the seminal reveries of Novalis are busy illuminating the dark night of the European romantic soul, that "thin flame" coursing beneath Sappho's skin[17] creeps everywhere—out of the absent-minded professor's file cabinets, along the shriveling rug, up the rungs of his chair, singeing his very beard—unnoticed, as he prepares the following lectures:

> From the calorific point of view, the sexual distinction is clearly
> complementary. The feminine principle is a principle pertaining
> to surface and outer covering, a lap, a refuge, a gentle warmth.
> The masculine principle is a principle of the center, a principle
> of power, active and sudden as the spark and power of will. The
> feminine heat attacks things from without. The masculine heat
> attacks them from within, at the very heart of essential being.[18]

A bachelor's reverie of unsatisfied desire, an alchemist's dream of uterine hegemony, a greenhouse made of glass while out-of-doors real nature runs rampant. After a busy day the floor of the woman's therapy studio is strewn with drawings of incendiary vaginas and uterine caldrons, burning with culturally imposed shame.

Because I owe much to the phenomenology of this jovial imagination, I will tangle with it here. All the arts of fire have been co-opted by Bachelard's men. "They are the work of a *father* [his italics] bearing the mark of primitive love," he says. "The forms created by fire are modeled in order to be caressed."[19] Perhaps, but by whose hands? As evidence of women working with fire we turn first to the potters of Koursalé, Mali. We have spoken above of the metalworker's mastery of the dangerous spirits of wind and fire. To the wives of West African smiths belong the mysteries of fired clay.

Koursalé. June 18, 1985. Early evening. Semourou came by. Charged with that crazy energy of hers, she insisted we go for a walk. She wouldn't say where. There was something she wanted me to see. Stopping to steal, with the laughing owner's tacit permission, two handfuls of *néré* fruits, clownishly she stuffed her mouth with them. (As head of Nyagwa, the women's secret society, Semourou gets away with bizarre behavior. She loves to play the fool. She is a gifted psychic who in the course of doing "readings" for clients is serious and insightful.) Back of the market she led me to that open space you cross on the way to the great plain. There in the mid-distance a huge, partially smothered fire was sending forth dense smoke through which could be seen silhouettes of women rushing about with skinny poles in their hands. The poles were perhaps three and a half meters long—like the antennae of excited insects. Now it was I who pulled Semourou forward, faster, against the fading light.

They were women from the *forgerons'* quarter, perhaps a dozen of them, though maybe fewer because their heightened activity multiplied their numbers. With those long sticks they were pulling huge blackened water pots out of the fire, racing to roll them away from the incredible heat as though playing with hoops. At the periphery of their space they would stop to beat them with bunched leafy branches dipped in water, which sizzled into pungent steam. Then, grabbing up her pole again, a woman would rush back into the density of the smoke for another hurried series of prods, which turned into rolls as the pot broke free from under its cover of partially consumed branches and smoldering grasses.

At dawn this morning they must have come out to carry the cooled pots home on their heads. When I passed by on the way to the river, only grayish-white ash was to be seen on the ground. No other trace remained of that incredibly vital scene. Maybe that's where Nyalé turned into Mousso Koroni ("The little old woman with white hair"): on a potters' field not three kilometers from the Niger.

Now, then, Monsieur Bachelard, let us go back to your childhood. It was your father, you say, who kindled the fire in the grate?

I could not imagine my father having any equal in the performance of this function, which he would never allow anyone else
to carry out. Indeed, I do not think I lit a fire myself before I was
eighteen years old. It was only when I lived alone that I became
master of my own hearth. But I still take special pride in the *art
of kindling* [his italics] that I learned from my father.[20]

Hmmm. Yes. But a woman does appear to preside over certain
fire-arts in your childhood. First she rekindles the fire, you say, then she
gets everything cooking at once in the stone open-hearth stove. Potatoes
both for pigs and for people bubble in the huge iron pots suspended over
the flames. When you are a good boy, she gets out her magical waffle iron,
enabling you to write, as a grown man, this remarkable passage:

> Yes, then indeed I was eating fire, eating its gold, its odor, and
> even its crackling while the burning waffle was crunching under
> my teeth.[21]

It was your grandmother who gave you the gift of fire, not that
withholding son of hers to whom in defiance of memory you grant all the
art. Hers in truth that fire "at the very heart of essential being."
    Among the Bemba of Zambia women don't usually kindle the
household fires either, for such work without flint or matches is tedious.
But the generative symbol belongs to them, and in ritual context they
demonstrate this ownership. On the seventh day of a Bemba girl's initiation, as Audrey Richards reports it, the eldest paternal aunt of one of the
initiates, an old woman "wrinkled and bent with rheumatism," dances
before the group, then lies down on her back so that the woman in charge
of the initiation can twirl a fire stick in the groove of her ancient thigh,
while the chorus of young women sings:

> *Scratch, scratch [sound of grating fire sticks]*
> *How many children have you borne?*[22]

After this symbolic action has been completed, the singing continues while the laborious firemaking process is transferred to the floor of
the hut. When the shavings catch, hand-clapping and ululations salute the
elder woman's accomplishment. When the fire gets going, a small "marriage pot" is set upon it to boil water and seeds. Thus is the power of
parenthood ritually transferred from elder to younger women in traditional
Zambia.

Now that we have the fire back in our hands for a moment, let's play with it. "Line up, girls," orders the headmistress. Tucking our blouses smoothly in, we line up. "Now," says the headmistress to our friend at the head of the line as she hands her a parcel of energy, "please transfer this to the end of the file any way you choose." Kathleen throws it neatly across all our heads to Edith. "Good," says the headmistress. "You have just seen a demonstration of radiation. Now everyone please move up." And she repeats the original instructions. Rachel is next. Gently handing the parcel to the girl next to her, who happens to be Margaret, she intends for Margaret to follow suit. And Margaret does. We all do. Eventually the parcel reaches Kathleen. "Good," says the headmistress. "You have just witnessed the conductive option. Please move up, girls." Margaret's turn. Seizing the smoldering parcel, she runs to the end of the line with it. "Good," says the headmistress. "A perfect example of convection. Can any of you think of another possibility?"[23]

One night in a dream the headmistress appears to Margaret. There's no one else in the old study hall, but obediently Margaret takes her seat, her knees locked up against the sloping built-in desk with its set-in inkwell and grooved pen-and-pencil holder. A bell rings. "Since ancient times," intones the steady voice of the headmistress, "man has used convective currents for heating and ventilation. Hot air and hot water, thus invisibly dispersed throughout structures, render them habitable in cold climates." The headmistress peers over the lectern at Margaret, who shivers in response. "Convection currents," the headmistress consoles, "also assist in the ventilation of mines."[24]

To Pacify a Tornado

Having visited the winds, having seized our part of fire, having felt those convective currents coursing through our own veins, we are ready to take on the thing itself—unaccommodated storm. In theory, it shouldn't be all that difficult for a woman to own the storm, essentially an invaginative process. When different streams of air meet, waves rise along the surface of contact; and eventually, as our globe spins, these waves begin to curl in. The crest of the wave becomes the eye of the storm: an occluded low-pressure pocket. The greater the thermal contact between the two streams of air, the more turbulent the eddies formed, the profounder the enfoldment. As the excited air mounts, further energy for its spiral ascent is released by the condensation process, during which some of this energetic updraft cools to form clouds that build up and up as long as the ecstatic air, whirling about the hollow center of the storm, fed from below the cloud column, maintains a higher temperature than its surroundings. And so long as contrasting dry air keeps moving it aloft, the momentum escalates. Inner and outer cloud boundaries form deflecting surfaces off which Oya the tornado wildly sheers. There would seem to be no form of the goddess that does not rise along the edges.

Surely this is it, the peak experience. But no, in time, even cloud space can come to seem confining to a cyclonic whirl. So much energy accumulated and released within the low-pressure core of that vaporous column inevitably leads to the generation of violent sub-eddies, bursting

OYA

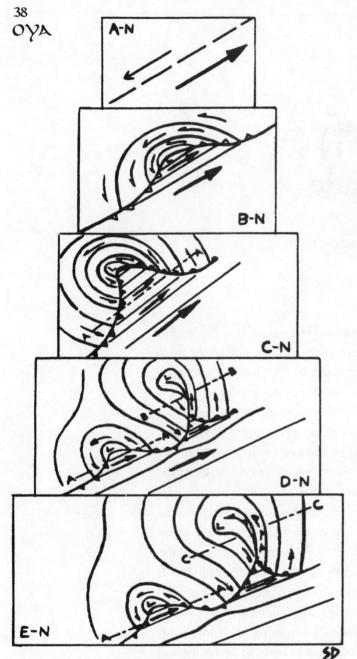

forth on their own into the open sky. Thus tornadoes are born—Oya's children, herself multiplied. No anemometer has survived to tell the velocity of their winds, no barograph to record how low the pressure at their center is. *Eeeeepa!* as the Yoruba say. What a goddess! Destruction shadowing their passage above ground, usually these runaway vortices shoot off horizontally or at a diagonal; but now and again they find the base of the home-cloud more congenial to their development. Darkly condensed, extending a hollow eye-on-a-stem (sinister telescope and suction pump combined), the reckless swirl descends for a more immediate contact with whatever happens to be on the ground. Then suddenly somebody's house, enveloped in a low-pressure casing, explodes from within and the roof whirls off, joints, struts, and all, to be deposited in somebody else's compound.

Domestic violence. Insanity. Despite the terror it inspires, there is something irresistible about that phenomenon, which, in the words of the meteorologist, "has a preference for warm and unstable air-mass parcels in preference to cool and stable ones."[25]

Formation of a dynamic cyclone between two air masses of different character moving in opposite directions with a cyclonic shear of wind velocities. The letters A—E refer to various stages of its formation. N refers to Northern Hemisphere. At stage A, the two air masses are flowing side by side, separated by a discontinuity or "frontal" surface. The action of friction and deflecting forces produces a low—pressure area and a wave in the frontal surface: stage B. The wave deepens, C, until the two fronts interlock or "occlude." D shows the warm front being forced aloft. E shows the reverse situation: an upper cold front. Source: Garbell, *Tropical and Equatorial Meteorology*, pp. 10–11.

Objects, or people, for such a little monster, whose girth rarely exceeds a kilometer, are to be compulsively seized, intensely toyed with for a while, only to be just as suddenly abandoned for a new possibility presenting itself upon the horizon. And we regard the playful, fateful creature with awe until it seizes, especially when it seizes erotically upon us, forcing us into its swirl, only to smash us down miles from where our delicate feelings were once complacently housed. Our culture provides labels, like "borderline," but no magic with which to civilize its conduct nor ritual with which to incorporate its scintillating energy.

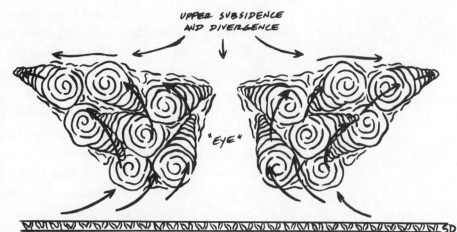

Schematic cross-section through the active portion of a mature tropical cyclone showing the eye and the anvil-shaped configuration of the cloud. Source: Garbell, *Tropical and Equatorial Meteorology*, p. 8.

The Yoruba, as we shall see in the story-poem to follow, approach the tornado first by calming the eye of the beholder. And how is the eye calmed? Paradoxically, perhaps, by arousal. The sacrificial ingredients placed upon the eye focus and empower the subject. Only then do the elders begin propitiatory gestures that will woo the object of

Typical distribution of the most violent convective activity and precipitation in a tropical cyclone. Arrow indicates direction storm is blowing. Source: Garbell, *Tropical and Equatorial Meteorology*, p. 91.

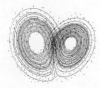

vision, the spun-off storm, into disclosing its compassionate, energizing side. The interchange is an intimate one: a mutual, even gently humorous process of recognition that establishes human relation to divine force without presumptuously seeking to limit it.

The following recitation from Ifa, the Yoruba oracle, describes how a conscientious, well-instructed young priest (equivalent in our culture to something between English professor and psychotherapist) comes to terms with natural feminine violence. At the sociological level, the wooing of storm with snails is a typically patriarchal gesture. But this is not the deeper meaning of the oracle, which ritually stages the bringing in or "owning" of one's own violence, thereby transforming its capricious, destructive aspects into creative, libidinal energy (represented in this story by goods and riches). The goddess is violent. The Yoruba diviners recognize her. And so, through them, may we. Our Western patriarchy, in turning away from the storm at the door, has raised the specter of catastrophic ire. We but toy with the darker side of the goddess.

how to pacify a tornado (with snails)

Now we shall explain what it is we call "Oya"
Now we shall praise Oya
By praising the second row of Ofun Osa
Which Orunmila says is called "Very White"
Meaning "Swept Clean."
Ifa, I say, Let her rip! *Hai! Lọ ya!*
Twist! Tear! They ask, Where?
It tore up the place of our friend Alara
Child of Established-wealth
10 Tore his house to shreds as he sat comfortably
Swept up all his money, all his clothes, everything—
So that his people wept
What sort of a thing is this? (*Hà á to ya bayi?*)
We looked around
Nothing to be seen
Aha! What sort of an invisible housecleaning?

Orunmila says, It's very white!
Ifa, I say, Let her rip! *Hai!*
They ask, Where now?

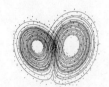

20 This time it cleaned out King Ajero
A peppery-tempered fellow, Moneybag's child
Son of Palm-oil-slick-on-the-surface-of-the-water
Turned that household into confusion
What sort of a thing is this (*Iru kini yi*)
Flailing the air with its cowtail switch
Massively, massively?
The whole wide world grew conscious of its strength—
Heaving things up, stacking them every which way
And everybody was afraid
30 Of being ground up in this terrible mortar
Meanwhile, whatever it was took off

Orunmila said for the third time:
It is very white! A clean sweep!
Ifa, I say, Let her rip! *Hai!*
Where? Any new reports?
Hold on, down she comes
Upon the town of Orangun
Hai! That one, master of tongues—
Crownbirds strut in his courtyard
40 Crownbirds fed by inherited servants
Hai! This thing forcibly thrust its way through the wall
Sounding its own drum
Stomping majestically, *whissh, swissh, thump!*

And all the hangers-on who had been sitting around open-eyed
Were blinded
Heh? What sort of a whisk is this?
What's going on?
Those on the farms cannot get in touch with their families
In town; those in the compounds are all rushing out to the
50 Farm plots, colliding with farmers returning, hurriedly
All's in confusion. What's going on? End of the world? Aha!
Orunmila said, quietly
And this time there were some who listened:
It is very white! A clean sweep!
Ifa, I say, Let her rip! *Hai!*
Its speed? Unknown. Direction?
Heading for young diviner's house
You had better warn him.

Greetings, apprentice of Orunmila

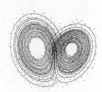

60 Something is coming. And when it arrives
It will bring you good fortune
If quickly you sacrifice
Two kola nuts, four sixpence
Touch each eye, saying:
My sight, don't go!
Sacrifice, in addition: snails, shea butter
Palm oil, and plenty of money.
Put those eye-protectors on Ifa's shrine
And let the adepts sing praises on your behalf
70 For whenever whatever this thing is
Arrives, it will bring you good fortune

The apprentice diviner did everything he was told
Atonement completed, somebody suggested:
Now have your wife prepare food for everyone
So they will stay on. Good!
As they were sitting leisurely around
Something tore! *Hai! Hai!*
Burst in, struck the ground with a roar
Just then Eshu appeared:
80 Tell me, in a thrice
Which of you did
Or did not sacrifice?
The assembled diviners answered with a single voice:
Our apprentice put himself upon the correct path
Hmmmm, Eshu said, Is that so? What did he provide?
Snails, shea butter, money, palm oil, they said
Furthermore, he touched his eyes with four sixpence
Two kola, then set his sights upon Ifa
Very good, said Eshu

90 Now that Something tore into the house
And paralyzed everyone with fright, save Eshu
Who gallantly stepped forward:
Hai! Hai! I greet you for arriving
Oya, I greet the elegant turbulence of your stride!
Then he offered her sixteen snails
A bowl of shea butter, and a flask of palm oil
All of which Oya swallowed in one gulp
Whereupon, with bulging eyes and a walloping sound
She began to vomit
100 What was she throwing up?
Everything collected from Alara, Ajero, and Orangun
Spewed forth upon Apprentice-diviner's floor

And he became wealthy at once

What shall we call her?
Can we not keep her?
Please don't go! (urged Apprentice-diviner)
All these things swept into my household
Might you not give the like to others?
I might, said Whatever-it-was
110 I will, if they but realize that:
She who stove in Alara's house and captured his goods
She who drove into Ajero's house and took what she could
She who tore into Orangun's house
Shook him up, sucked him dry, blinded his eyes
She am I who came down just now
And I will never depart from your house
If you know how to take care of me
Feed me correctly and you will become the
Richest man in the world
120 For I am Oya!
Who knows how to calm me down
Knows how to prosper

Heu! said Apprentice-diviner,
What wrecks your house also makes it thrive!
The Father-of-secrets knew this all the time

[*Reprise*]
Orunmila says, Very white! A clean sweep!
Let her rip! say I
Watch out, Apprentice-diviner
You have but two alternatives:
130 Two thousand enemies waiting to put you down
Two thousand charms for avoiding death
Sacrifice! How?
Cover your eyes with four sixpence and two kola
Then snails, shea butter, and palm oil will calm her down
So Eshu welcomed Oya
Offered her food
Made her feel at home
And she vomited
Aftermath of the storm upon the floor. . . .

140 Travel to Ifa often
And see the blessings of Oya.
On that day Oya blew into the world she exaggerated.
Suddenness means tornado.

Swept-clean means Oya
The explanation has been given. Greetings
For the sacrifice prescribed and accepted.[26]

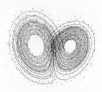

A preliminary note on the supernatural characters: Orunmila (who enters the narrative at line 4) is a way of personifying the oracle as its own divine spokesman and, occasionally, as its paradigmatic client, whose role here is assumed by the Apprentice-diviner. Eshu (who does not appear until line 79) and is the Yoruba trickster-mediator between human individuality and the vast energies of the gods. Eshu is the messenger who carries the sacrifices we make to their appropriate loci in spiritual space.

As above, so below. It is the premise of all geomantic systems of divination, like Ifa, that lived-in world and cosmic domain are mirror images of each other. The diviner who recited these verses provides an ingenious depiction of this situation in his verbal image of the confusion (lines 48–50) going on in the human community—people rushing back and forth between habitations and farms—while the converging air masses overhead are generating a mysterious tornado. Of course the same confusion is going on in the Oya-struck client's psyche. Nor does the oracular imagination shirk the task of conceiving a way to represent that which is "outer" and unseen as "inner" and visible.

Until this wind-force enters Apprentice-diviner's compound to be fed, since only the results of its fury are known, the tornado naturally proposes itself in the form of a question: "What sort of a thing is this?" (All we have is the symptom; what's the cause?) The preparing of the client's eyes with coins and stimulating kola nuts will enable him to look at whatever it is without becoming blind in the face of its divine otherness or cowed by its superior power. The tornado cannot be conceived of as enemy by the desiring eyes that take it in, as a projection (in psychological terms) is "withdrawn." But a mediating principle at the threshold (of the house, of consciousness) is needed. Therefore, it is the client's personal Eshu (his principle of individuation deified) who welcomes the storm and names it acceptably, "Oya."

At this point the weather of the narrative turns around. What had been conveyed in broad, heavy strokes (the wrecking of compounds, people running around) becomes more focused, engagingly humorous. What Oya is fed causes an inversion of behavior. The sacrificial ingredients, which the wild creature slurps up in an undifferentiated primal gulp, act

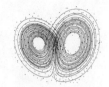

as an emetic. Low-pressure suction becomes high-pressure vomiting, and to the pious man's compound are attracted all those riches that had been playfully lifted from the three worldly kings blind to Oya's majesty. Now, why did these particular substances trigger Tornado's peripety?

According to the Yoruba system of correspondences, shea butter and snails are most efficacious in the calming down of heated behavior in women. Numerous are the mythic instances in which one of the so-called white forces of reason and balance feeds "white" substances to overenergetic female forces. Although Orunmila often employs them, shea butter and snails are basic ritual foods of Obatala (literally "King of the White Cloth"), the Yoruba god who exercises the principle of creativity within the context of male generative power. More inclusively, then, the appeal is to reason—clinically not a bad function to build up in someone overwhelmed by primal terrors and vortical depression. On another level, the sacrificial ingredients accomplish a sort of libidinal transfusion. Obatala's ritual snails contain quintessential semen, which the Yoruba, like the ancient Greek mythobiologists, associate with spiritual refinement, as opposed to the rowdy blood of animals and women. Thus, to give snail-liquid to a hot female force is symbolically to impregnate her. Should she be strident, this should calm her down. It will also bring out the soft, hidden aspects of her temperament. In turn, the negotiating male (for it's really his story) is acquiring confidence.

The oily paste made from the kernel of the shea tree (*Butyrospermum parkii*) is the product of a laborious process of refinement engaged in by women as a cottage industry throughout West Africa. And it is the process as well as the product that is implied; for a tornado can't come into a person's consciousness overnight. Apart from its culinary use, shea butter provides illumination in traditional clay or iron lamps. Passion, refined, illuminates. Palm oil, on the other hand, is a condiment with a very strong flavor. Ontologically viewed, it is a "red" substance favored by vital woman-power, which the male establishment construes as witchcraft and makes every effort to conciliate. The palm oil signifies that Oya is being welcomed as a Great Witch whose powers are necessary to render divination efficacious.

An inchoate natural force enters the house/head and, although still rather amorphous, finds a voice comprehensible to men. Treated to a balanced sacrificial diet of white medicines with a dash of red, the tornado—generative power of the feminine, promising loyalty in return for

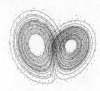

continued homage, will bracket its destructive potential and move in. Even the best-intentioned men sometimes forget that continuous need for homage, lack of which is apt to send Oya off into a tailspin. The Yoruba, like all traditional African cultures, deeply reverence the mother.

The name of the oracular configuration, Ofun Osa, reflects the balance of white and red. *Ofun* means "white," more specifically "white chalk," a sanctifying and cooling substance. But the tornado, as Orunmila insists, is also "very white"—an agent of purification. Thus, reddening our eyes, we appropriately desire it as it best is. *Osa* is associated with red camwood paste, a beautifying and fecundating agent. As a verb, the word *oṣa* means "to ventilate," which is exactly what Oya, properly reverenced does: clears the air.

The tornado's entrance is a cathartic event. Oya's whisk, her *ìrùkẹ̀* (see lines 25 and 46), cleanses. To whirl it about with upraised hand, thus dramatically to represent her whipping up of a storm, is at the same time to perform a ventilating action. Storms clear the air and dispel pollution. To wield Oya's *ìrùkẹ̀* with a series of down-stroking flicks is to get rid of negative energies clinging to whomever is thus whisked. The first human sound to be heard early in the morning in an African compound is that of a woman sweeping the place clean of the previous day's refuse. Oya is with her then.

Oya's River

I

According to Ifa, the Niger River was produced in the following manner. The king of the Nupe (northern neighbors of the Yoruba) consulted the oracle in time of war. How might he prevent invasion? Ifa replied that the besieged king should procure a length of black cloth and appoint a virgin to tear it. The king's choice fell upon his own daughter. Summoned by the elders (her father, the oracle priests, the generals), the young woman took up the black cloth. O-ya—"She tore"—it. Then she flung the two pieces upon the ground, whereupon, before the wondering eyes of the assembled Nupe, the cloth turned into black water, which spread out and began to flow protectively around the nucleus of the kingdom, now become an island.[27] Though the Nupe eventually transferred their capital to the mainland, Jebba Island remains in the midst of the Niger. Descendants of the Yoruba in Cuba speak of Oya's Island as Haitians speak of Guinée: it is the place of return, the place where the souls of the dead go, from which they may be called back spiritually to bless the living.

What strikes one upon inquiry as odd is that the Nupe themselves, particularly those few elders who still live on Jebba Island, have no knowledge of the event. The tearing of the black cloth is not a Nupe story. The Nupe do not practice divination by means of Ifa's oracle. They do not call the river "Oya." It is a Yoruba story, projected, as we would say, upon the Nupe. It is a story of a foreign princess from a bordering kingdom, which presumably the Yoruba themselves were preparing to invade. A subsequently unattainable kingdom, therefore, was Nupe. But the princess was not entirely out of bounds. She could be brought across, she and her black-cloth power. At a later stage of legendary history, Oya crossed the river to marry Shango, the thunder king, whose mother was also reputedly Nupe.

The thanatological import of the cloth-tearing story is intertwined with the political. Limitations are set upon human endeavor that geographically coincide with limitations on the expansion of Oyo-Yoruba power. The landsmen of Shango have been privy to certain magical techniques by means of which spirits may be empowered to return upon ritual occasion to greet the living human community, but politically they never succeeded in controlling the segment of the Niger River that formed the northern boundary of their empire. Neither, for that matter, did the Nupe, even though they were able to exercise a certain indirect control by contractual arrangement with those who ran the rapids and maneuvered the currents.

All along the river, rain magic and the prerogatives of transport traditionally belong to a special caste of canoemen who, in the region we are concerned with, are called Kede. (Upriver they are called Sorko, and even farther upriver, Marka). Upon these technicians of river travel both the Nupe and downstream commercial kingdoms allied with the Yoruba were economically dependent. Besides carrying trade goods and transporting officials, the Kede also used to serve as tax collectors for the Nupe and as carriers of tribute, in which they shared. The suspicion arises that the princess of the black cloth belonged to this group. Were water magic to be performed to ward off invaders, who but a Kede could do it? Perhaps the black cloth could generate storm clouds as well. Rip it, and there's a cloudburst; rip it again, a flood.

As Oya moves in the ancient stories from virginal daughter to king's partner, Oya's magical water turns back into cloth. From a Yoruba religious perspective, the island kingdom surrounded by water looks like a topographical metaphor for Oya in masquerade form. Behind the cloth is a secret "island" of transcendent consciousness. But how about the "Kede" aspect of Oya? In what ways does this survive her various permutations? Throughout West Africa the dead are believed to be ferried in canoes

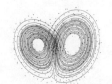

across the three rivers separating this world from the other world. In certain instances and locales the Yoruba, a people of the land, actually bury their dead in canoes. As goddess of transition between life and death, death and life, Oya owns this fleet plying her waters. Furthermore, turning back to the "Traditional Praises of Oya" (page 8, line 15), we now may behold her in a new light, standing like a Kede:

> . . . *at the frontier*
> *between life and death*
> *Customs officer of multitudes!*

Thus, to a now obscurely remembered, frustrating politicoeconomic situation is wedded a theology of the dark, transformative goddess who answers to the Yoruba name for the Niger River. Since the Kede were masters of river trade and river ritual, all either Nupe or Yoruba could hope to control was the crossing at Jebba Island. There land caravans from north to south would have to pay tribute. To stage the oracular cloth-tearing story in Nupe implies that death's realm (represented by one's hostile neighbors), besieged by life (represented by one's own people), was bound to win, although an alliance could be made and death's daughter brought from her impregnable island to the mainland we're all a part of. Thus she will continue to perform her original act of severance, but with a different intention. She will tear the cloth in order to produce a fluid boundary; and death will remain an invisible kingdom, secure from human invasion, though not, if tribute be paid, hostile to travelers passing from one mode of existence to another.

Ọ-ya. The vulnerable kingdom of the self is under siege. Warlike pressures within and without threaten to overwhelm its integrity. They seem to be outside only, though, these perilous invaders. Personal existence flickers dangerously as a candle niched in a windy tunnel. Now or never! whispers an oracular voice. Virginal hands grope for the infinitesimal flaw along the selvage edge and rip, rip the black cloth. And it happens. In a flood Oya's dark river comes to surround that nucleus of self with vital flowing power.

The ripping of the cloth by the Nupe princess was an act of deterrent magic to render a high-risk kingdom not only out of bounds but invisible. It seems that the others have vanished, flooded out. But from

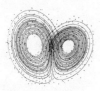

the mainland no one sees the island anymore. It has, like the old-fashioned photographer, disappeared behind black cloth. The image enters through the lens and dies in the heart.

Oya's protective gesture with the black cloth tears social reality to shreds. Like a glandular secretion, it touches us at the instinctual level of defense. It renders us temporarily "beside ourselves" and therefore impervious to attack. It is the goddess herself who will magically meet the threatening situation for us. She will deflect the enemy's attention so we can escape. Or, awestruck by the sudden apparition of the cloth, the opposition staggers back. The war no longer exists. Whatever drama there was takes place on a different level, as when a child's refusal suddenly escalates into tantrum.

The goddess in such situations behaves like an octopus who, during her fecundation period, emits a dazzling display of colors. Males rush "like luminous arrows" toward the brilliant female octopus. But when she is alarmed, this same creature injects into the troubled waters a cloud of black ink, which does not diffuse itself but rather retains its shape, persisting as a dummy double of the anxious cuttlefish. The black likeness engages the enemy's attention while, changing its color, the real thing takes off in a different direction.[28]

Chemically, what the octopus secretes is melanin, resistant to analysis on account of its density.[29] Psychiatrically, its inky behavior would be diagnosed as an omnipotent maneuver out of stress. Suggestive hypotheses link such strategies, including possession-trance, to the neuroendocrine system.[30] I wonder, when the news about endorphins is all in, whether in the nether regions of pituitary and hypothalamus the triggering and secretion of melanocyte-stimulating hormone will not turn out to be in some way linked to these natural painkillers. For Oya recognizes no barriers between geography and physiology. She tears her black cloth anywhere circumstances dictate. However the threat materializes, her protective process answers inkily.

Like the octopus, Oya is a creature of many colors, but nine rather than eight tentacles distinguish her from her counterpart in the invertebrate kingdom. Nine brilliant streamers adorn her ritual standards propped on the floor beside offerings to the local dead. The masks worn by her children, those who return to life after death, are multicolored, Medusa-shaped creatures. Her preferred colors, though, are crimson, brown, and purple—the hues of flowing blood, vital animal spirits, and royal prerogative. The black cloth is only a shape she assumes when those she's partial to find themselves hard pressed. Behind it she herself gets away. Look what happened when Jebba Island was besieged. She tore, and the next thing we hear of Oya she's gone over to the enemy, as queen. Behind the blackness of death, the image of the corpse displayed as decoy, the soul too, changing its colors, slips away, to return, it may be, at some future time upon that red stream leading into the womb of a different mother.

II

So we allow the imagination to drift upon backwaters of the torn cloth story. Yet these black waters we have envisioned spreading out and rushing by are an aspect of her river's hydrology. Oya the goddess may be metaphysically positioned upon an island between this world and the next, but the river she made really does have a double flood: a normal and an anomalous runoff.

If you remained on Jebba Island for an entire solar year, you would see the first spate, fed by streamlets from the Atakora Mountains on the right bank and by the Sokoto affluent on the left, arrive in late summer—August or the beginning of September. Then, beginning in December and continuing into March, the still relatively swollen river would rise again. This is the mysterious "black flood," as local observers have always called it. Laden with decaying organic matter, this second, surprise flood would be an excellent cloak of inundation to throw down before the horses of unsuspecting invaders.

This double flood bears witness to a curious history undergone by Oya's river, as does the twisted trajectory that baffled European explorers for generations. The course of the Niger is so complicated that its source was sought in a variety of directions. All this chasing about on expeditions to track her to her hidden origins must have amused Oya in the old days, for as a river her own experience had been the opposite—a refusal not of opening but of closure. The rapid shifts of direction along her course were once strategies for death-avoidance—a desperate search for outlets and replenishment, new life that the dying river found. Oya is a conundrum. She is a double goddess: not here but there, not there but here; on the side of death, on the side of life. As a river, the seemingly integral Oya is actually composed of two streams, each with a radically different origin, flowing together now.

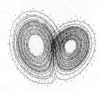

The southeastern slope of Oya's river began its hydrolic life as a Pleistocene wadi in the Sahara. Rains came and the river flowed. Rains abated and the river recoiled. The first pluvial age pushed the river across the Badjibo Sill, where rapids formed (only recently tamed by the Kainji Dam). Beyond the Sill the river followed the path of least resistance to the sea. Sloping through land now farmed by the Yoruba, the river, joining with a powerful affluent from the east, the Benue, sought peace in the salty Bight of Benin. Then, at a certain moment of what surely seemed an endless flow of time, death struck. High-pressure anticyclones evaporated the Saharan tributaries out of the ancient wadi. These streams now look from the air like the imprints of leafless trees. Occasionally in summer these fossilized remains of the river's upper reaches are flash-flooded with Pleistocene memories, which quickly subside into sands of today.

Meanwhile the northeastern slope of the great river was having its own contrasting hydrological problems. The sources of the Pleistocene Djoliba (as this part of the river is locally named) remained fresh in the Guinée highlands. However, a shift in the earth's crust during the Tertiary period deflected the flow of this stream from its original course across the Bara plain. The river had been accustomed to flowing across this plain on its way to a deep trench, which aeon after aeon it filled to create an inland sea (a long way east of the wadi mentioned above). Then dry winds, those we have already witnessed drying up the sources of the other stream, formed a series of sinister ergs barring the Djoliba's path to its inland sea. Unable to get out of the plain, the river from Guinée's highlands had no alternative but to back up. The Djoliba flooded the Bara plain. The rains persisted in the highlands. The Bara plain itself became a dune-blockaded inland sea. More rain. Finally, in the process of submerging every low-lying parcel of earth within reach, by chance the engorged and frantic Djoliba stumbled upon the narrow Sill of Tosaye, across which it could discharge its nourishing flood into the starving riverbed below.

Thus both rivers were saved. Geologists speak of a "capture." Perhaps reciprocal, sudden bonding is more in tune with the mood of those needy forces at the Sill of Tosaye. The overflowing one received channeling. The deprived, incisive one was provided with luxuriance, to which it thankfully yielded. At that juncture Oya's river as we know it came into being.

For millennia thereafter the Bara plain continued to flood in response to the rainy season. Having reached its peak, the inland tide would then turn and begin to run out through the river's main channel and over the Sill of Tosaye as across the granite commissure of a torrential brain. The receding of these bounteous waters revealed lush pastures of borgu grass for future herds of the nomadic Peul to graze upon and ponds of breeding fish for future Bozo fishermen to trap at the drainage points. This,

redolent with experience of mud, grass, and cow dung, is the "black flood" that pours past Jebba Island during the cold months of the year.

At the end of the Niger's complicated trajectory, the two floods—local run-offs and drainage of the inundated plain— coincide at the outer, brackish delta. Together "white" and "black" floods fill the swamps and overflow the creeks where the Ijo people live. Upon one full surge the water spirits, so they think, are swept into their villages. When the tide recedes in late December/early January, it carries away the accumulated sins of these Ijo villages. In certain communities these pollutions are sped on their way by seagoing

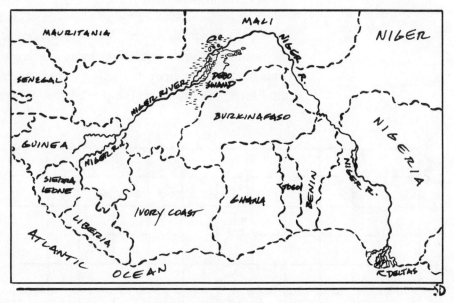

Map of the Niger River showing the inner and outer deltas and Jebba Island.

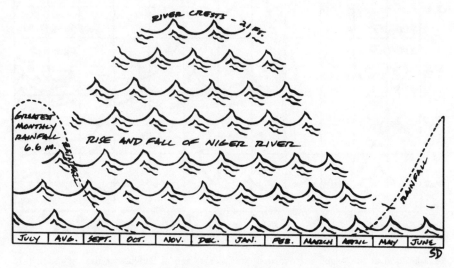

The flooding of the plain whose draining waters become the "black flood." Source: Pascal James Imperato, "Nomads of the Niger," *Natural History* 81, no. 10 (December 1972): 62.

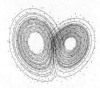

canoes into which they are ritually transferred. In the old days a human scapegoat used to carry them in a canoe-shaped vessel upon his head until the cleansing flood pulled him under the ocean.

These purificatory floods merging in the estuaries of the lower Niger delta are actually three thousand miles and an entire rain-year apart in origin: Oya's time warp. To bathe in them, as is customary on New Year's Eve, with a certain geological awareness is to be buoyed by a sense of mystery comparable to that felt by one's fellow bathers, who dream of water spirits and underwater voyages to the great python's kingdom. But at this moment, far from its healing waters, one's Niger thoughts autumnally turn to reflections on the precariousness of all existence—even that of rivers.

Double flood of the Niger, as recorded ninety years ago at Badjibo, at the rapids, slightly upstream of Jebba Island. Source: Capitaine Lenfant, *Le Niger* (Paris: Librairie Hachette, 1903), p. 230.

Because of failure of rain even in the mountains, at the sources of Oya's river, for the first time in human memory the Bara plain did not flood. The cattle, accustomed to grazing on the borgu grasses there, have died. The itinerant fishing communities have been moving farther and farther upstream in quest of slim fish blocked behind a new dam on one of the Niger's affluents. The lakes at the apex of the river's northerly trajectory are sandy depressions. In early 1985 the affluent called the Bani, which should have been

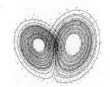

flowing along the eastern edge of the great plain past Segou, San, and
Mopti, had given way to rocks, sand banks, and evaporating puddles.
Some said the active waters of the Bani had slipped into a fault and gone
underground. Over the rim of Tosaye, however, water from the Niger's
principal channel continued to flow down into the rocky streambed engraved aeons ago by vigorous streams leading out of the Sahara. At Gao
the river, still alive though drastically diminished, had shifted its course
three kilometers in search of a more efficient fall line. To swim in that
faithful remnant of flow was a prayerful act of body. That year's end,
impossible to believe, there would be no black flood at Jebba Island.

III

The river is matrix of memory. All along the Niger from Kangaba
to Jebba Island, those with ritual and psychic access to the invisible world
will tell you the same thing in different words. Already in the course of
these pages it has been said that the river is a bard, endlessly transmitting
the old stories, and that Faro the water spirit encases the burning word of
impulse in intelligible moisture. Water contains and conducts utterance.
Here is a further ramification of this belief.

In Niamey, Niger, a water-spirit priest whose family for centuries
has been the custodian of esoteric knowledge of the river spoke to my
concerns about secularization of the spirit and exploitation of traditional
ceremonies by foreign photographers. His family's competence in such
matters derives in part from their symbolic alliance with the silurian, an
ancient mudfish. Indeed, they consider themselves in some way consubstantial with this deep-burrowing creature, which need not rise to breathe.
He told me that the danger of exposure of magical wisdom was less than
I feared because it was substantially stored in the bodies of the possession
cult dancers, who traced certain concepts of cosmic organization on the
sand with their feet. Of these patterns most of the dancers would not have
been able to give a rational explanation; but highly initiated elders were
even able to read invisible points in the dancers' patterns—spaces representing spiritual beings too ancient and august to possess human beings
and be danced by them. To perform such dances before the camera, therefore, would be in no way to disclose their meaning, to which even the
dancers themselves were not privy. "All along the river," he said, "from
sources to sea, religion—Islam, Christianity—will not be able to destroy

tradition. All people who live near the water defend it. Contact with water by its very nature safeguards the primordial secrets."[31] I have often thought of these words, hoping that cultural history—the persistence of a magical world beneath the various monotheisms and materialisms imported into Africa—will continue to bear them out. Persuaded of their subjective truth, one who does not live along the banks of Oya's river stubbornly seeks confirmation of these words from the element itself. For our concept of the unconscious is only an analogue of that intrinsic persistence which those who speak thus of the river are guardedly conveying.

How does the river remember? And how does it transmit sacred information without profanely disclosing it? And why can this process be suggestively compared to sacred dancing? How does the river itself "dance"?

Stand in the river facing upstream. Look closely: a translucent buffer is continuously forming about your obtrusive knees. A protective pattern is being "spoken." Turning to face downstream, you notice a pattern of vortices reverberating from that buffered place where your knees have obstructed the river's flow. In liquid embroidery patterns the little spirals to the right of each knee are rotating left; those to the left of your knee spin right. Both chains are swirling from the outer edge of the pattern inward. The message is involutional.

Meanwhile, both banks are exerting a steady pressure to which the water responds in grander whorls, setting up a double circulation of currents from midsurface to shore. Down and under and toward the center "dances" the flow, before rising and bending shoreward again. Out of such encounters with warm shore and obtrusive objects (rocks, canoe prows, wading creatures) are created periodic, interpenetrating forms that persist through time despite displacement of one spate of water drops by another. The patterns recall themselves. The forms recur—whatever new objects may occasion them. The river's energy gives impetus to their formation, these patterns, which, however they may vary in scope or intensity, remain constant.[32]

Thus the intricate sacred dances are repeated by generations of dancers. Freed by the spirits entering them to become like the element that primarily composes them, the bodies of the dancers trace intricate patterns upon the ground and in the air, which are intelligible only to

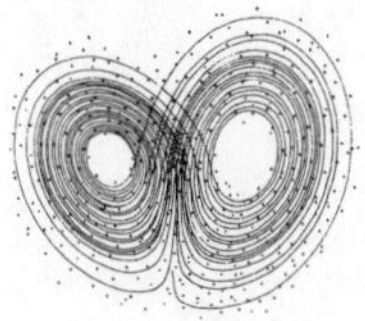

those of "high degree". The patterns replicate the beginnings of things, the interplay of stresses, and discrepancies of temperature. Similarly, the mind of the bard is freed through attunement with water to elaborate heroic songs whose circulating rhythms and refrains give fluid forms to the details he partly recalls, partly invents. Feeling the pressure of time upon him, the bard creates periodic, interpenetrating forms to express the larger patterns of human experience it is his special competence to pass on to us in flow of speech. Through spiraling apertures we hear his music inwardly.

The patterns of the dances performed in ancient Crete were reflected in the intricate metrical patterns of songs accompanying them and stylized into stone pavements. *Labyrinth* is a word "of unknown origin."[33] I like to think of it as a watermark—trace of a flowing secret, never divulged, whose meaning through introversion can be replicated.

Upstream of Jebba Island there is a bridge to accommodate the modern equivalent of that traffic to and from north and south over which kings of Yoruba and Nupe lineages vied for control. Not properly taking into account those swirling, downward-sucking currents about the giant, concrete stride of the bridge, I risked drowning there. It was December 14, 1976. I remember making a great effort to reach a thick line of reeds, which, had the river not been so swollen, would have marked the shore. The reeds broke the speed of the runoff, but exploring feet could find no firm ground, only viscous mud. A fishing canoe that had put me off on a rock above the bridge came back to pick me up. The fishermen suspected, correctly, that the swimmer was not so competent as she assured them she was.

Later that evening, the oldest man on Jebba said that they no longer sacrifice a cow from the jutting rock as floods, both white and black, fling past the island. The island isn't what it once was, he said. Most of the fishermen have gone upriver to the lake that has formed behind the Kainji Dam. But it is Islam rather than underpopulation that is responsible for neglect of the propitiations. Then followed a curious discrepancy in the old man's talk. Though as a Muslim he spoke of the river as a male force, the offering they used to give to the river was a cow, he said. One does not throw a female animal to a male divinity.

Upriver the Sonrai, who perform the dances mentioned above, still give a cow every year to Harrakoi Dikko (Mother of the Waters).

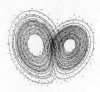

Downriver from Jebba, at Onitsha and Ida, towns from which the ruling class of Nupe are thought to have migrated, at the purificatory turn of the year when the black flood rushed by, it was not a cow but rather an obedient king's daughter who used to be thrown to the river.[34] So whatever negligence of custom or verbal cover-up, the pattern persists. A female animal appeases the goddess of the river.

Thinking Lightning

A river makes its own model. First a few drops, then a filament of water, and eventually a route is engraved for greater surges to follow. Water-fingers, feeling their way along earth surfaces of least resistance, instantly actualize their own premonitions. Unimpeded on flat ground, rivers trace periodic meanders—serpents of currents. For a long time, following Kenneth Craik,[35] I supposed that in all the realms of so-called inorganic phenomena, rivers must be unique in this regard, only belatedly to discover with astonishment what must be common knowledge among meteorologists. Lightning also makes its own model. Thus, from two correlates arose the possibility of a unified field theory of the natural intelligence of the goddess. And sure enough, confidently picking her way through the densest of forests, the old female buffalo (Oya's animal avatar) at the head of a file of young males, heifers, calves, and their mothers, she too etches out an itinerary.

Lightning was discovered rather belatedly in Oya's anthropomorphic career. Virginal river, tornado witch, buffalo-woman, all these phases had been mythologically accomplished before she settled down to become the senior wife of Shango, legendary founder of the Yoruba equivalent of "divine right of kings." Oya's role in empowering this dynastic succession will later be seen as crucial, her mask providing the *sine qua non* of ancestral validation. By the same token, Oya's electrical charge is so intertwined with Shango's that it would be perilous to speak of it without first introducing the great thunder god and paradigmatic Yoruba king to any who may still be unaware of his existence.

Kabiesi! Greetings to Majesty! When Shango dances—and no Yoruba god dances with more vitality and excitement—he gestures alternately to the heavens and to his balls. The dance "talks" of his thunderstones, seeds of his fecundity. Thus, as a divine force, Shango exalts; but as a human being, he found life unendurable. To begin with, his parentage was questionable. Estranged from himself, challenged by rival factions within the city and by warring kingdoms without, he understandably sought magical means with which to consolidate his power. Rumor had it that the king of Bariba (part of the Borgu federation) possessed a certain medicinal preparation enabling the owner (who places it beneath his tongue) to spit forth thunder-stones with voltage sufficient to knock whole armies out of commission. So from his capital at Old Oyo, Shango dispatched his favorite wife, Oya, to Bariba. Charm to the charming, Queen Oya accomplished her mission. Secretly, though, she kept as "dash" for her work a little parcel of lightning all her own.

Unfortunately, while experimenting from a mountaintop with his new power, Shango misdirected a gross bolt toward the precincts of his own palace. There were few survivors. Horrified at having thus annihilated those whose preservation should have been his profoundest concern, Shango fled the capital. On the way to an unknown destination, he hanged himself at a place subsequently called Koso. *Kòso* means "He did not hang," for therein lies the mystery. Shango disappeared into the ground and became a god (*òrìṣà*). (The *àyàn* tree from which he attempted to hang was divinized as Ayan, patron of drummers.) Oya, who had faith-

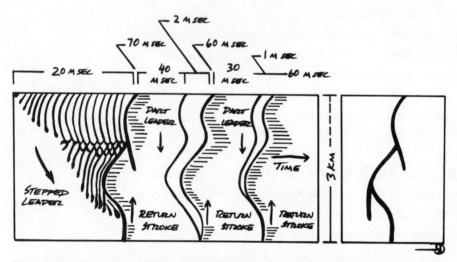

The luminous features of a lightning flash as would be recorded by a camera with a fixed lens and moving film. Time increases to the right. At far right is the same lightning flash as would be recorded with stationary film. Source: Martin A. Uman, *Lightning* (New York: McGraw-Hill, 1969), p. 6.

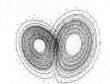

fully followed her husband from a distance, was so overwhelmed with grief that she too disappeared, into a swampy marsh at Irà. Together they now rule the stormy sky. Oya's winds precede thunderstorms. Shango's rain-seeds fertilize the earth. In between is the problematic provenance of lightning.

Although the Nigerian government placed a statue of Shango at the Kainji Dam to celebrate its dynamos and power lines, and although in the New World, Shango is often syncretized with Santa Barbara, patron saint of electrical storms, lightning is also iconographically associated with Oya, whose Catholic counterpart is generally considered to be Candelaria, Our Lady of Candlemas. The zigzag borders of the ancestral masquerades over which she presides speak lightning. And, closer to home, when a folkloric drama about the Yoruba gods was recently staged by a Latino theater company in New Jersey, Oya made her entrance in a purple satin turban from which sprouted a single jagged bolt.

Since Shango's meteorological competence clearly resides in the fertile thunder-stones themselves rather than in his aim, which can go awry, since it's the rumble and thrust that characterize his presence in the heavens, why won't the sacerdotal establishment (if not the obviously confused Nigerian government) come right out and say that to Oya belongs the light and to Shango the sound of nature's most theatrical production? Or could there be after all a modicum of poetic justice in the old story about Oya's trip to the foreign king on behalf of her harassed husband? She herself was harassed as well, one imagines, by her situation as a royal wife with its cumbersome protocol and moody, frightened household. For she stole the lightning, and one steals what one deeply needs.

A scientific truth is reflected in the apparent contradictions of popular iconography and cult dogma. Obviously, lightning precedes thunder. But small spurts (of the sort Oya put under her own tongue), invisible to the naked eye, in turn precede the brilliant flashes we actually see. In other words, as suggested earlier, lightning too makes its own model, but at such tremendous speeds and at such great distances from the observer that this pioneering behavior has gone unnoticed save by the inspired intuitions of African mythologues and, more recently, by various ingenious recording devices developed by the Western scientific community.

During the convective buildup of cumulonimbus storm clouds, an enormous electrical tension develops between the negatively charged central region of the cloud (undergoing rapid condensation) and the ground.

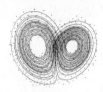

When this powerful attraction exceeds the breakdown potential of 25,000 volts per inch, discharge must occur, beginning near the ground-beholding base of the cloud. But no matter how irresistible the pull, its electric potential simply cannot support a spontaneous arc thrown across five kilometers of atmosphere—under normal conditions a rather indifferent conductor. An ionized path through the air has to be tried out by a relatively low-charged series of impulses known as the "stepped leader."

A modest cascade of electrons descends about 300 feet at a time, pauses after each "step" about fifty microseconds in order to scout for a semi-ionized path of least resistance, then continues along its tortuous way by fits and starts, in the process forming numerous lateral branches as contiguous pent-up energies are suddenly spurred to uncover themselves to the parent stream. All these "decisions" in our time-frame seem instantaneous. But to Oya they are the reflexive positioning of one fairly sure guess at a time. Only a faint series of glows mark their accomplishment upon the black screen of telephotographed night, but to Oya a vast candle path explores her darkness.

As the forward tip of this leader nears the ground, anticipatory streamers rise to meet it. (Synchronicity! Now we're getting somewhere, thinks Oya.) From treetops, from pointed pieces of metal, they tease acceptance from the descending charge, which quickly bestows its favor upon the most prominent; and the conducting channel is accomplished. A sudden sucking action pulls all loose electrons in the vicinity of the leader down to the ground. (Now look what I've done—too much of a good thing, thinks Oya.) Called the "return stroke," because the process begins at the bottom of the channel, this is the brilliant flash ev-

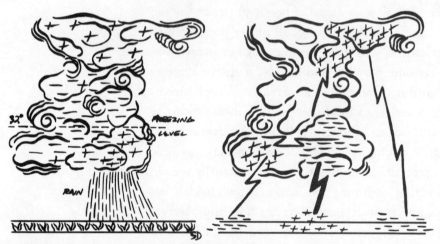

Distribution of electrical charge in thunderstorms shown in relation to altitude and freezing level. Source: Louis J. Battan, *The Nature of Violent Storms* (New York: Doubleday Anchor, 1961), p. 69.
A spectrum of possible lightning flashes. The heavy jagged line shows the most common cloud-to-ground type. After Peter E. Viemeister, *The Lightning Book* (Cambridge, MA: MIT Press, 1972), p. 111.

erybody sees: "Lightning!"—publicly acclaimed. It may strike again and again thereafter, rapidly down the prepared channel, as intercloud tributaries created by the same intuitive method liberate other densely charged sectors. Though Oya's heart is no longer in this work (I've done it once), the attractive path perpetuates itself. Each strike remains a two-way process. The "stepped leader" is replaced by a "dart leader," which re-ionizes the way for luminous suction motions to follow. The pump is primed; light gushes up the spine of the cloud; then and only then comes royal thunder—loudest natural sound in the world—to speak in praise of the consummation.

But what moves thunder to come forward? The unimaginable heat inside the channel (as much as 30,000 degrees centigrade), pressing against its walls, forces expansion in the form of a shock wave that, after each lightning stroke, relaxes into an acoustical follow-up of much lower amplitude. So Shango's sound is really an expression of cosmic pleasure in release rather than anything like a tumultuous threat of chastisement—as popularly promulgated by thunder-priests of all times and denominations. What we hear depends on where we're standing. In general, the crash comes from the base of the channel and the ensuing rumble from within its molten twistings and turnings. But "crash" and "rumble," besides being inadequate to describe the magnificent timbre of thunder, far from exhaust its sonorous possibilities. There's the *boooooom* followed by silence, for example, which reflects an energetic high-altitude flash. And, seldom heard but extraordinarily significant in our context, there's that "rare ripping noise that can be imagined as the tearing of some cosmic cloth."[36] Indeed. Meteorologists who have heard this sound don't know how to account for it. Perhaps, they say, it is an acoustical record of a stepped leader that didn't make it (all the way to the ground).

It would seem impossible to describe electrical storms without falling into the language of reciprocal desire. Apart from what goes on in the molten channel, and leaving aside the stepped leader's brief flirtation with pointed objects on the ground, there's the fundamental pull between earth and sky, which the Yoruba symbolize as two halves of a closed calabash. This great container of all existence is calm. However, there would be no passion in the eternal embrace in whose midst life flourishes, were it not supplied by fiery Shango and Oya. Meteorologists, avoiding erotic overtones as best they can, speak of the ionosphere and the earth's surface as plates of a spherical condenser, the top of which must always maintain a

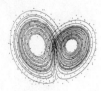

residual plus charge (masculine) and the bottom of which must always display a negative (feminine) propensity. Even though the atmosphere separating these "plates" is an indifferent conductor, some leakage (sublimation?) does occur. A perpetual current of about 360,000 volts escapes, a voltage sufficient to discharge earth's "condenser shell," were it not for thunderstorms, which wondrously generate enough supply current to maintain the electrical balance.

About two thousand thunderstorms must be taking place at any given moment of earth-time in order to satisfy the positive yearnings of those immobile electrons on the ground. But some hours of the global day-night continuum are more fruitful in this regard than others. The recharging process peaks between fourteen and twenty o'clock (Greenwich time) because of the stupendous effect of late-afternoon and early-evening action along the West African and Latin American portions of the intertropical front.[37] *Kabiesi! Eeeepa!*

The reciprocal desire of earth for sky and sky for earth realizes itself as fertility. For the Yoruba, fertility's paradigm is gemination. Inseparable companions of the sweltering leader core, Shango and Oya mythologically produce twins. That is, over and over they reproduce the collaborative identity established in the creation of their regenerative storms. Under the patronage of Shango and Oya, the Yoruba people themselves give birth to an astonishing number of fraternal twins (as many as 42 per 117 deliveries) as the skies over their heads produce thunderstorms at the second highest rate in the world.[38] Apart from the exemplary behavior of their royal gods, what could possibly be the connection? Lightning, as every schoolchild knows, causes some of the nitrogen in the atmosphere to combine with oxygen. The result, nitric oxide, is dissolved in rainfall and brought to earth as nitrates, which, absorbed by the soil, nourish vegetation . . . and subsequently "nourish" whatever genetic program opts for twins in the womb? On this question the goddess remains silent.

Although women are decried in the Yoruba folklore for their talkativeness (ranging from betrayal of sleeping-mat confidences to noisy and bitter squabbles among co-wives in the compound), actually they well keep their own counsel. It is the secrets they won't tell that exasperate men into the creation of a counterimage of irresponsible loquaciousness, invoked as a rationalization for excluding them from highly sensitive discussions of political and religious issues. Yet, as we shall see in the ensuing chapter, women's capacity for realizing projects (a virtue linked to the irrepressible vigor of their reproductive process) is always at least covertly called upon whenever concept verges upon transformative action. At this juncture, words, becoming magically efficacious, secure pointed results. And it is Oya who speaks, through her human surrogate, with an infinitesimal spit of conduction—enough to ionize whatever copulative corridor.

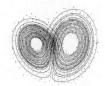

This little bit of lightning that Oya kept for herself, hidden under her tongue, is represented upon her altars by a small pair of swords, by an ornamental saber, or, in the Americas, by a heavy-duty machete. She stole it originally, one supposes, out of deep foreboding that one day she would be swamped. But when that day came, she figured, why not? This weapon won't rust. One can skewer options anywhere. Stepping out into the dark hiatus between cloud and treetops for the first time gave her rather a shock. It is not so easy to ground one's impulses along a considered train of thought. But she persevered and greeted those anticipatory streamers like long-lost premonitions from another life. And with what sonorous satisfaction her now jovial consort greeted the coruscating accomplishment. Not that she took credit for such flashiness. Let admiration fall upon mere repercussion—the better to protect the hidden randomness of her enterprise, the nervy fun of it.

Notes

1. Pierre Verger, *Notes sur le culte des oriṣa et vodun* (Dakar: Ifan, 1957), p. 29.

2. Northrop Frye, "From Words of Power: Being a Second Study of the Bible and Literature," *The American Poetry Review*, November/December 1990, p. 7.

3. Mary Barnard, *Sappho: A New Translation* (Berkeley: Univ. of California Press, 1958), p. 44.

4. *The Notebooks of Leonardo da Vinci*, vol. 2, compiled and edited from the original manuscript by Jean Paul Richter (New York: Dover, 1970), p. 220.

5. Léopold Sédar Senghor, *Poèmes* (Paris: Editions du Seuil, 1964), p. 11. "L'ouragan" from *Chants d'ombre*. English version by Judith Gleason.

6. "Scientists Hope to Forecast Lightning Strikes," *New York Times*, July 8, 1986. The article, by Walter Sullivan, begins, "Wires trailed by rockets to trigger lightning flashes, cables between mountains to create 'upside down' thunderheads, computer-linked networks of observatories and other devices are helping scientists learn what energizes lightning and controls where it hits and how much damage it does."

7. Sullivan, "Scientists Hope."

8. Richard Broxton Onians, *The Origins of European Thought* (Cambridge: Cambridge Univ. Press, 1954), chap. 3, esp. pp. 50–51.

9. Camara Laye, *The African Child*, trans. James Kirkup (London: Collins, 1955), pp. 24–25. (*L'Enfant noir*, Paris: Librairie Plon, 1954.)

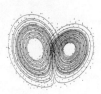

10. Laye, *African Child,* p. 26.

11. The literal translation of Djoliba is "River of Blood." But in Malinké and Bambara "River of the Bards" or "Bardic River" is homophonic to the first meaning, and many legends correlate the two. The interplay of words for *blood, word,* and *water* is part of the texture of heroic song. See Hugo Zemp, "La légende des griots malinké," *Cahiers d'études africaines* 6, no. 24 (1961).

12. I talked to a master kora player once, in 1970, who told me that when the Malian government sent him on tour to Zaire, he tuned perforce to the Zaire (Congo) River, who obliged by animating his strings with local mysteries and nostalgias, thus endowing the Malian with the power to move his foreign audience.

13. Madame de Ganay's account of Nyalé was subsequently published as "Un enseignment donné par le komo," by Solange de Ganay and Dominique Zahan, in *Systèmes de signs* (Paris: Hermann, 1978).

14. Aeschylus, *The Eumenides,* first stasimon, ll. 299–396.

15. Because the earth's surface rotates eastward at greater speed near the equator, any moving body on or above the earth's surface will tend to drift in accordance. Air moving toward the equator with the slower rotational speed of higher latitudes will tend to fall behind and veer west. Air flowing east will feel an additive pull—that of the earth—and flow faster. There is also a longitudinal drift due to centrifugal force caused by the earth's rotation, a force that exerts itself at right angles to the earth's axis. Thus, winds flow westerly toward the polar regions, the *-ly* suggesting a diagonal direction; and they flow northeast and southeast toward the equator, as illustrated in Figure 2.

16. C. G. Jung, "Psychology of the Transference," *Collected Works,* 16, p. 211.

17. Barnard, *Sappho,* p. 39.

18. Gaston Bachelard, *The Psychoanalysis of Fire,* trans. Alan C. M. Ross (Boston: Beacon press, 1968), p. 53.

19. Bachelard, *Psychoanalysis of Fire,* p. 56. Here he quotes Valéry.

20. Bachelard, *Psychoanalysis of Fire,* p. 9.

21. Bachelard, *Psychoanalysis of Fire,* p. 15.

22. Audrey I. Richards, *Chisungu: A Girl's Initiation Ceremony Among the Bemba of Northern Rhodesia* (London: Faber & Faber, 1956), p. 77.

23. I owe the idea for this game to William L. Dorn, author of *Meteorology with Marine Applications* (New York: McGraw-Hill, 1951).

24. The headmistress is quoting from *The New Columbia Encyclopedia* (New York: Columbia University Press, 1975), p. 647.

25. Maurice A. Garbell, *Tropical and Equatorial Meteorology* (New York: Pitman Publishing, 1947), p. 95.

26. This version of the text and commentary was published in *Parnassus: Poetry in Review,* Spring/Summer 1985. An earlier version was published in *A Recitation of Ifa, Oracle of the Yoruba* (New York: Grossman, 1973). The diviner who recited the text was the late Awotunde Aworinde of Oshogbo. The late John Ogundipe of Lagos and New York transcribed the text and worked with me on the first English version.

27. Chief Fagbemi Ajanaku, Araba of Lagos, personal communication, February 2, 1976.

28. David Tomtsett, "Sepia," Publications of the Liverpool Marine Biology Committee, *Memoires,* no. 32, September 1939, pp. 144–45. Cited by Edward C. Whitmont in *Psyche and Substance.*

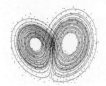

29. Dr. Frederick Holley, personal communication.

30. Raymond Prince, "Shamans and Endorphins," *Ethos* 10, no. 4 (Winter 1982): 420.

31. This interview took place in Niamey in April 1977. For an exoteric discussion of the choreography of the water spirits, see Judith Gleason, "Out of the Water, onto the Ground, and into the Cosmos," *Spring,* 1982 (Dallas).

32. I would like to acknowledge my indebtedness throughout this section to Theodore Schwenk's *Sensitive Chaos: The Creation of Flowing Forms in Water and Air* (New York: Schocken Books, 1976).

33. According to *The Oxford English Dictionary.*

34. See Richard N. Henderson, *The King in Every Man* (New Haven, CT: Yale Univ. Press, 1972), pp. 390, 402; R. S. Seton, "Installation of an Attah of Idah," *Journal of the Royal African Institute* (1928), pp. 255–78.

35. Kenneth Craik, *The Nature of Explanation* (Cambridge: Cambridge Univ. Press, 1967), pp. 255–78.

36. Arthur A. Few, "Thunder," *Scientific American* (July 1975), p. 90.

37. C. R. Wait, "Aircraft Measurements of Electric Charge Carried to Ground through Thunderstorms," in H. R. Byers, ed., *Thunderstorm Electricity* (Chicago: Univ. of Chicago Press, 1953). F. J. W. Whipple, "Modern Views of Atmospheric Electricity," *Quarterly Journal of the Royal Meteorological Society* 64 (1938): 199–213.

38. Robert Farris Thompson, "Sons of Thunder," *African Arts* (Spring 1971), p. 8. G. J. Afolabi Ojo, *Yoruba Culture* (Ife, Nigeria: Univ. of Ife Press, 1966), pp. 170–71. Ojo cites C. E. P. Brooks, *Climate in Everyday Life* (London, 1950), pp. 216–17.

part two

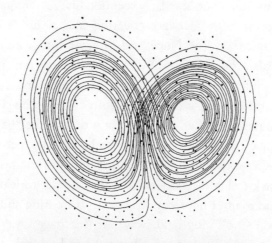

# of masquerades and woman-power

[There is] a double affirmation without limit which says a measureless, excessive, immense yes: both to life and to death. . . . The chance and the probability of such affirmation—one that is double and therefore limitless—is granted to woman. It returns to woman. . . . It is "usually" woman who says yes, yes. To life, to death. This "usually" avoids treating the feminine as a general and generic force; it makes room for the event, for the performance.

—Jacques Derrida

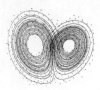

All female Orisha are not only rivers but witches. Oya is no exception to this rule, but she is, exceptionally, a masquerade. By "masquerade" is meant both face-lace-covering and a full-length costume. When first "tamed" by the Nupe and brought into culture, Oya was a purification ritual. To this day Orisha Oya cleanses and purifies the immediate surroundings. What you would have seen and can still occasionally see in Nupe country is a swirling cloth cylinder, magically empowered to rid the community of all ills, including that of the "bad mother." Later this Oya-apparition crossed the Niger to become the genesis of the Egungun cult—a secret society historically consecrated to the task of bringing the Ancestor back to life in masquerade form in order to legitimatize reigning authority and to utter imprecations against dissenting and corrupting elements wherever Oyo's king held sway. At this stage Oya's masquerade cloth became red in the service of Shango, her husband, the one who brought Oya across the Niger.

Vital red cloth is apotropaic against death. Thus, when the Ancestor appears behind red cloth, or behind panels of various colors bordered with red, (zigzagged to convey further energy), death is momentarily defeated.

Although originally called in to perform on behalf of the king of Oyo, Egungun masquerades were developed by the so-called Nupe lineages, such as the Igbori, Ologbin, and Ologbojo. (Probably these families were "Nupeized" Yoruba who returned across the river in order to involve themselves in dynastic struggles going on in old Oyo.) These families have traditionally been associated with praise-singing and entertainment. Their productions for the king of old Oyo are considered to be the genesis of Yoruba theater. Eventually the Egungun concept spread to other lineages and, primarily under the aegis of those "theatrical" families who first brought it into play, Egungun's repertoire of miracles and the costumes used to facilitate their performances expanded also. Among the wondrous performances to be seen today are acrobatics of cloth turning itself inside out, cartwheeling, flattening into apparently disembodied screens of vivid color. Each of these types have names and praise-pedigrees. Their antics delight Oya. But I will here limit discussion to those with whom I have had direct contact, the old ones, the heavy founders called Agba.

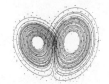

In lineage praises chanted by professionals of the Igbori, Ologbin, and Ologbojo clans, stories of how Egungun was first performed in mythological time, including bizarre genealogies of dignitaries, spirits, and cult symbols, are kept vibrantly alive to this day. Versions of these songs have entered the Ifa divination literature, which incorporates lineage-based etiologies into the oracle's own broader vision. It is in Ifa recitations that one learns of Oya's first appearance "with red cloth over her head" and of how she gave birth to the original returning ancestor, who in turn united with a mysterious mound-mother to produce triplets. This "family" and their successive generations of representatives became the sacred custodians of Egungun cult practice.

In attempting to give as full a picture as possible of Egungun-Oya, both diachronically (insofar as this is possible) and as she appears today, we will have recourse to the oral traditions mentioned above in addition to direct field experience. As an Ato (the lesser of two female officials of Egungun) from Oyo, I was in a position both to be privy to the secrets and to be excluded from them, depending. Because the tension experienced seems paradigmatic with regard to Egungun cult officialdom in general (not the individuals, most of whom were always gracious and charming), I have used that modicum of frustration as means of emotional learning and as vantage point for what ten years ago would have been called deconstruction. Because what I have always personally admired about Derrida is his playfulness, I hope my critique of the institution (never the idea, never the performance) of Egungun will not come to seem heavy-handed. The original "little Ato" was equipped with sharp tongue and sword. In this work she, Oya's granddaughter, must be the writer's role model.

Because Egungun involves much overlapping and borrowing, I have structured this section to resemble an Agba Egungun costume: a series of "panels" of verbal cloth, some plain, some variegated, some rich in implication, some the worse for wear. Contributing to the sizable garment are segments recalling Yoruba funeral rites, remnants of Oya's masquerade in Nupe, and cross-cultural reflections, as well as allied "coverings" of the mystery like Obatala's white cloth, Shango's crown, and the ubiquitous palm fringe. Oya interfaces with all these vestments, some very intimately. One red panel focuses directly on the question of womanpower; other chapters are simply edged in red.

The Cloth
of Contention

All things were created double, they say in Africa. Visible/invisible, male/female, the calm/the violent, the life-enhancing/the life-depleting, right hand/left hand; all phenomena partake of such dichotomies. When it comes to the balance of social institutions, there's masquerading for men/witchcraft for women.[1]

What woman from the outside would not initially bridle at such allocation? Masquerades are exciting entertainment. Witches are dubious beings. Surely this is a trap set to capture our doubts about ourselves as mute, ambivalent participants in male ideological systems that, were we to take them overseriously, could sink in, thus threatening our redemptive perception of the whole.[2] And yet, in search of Oya, it is necessary to enter as deeply into the masquerade phenomenon as possible; for at the center of it, beneath layers of fabric, she presents herself as an essential exception to the either/or rule.

Patron of strong women in the marketplace, Oya's power to effectuate advantageous transactions—the primary (value free) meaning of àjẹ́ or "witchcraft" is hidden in the textile section, for such power must always be kept from jealous eyes and suspicion of evil design (which its very hiddenness will paradoxically amplify). Patron of the masquerading tradition known as Egungun, Oya's representation in Yoruba religious culture is that of a great mask. When the ère, or wooden images of the various Orisha worshiped in a particular town, are paraded before the local king,

Oya's is liable to be missing, for she isn't properly depicted that way. But when the Egungun ancestral masks come out at the annual festival for the dead, they will make their way to her shrine in order to salute her apparition in cloth, as sons enter the compound to beg their mother's blessing.

But we anticipate. At this state of inquiry Oya is not yet Oya specifically, but rather a syndrome, a ubiquitous performance cyclically enacted in innumerable village and town squares throughout Africa. The masquerades come out. Women, driven by custom into the house, emerge contingently, dressed in their festive bright wax prints or local weaves, when the masquerade officials solicit their support along the fringe of the performance space. There the women clap, sing, perhaps play shekere (a

Egungun-Oya of Igbeti, Nigeria, March 1977. She is not performing but only presenting herself to be photographed. Igbeti is close to the ruins of Old Oyo and the Niger River at Jebba Island where Oya entered culture (as a masquerade ritual).

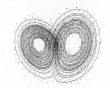

beaded, netted gourd), and playfully get out of the way when a masquerade lurches into the crowd.

In the old days, an explicit witch would be "devoured" on the spot by a certain type of mask embodying an avenging spirit. And yet the full-length costumes worn by the masqueraders recall women's figures. Sometimes this resemblance becomes literal, and womanly bulk (especially the buttocks) and gait are parodied. The players are satirizing woman's misbehavior—her promiscuity, her big mouth, her bossiness. Other times it is the expansive, inchoate power of motherly presence that is being awesomely suggested. A closer look at the carved faces of the masquerades may reveal delicate feminine features set amid a turbulence of raffia.

There are signs of a more collaborative relationship between the two factions, masqueraders and witches. A group of singing, dancing, calabash-playing women may occupy a secure space within the performance area as though necessary for the event's successful outcome. Maybe some women will be partnering the masquerades—dancing opposite their grosser reflections. Furthermore, in every community there will be a few older women accompanying the masqueraders into their sacred forest or cult house. Supportive of these observable affiliations—the token women participants in masquerade performance, the seemingly inescapable use of the female body image in theatrical representations of the mysterious—are "likely stories" about the feminine origins of these fabrications.

All along the Niger River axis of West African culture, myths testify that masquerading was once a woman's art used to terrify and dominate men, who managed to wrest away the mask-making secret and boomerang its power back upon its resourceful originators as a means of controlling them. As though in atonement for this theft, one or two leaders of the offending women's group of celebrants were retained as officers of the otherwise now exclusive confraternity. The titles of such women, like Sigine (Dogon) or Peleba (Ijǫ), perpetuate those of the eponymous founders.

Were masquerades literally seized from women? The core motive behind the takeover myth is, again, ubiquitous, cropping up all the way across the Atlantic on the op-ed page of the *New York Times*.

Motherhood has a visual reality: We can see pregnancy and birth, whereas "Fatherhood, in the sense of conscious begetting, is unknown to man . . ." This dichotomy causes male

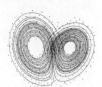

insecurity about potency, paternity, and, apparently, even male *raison d'être.*[3]

No African woman, no matter how sharp her tongue, would ever publicly formulate such an attack. The masquerade-witchcraft dichotomy ritually kept alive subsumes (dialectically "sublates") it. And in examining the Egungun cult as one instance of this play between the sexes, perhaps we can move our understanding of "mother-right"[4] closer to its probable psychosocial genesis as a quadruple yes said by women to life, to death, to themselves as containers of secrets, and to the men of the subsequent generation. For that long ago when we were in charge is only yesterday when our sons were infants.

The masquerade-witchcraft dichotomy was formulated in polygamous societies where the bond with the mother is reinforced by the quandary of a father shared with children of other mothers. One's own mother resides in her own space, a little house from which one issues forth into peer community. If one is a boy, one's male role model will probably be that of maternal uncle rather than engendering father. (This is always true in matrilineal societies.) A boy shares food with father or uncle and many brothers, half brothers, male cousins. To recapture a sense of uniqueness and self-affirmation, such a boy will have to return (in thought and dream at least) to mother. Further, in traditional African societies one is never cut off from elemental matrices. Feminine qualities lodge, as we have seen, in fire and wind as well as in earth and water. The natural symbols of creative energy and accomplishment are feminine. So already behind both myths and masks one will assume a complicated identification with the mother and a problematic sense of paternity. Women permit the takeover myth and generously accede to their estrangement from the process of masquerading because theirs are the real wombs.

The Yoruba word for "theatrical performance," *ìrọn*, also means "vision," that which can be seen with imagination's inner eye and which the verbal and presentational arts, notably masquerading, can bring before us. Deidre LaPin, an authority on Yoruba storytelling, synthesizes various connotations of *ìrọn* as implying "a mysterious, permanent dimension of reality which, until revealed, is shut off from human view."[5] That which paradigmatically contains such essential secrecy is woman's body. As it happens, *ìrọn* is also a collective noun meaning "generation." Along the invisible continuum of family lineages, which include those who have

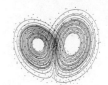

gone before and those yet to be born on earth, a generation is one contemporaneous segment—visible manifestation of the "permanent dimension" of lineage. It is this multifaceted image of generation, with a unifying spirit-ancestor at the core, that Yoruba Egungun masquerades place before the eyes of all spectators, importantly including women.[6] To do so they have borrowed the female body's bulk and secrecy. Furthermore, in ritually empowering each masquerade before it goes out of its sacrosanct enclosure, they "borrow" the generative magic of women—that which conceives and carries to term. Only a woman can bestow this accomplishing power.

The *ìrọn* is ironic. It is an illusion. Yet magical substance animates it, and truth inhabits its core. If things are done correctly, the male ancestral force thus being embodied, possessing the carrier of an Egungun masquerade, will blot the husky young man out and take over. The cloth construction is a denial of death. The spirit it summons is doubly charged with chastisement and blessing. Magically, male potency is ensured by the masquerade ritual, paternity is affirmed as the basis for patriarchal organization of society through male lineage groups, and harum-scarum women are brought into line, thus to cooperate in the grand round of lineage renewal.

Enter Oya. The first Egungun myth, the most ancient, defies expectation by being markedly at odds with the prototypical West African "takeover" story. It shows the original masquerader, in this case, the goddess, triumphant, after a struggle.

There is a cloth called "Grant-I-may-live-long." Agan, senior brother to Egungun, quarreled with him over this cloth—their father's legacy. Dispossessed of what he considered rightfully his property, Agan swore that if he saw anybody wearing this cloth he would seize it. Along came Oya wearing it. Agan attacked her; but Oya resisted and conquered. Allying herself with Egungun, Oya became leader of the masquerade cult. Feminine-Agan-wielding-the-sword was the title bestowed upon her. As a result, Agan has no cloth. He is only a voice.[7]

How did Oya manage to get hold of the cloth?

Here's a "likely story" from the Ifa divination oracle under the sign Ìrosùn Ọsá.

oya puts red cloth over her head

Owner-of-camwood-thunders-violently-as-though-to-devour-us consulted the Ifa oracle on behalf of Oya, the Ọkara of Itile, on the day

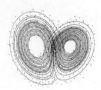

she was weeping for lack of children. She was asked to carry the following offerings outside the house: nine whips on the right side, nine whips on the left side, and nine cocks able to crow. She was asked in the process to cover her head with red cloth.

Oya carried her offerings to the marketplace. Arriving at the marketplace, Oya covered her head completely with red cloth. People were amazed. They had never seen such a phenomenon.

In the course of time Oya gave birth to nine children. They liked to play with cloths over their heads. She told them not to, but when their mother wasn't looking, they did so anyhow. They would frighten people. They even went to market with whips in their hands as well as cloths over their heads. In the "*segi*" Egun voice they would say, "*Ago ẹ yà l'ona e!*" ("Watch out, turn aside, you people, clear the road!")

Oya said, "No more of this!" And she called a halt to their grandiose game.

Then illness alighted on these children of Ìyágán. She went to call a second set of diviners, whose names were "It-is-a-great-occurrence-when-rat-is-found-in-a-hole-of-water" and "It-is-a-great-occurrence-when-fish-is-found-in-grassland."

The diviners said, "Quick, Oya, sacrifice a cock to each of the cloths they've been wearing on their heads and let them go about the marketplace just as you told them not to."

When they had killed their cocks and cooked their stew, these children became well. They were going out; they were coming in; they were dressed in their red cloths and going about the marketplace saying, "There is no doing, there is no leaving undone," meaning, "No other choice is available." Oya asked them each to take a whip along. This whip is called the "death stick" (*ìṣán ni ọ̀páku*). Nine of them must be placed in the corner of the house and carried into the sacred forest when sacrifice of ram or goat is required to be made upon them.

"What has happened is *gùn*, meaning 'long,'" said Oya, meaning "good for perpetuation." So it happened that this Egun became a family festival.[8]

Oya Ọ̀kàrá Itílè means "The one who buys guinea corn (in order to make the special wine drunk at Egungun celebrations) House-post (which holds up the roof of the house)."

Tell me, in your view, how did Oya come by her red magical cloth? She had it from the beginning, as a gift from the creator, said the Araba, who had recounted the first story. So did Shango, he added. (In the second story the diviner called "Owner-of-camwood-thunders-violently-as-though-to-devour-us" is Shango in disguise. Though Shango, the diviner, had the idea of the red cloth, Oya was the one who first wore it). "They each received the cloth before the death of the father," Fagbemi Ajanaku said.

Then he went on to transpose the myth into legend—that is, to place it in pseudohistorical context. In this more popular story of how Egungun really could have happened, the "characters" become titles given to certain Egungun cult officials. And already the takeover has happened. In Oya's place we see "the female child," named Ato—role unspecified. Ceremonially, the "little Ato" (a grown woman official) does wield a sword, so someone privy to Egungun ritual could make the connection back to the Oya of the first story. Otherwise, behind the face of the text, Oya, owner-of-the-cloth, is already hidden, as is her (grandchild's) sword.

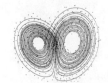

> Ogogo Onigbori was the first Egungun. He bore three children: Agan, Amuisan ("The Whip"), and Ato, the female child. When Ogogo Onigbori died, the King of Oyo asked Agan, the senior son, to come dance before him as his father had done. But Agan failed as a performer. Therefore the second son, Amuisan, was summoned to entertain the king; and he danced very well. So the King of Oyo decided he should inherit his father's ẹkú cloth. To mark this incident, when the Egungun festival is about to begin, Agan shall dance first, on the eve of the celebration, and Egungun the following morning.[9]

Women are forbidden to see Agan dance, the Araba expatiated, because the cloth he should be using was taken away from him. Furthermore, the clothless Agan went on to found his own witch-punishing Opa cult (of the "Rod").

Already paranoia, or at least anxiety, has set in, for there is the undeniable implication here that women were responsible for Agan's bad "performance," and thus for his clothlessness. (However, Agan, as initiator of the festival, aesthetically bridges the gap between nothingness and representation. The legendary rationale already focuses on Egungun as a means of social control.) Shango has been translated into a nameless, generic king of Oyo who wants to be mirrored by a cloth-dancer whose message will be fertility—seed planted in defiance of death. This second version also suggests a change in the character of the cloth. In the beginning, one assumes it to have been whole, whereas now (having been contended for) it is tatters.

An Assemblage
of Boundaries

Most Yoruba celebrate their yearly Egungun festival during the short dry season between rains. The intertropical front has moved north with the sun toward its summer solstice. In Oyo state, when the masks come out, it has already been raining for three months, and the harvesting of first crops is not far distant. Suppose you happen to be staying in a medium-sized town not far from Oyo's capital. Maybe you're closeted with your work on the second floor of a storied house. Suddenly the clamor of bata drums announces the visit of a great Agba masquerade to the owner of the house, who will receive the impressive guest in a private shrine room on the first floor. You jump up and peer over the stairwell. Maybe you catch a glimpse of its bulk or hear its thick, gravelly voice bestowing blessings, but chances are, all you'll see are its numerous retainers. Evenings, along the street will come acrobats and satirists of the cult. They perform—turn themselves inside out, dragging their strange sackcloth in the dust. Some dart erratically after pretended miscreants. They are accompanied by young men wielding branched sticks flexible as willow wands. They are like trick-or-treat pranksters. You dash them small amounts of money, and they dance off to the adjoining compound. Then the day comes when the great old ones all convene to greet the traditional ruler, the Oba. Several bata drum threesomes are playing at once. The yard is so tightly packed with celebrants that it is difficult to see what's going on. From the crotch of a nearby tree looking down, their huge

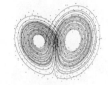

cowrie-studded heads rise like white hillocks above the colorfully coiffed crowds.

It is these great old ones, the Agba Egungun, those who carry heavy "loads" on their heads, who are of primary metaphysical importance in the cult; indeed, they are invested with the highest magicomoral authority of any visible personages, outranking even kings in full regalia—their closest counterparts. These living ghosts of lineage founders, whose frames support multiple generations, are corporate entities reinforcing group values. Yet all these assemblages, rather like concrete universals, have names, which permit a distinguishable "character" to be acted out by the hidden impersonator. Even propped on poles in a hidden shrine room awaiting the next outing, these Agba costumes get to seem like weird great-uncles, to be recognized and greeted with respectful affection. The Agba I know in this way are Jenju (A-restless-person-who-devours-in-the-bush), Ologbojo (The-bard-who-controls-rain), and grandmother L'Aiye Wu, Egungun Ode, Orisha Oya.

Now it is time to brave the tight-packed crowd and take a closer look at these old ones as they converge with their followers upon the local king's palace. See how bulky they are, how disheveled in their finery, how swollen their heavy heads, encrusted with centuries of accumulated power! Such senior ancestors, though they may function at times like retributive superegos, are gowned chaotically like the unconscious. They come on like beggars in a grand comic opera: top to bottom accommodated in a cumbrous multilayered garment made up of panels of bright cloth, some of it patchworked, edged with red rickrack borders that express both lightning energy and the dynamism of surface boundaries. Some of the strips are pure "Grant-I-may-live-long" crimson. This death-repelling red empowers their defiant return to this world. Some of the strips are snakeskins and pelts of powerful animals like the leopard. Still others—the blue brocades, the purple velvets, the gold satins—signal lineage wealth. Although the lappeted construction of this spirit tent in motion is thought by some connoisseurs of Egungun to derive from the palanquins in which Bariba kings used to make concealed public appearances, although the stunning appliquéd segments and the borders are tributes to the sartorial imaginations of Hausa tailors hired to make them, whatever the artistic models—all are at the service of the spiritual conception to be realized. When the attendants clear space for these costumes to dance in the open, strips of the very fabric of existence fly out whirligig-fashion in praise of Oya. What seemed strata of something oppressively solid are revealed to be naught but an explosion of boundaries.

The faceless face of these senior Egungun is a rectangular window covered with woven mesh, often black-and-white striped, occasionally beaded. Atop the head a mask or masks of clay or wood may be set among spiky animal horns. Alternatively, animal skulls thickly encrusted with dried pond mud, blood, indigo, and herbal medicines may be displayed together with horns and clusters of small sticks (like Roman fasces) on a sort of mortarboard tray—as if these masquerades were carrying summations of sacrificial offerings. (The animal skulls are most often of the monkey sacred to the cult.) Here and there brilliant white cowrie shells decorate the "offerings." There is an alternate domed head construction: a mound of resinous medicine so thickly paved with cowries that the beholder imagines cells of a giant brain beneath it.

Attendants of the masquerades keep back the crowd with whips known as ìṣán, made from the flexible stems of the àtòrì bush, which are of more importance than at first appears. Unlike the switches that African elders routinely pick up to discipline unruly boys, the ìṣán are ritually incised. They dramatize the existence of a repellent magnetic field already created by the apotropaic cloth (which in the old days it was certain death to touch) and intensified by chants activating medicinal preparations applied to the carrier during his costuming. The ìṣán, are also visible representations of lineage segments. Slightly more substantial stalks of the same àtòrì bush are used as Egungun cult staffs of membership. Placed in shrines, along with the akòko branches (to be discussed later), these staffs symbolize ancestral continuity through the male line. Similar sticks of wood may be observed in household shrines throughout Africa as loci of progenitorial power. Amuisan, the effective dancer who was awarded his deceased father's cloth by the king of Oyo, is this flexible stick personified. The apparently dry, leafless wand promises continuity. The mystery, how it happens, the illusion that must sustain us, resides in the cloth. Thus does art out of nothing, dancing in defiance of the ordinary, dare triumph over disintegration.

Collaboration Between Cloth and Soil

The Reverend Samuel Johnson's *History* of his people, written almost a hundred years ago, contains a description of a traditional funeral that highlights the contribution of cloth as token of kinship and connects with agricultural process the ancient impulse to make a clothed image of the deceased.[10] His account also includes mention of certain ritual details providing important clues to the meaning of a cult that, however much panoply it may owe to kings of Old Oyo and the Nupe lineages collaborative in its development, is surely grounded in customary funereal practice of the ordinary Yoruba.

Johnson tells us that the Yoruba traditionally bury the dead in the floors of their own houses with an abundance of cloth—each near relative being expected to contribute a piece, just as everyone who belongs to the Egungun cult is expected to donate new strips for the particular lineage masquerade thus served and serviced. Before there were coffins (a colonial influence, Johnson says), the shrouded corpse was wrapped in mats upon which were placed a few sticks of the *akòko* tree. This tree is perched upon and its magical properties controlled by the Great Mother of those birds-of-the-night who are witches' avatars. But the tree is sacred to Orisha Ogun, god of the out-of-doors, who sacralizes all fraternal bonds and oaths of fellowship. From this tree is cut the wood from which the most sacred ancestral staves are made.[11]

Alakòko (Owner of Akoko) is one of Oya's praise-names in Egungun cult discourse. Long before the Egungun costumes familiar today were sewn and danced in in the palace precincts of Old Oyo, Ogun and a generic Witch-Woman were patrons of Yoruba funereal performance. As the religious concept of Oya developed, this generic Witch-Woman acquired the name and complex personality of Oya: goddess of death from across the river who by the Creator was endowed with that vital animating power (àjẹ́) with which many human beings, mostly women, are similarly endowed. Upon Akoko, Oya was grafted and grew. In myth, Ogun became her husband, from whom she borrowed more than Akoko.

The final funeral ceremony, says Johnson, performed several odd-numbered days after the burial, requires the following sacrificial ingredients for completion: cowries, yam (pounded or roasted), local "hot" (distilled) drinks, parched corn, a dog, a hoe, and a cutlass, plus two pieces of locally woven cloth. One always feeds dog to Ogun. The hoe and the cutlass, forged by sons of Ogun (patron of blacksmiths), are sacred emblems of the jural-fertility cult called Oko, which summons the power of Iron to prevent sorcery and witchcraft directed against human fertility and analogous yield of soil.

The deceased's name is called three times to the sound of that iron cutlass striking that iron hoe. A hidden voice (ventriloquism, says the Reverend Johnson) eerily answers. Next morning an impersonator appears in the deceased's clothing. Intrinsic to the process of bringing the otherworldly into human view is the mediating voice in the night (invisible "Agan") as prelude to daylight envisioning (clothed "Egungun").[12] In a rasping ghost-voice this apparition blesses his survivors in exchange for gifts. He then departs for the sacred grove, to be seen no more until the next year, when hopefully he will return decked out more splendidly in contributed, generational cloth segments. Were there no progeny to make arrangements, this and subsequent materializations of the spirit could not happen. The deceased person's Egungun will not appear at annual festivals of the dead if lineage lands do not continue fertile and the living prosperous. Conversely, it will be the tended rather than the neglected ancestor who is able in masquerade form to combat the threat of aridity from witches that would ultimately mean his own effective disappearance as progenitor.

The Cloth of Containment

What is being asked of the bereaved at funerals is moral vision of life as a whole. The dramatic potential of cloth is summoned to posit continuity in the place of absence, whose horror, thus hidden, may be gradually "worked through" in the course of rededicated tending of the living soil. Anger naturally felt toward the deserting parental provider is absorbed by the Egungun cloth, which, belying crass loss, urges reconciliation with cyclical processes of nature.

Funerals may dramatize the need, but the achievement of such philosophical poise is a continuous life task overseen in an exemplary way by a Yoruba Orisha we have thus far only mentioned in passing: Obatala, whose name means King-of-the-white-cloth. Character (ìwà) is the quality in us for which Obatala's energies are responsible, and at the same time "character" puts the responsibility for the quality of our lives within our own competence. Whatever twists and turns our prenatally chosen road may compel our feet along, whatever passions may strike, whirl, or rivet the backs of our heads, vital functions can be aloof to such vagaries. Our delicate inner organs can nourish self-worth or starve it with the slim pickings of misguided endeavor. Those who cannot pause to listen to the "oracle of the heart," those with "malice in the bowels," those with a sour stomach, gripped by fear, rush about generating mistrust, havoc, and bad luck, and end up severing "the rope of life," which gentle character alone can keep unbroken in our hands. But those who resolutely center them-

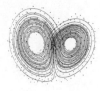

selves in calm are able to behave with generosity toward others. And so, inevitably, good character extends itself into good reputation, which the Yoruba refer to metaphorically as "white cloth" (àlà).[13]

Obatala is a sculptor in clay whose compassion extends to those whose bodies he once in mythological time inadvertently deformed while drunk on palm wine (which his priests take care to avoid). Obatala's magical powers, through substances sacred to him, may help to cool our heads and sweeten our insides so that good character is given time to develop. They may also be used to pacify serious mental disturbance, even to civilize, as we have seen, an outrageous tornado. Yet like all Orisha, Obatala can be lethal. His white cloth is highly charged with what we call "passive aggression," and even when unprovoked, Obatala's "shadow side," grandiose, wants to take over.

Obatala might be viewed as a feminine presence in masculine space. His inwardness, the clay with which he works (in Africa, women are potters), his killing by smothering rather than by means of a pointed weapon, his all-inclusiveness suggest a maternal imprint upon god-consciousness. In Cuban Santería, Obatala is sometimes popularly anthro-pomorphized as a woman, in cultural opposition to a *macho* image of Shango. The civic analogue of the Obatala-Shango polarity is that between Ife and Oyo cities. Historically the spiritual capital of the Yoruba, Ife is the headquarters of the "white" divinities, Obatala first of all, as well as of the Ifa oracle, which, though practiced throughout Yoruba territory and beyond, is centered in Ife and reflects the "cool," "white," "reasonable," and inward-looking ethos of that city. (Of the major female Orisha, Yemoja, mother of the waters, was originally located in Ife, before her worshipers fled to the southwest, toward Abeokuta.)

What follows is an "Ile Ife" version of the contended cloth or masquerade-takeover story. Gone is the red cloth Oya shares with Shango. It's as if the Obatala people and the Ifa diviners were trying to take Egun-gun away from us expressive Oya types—which, of course, they never really did. What is the meaning? White cloth *is* worn by all Yoruba religious celebrants during the sacred parts of their ceremonies, Egungun-Oya members included—though not when Egungun masquerades go out on the streets to perform their miracles publicly. I take its meaning as having to do with the requirements of the *temenos* (sacred precinct) generally, and with the equivalent of that space in the human psyche. What is being projected upon women here is restless extroversion, a hyped-up perversion of women's relational and communicative skills.

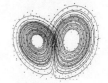

taking over odu's cloth

Osa Meji-is-wealthy Making-a-lot-of-noise Bell-sound-come-down-to-earth consulted Ifa for Odu that day she arrived, also for Ogun and for Obatala, Odu being the only woman.

"What will happen on earth when we get there?"

Creator said, "Whatever you want to accomplish, I'll give you the power, that the world may be a good place."

Ogun marched ahead, Obatala followed, Odu lagged behind. Retracing her steps, "O Creator," she said, "down there Ogun will have warpower. He has saber, he has gun, he has everything for fighting. Obatala has authority to rule. What about me, the only woman among them? What can I do?"

Creator said, "Yours is the power of motherhood to sustain the earth. And this bird-power is yours. I gave you a big gourd full of it. Odu, come back. Tell me, will you know how to use it?"

Odu said, "If people don't listen to me, don't even ask my advice, I'll fight. If people ask me for money, for children, I'll be obliging unless they become impertinent; then I'll take everything back."

"Good," said Creator, "but use your power with calm, not violence, or I'll take everything back from you!"

Since that time, because of Odu, women have power to say what they please, for in the absence of women, men can do nothing.

Odu came to earth. All forests sacred to ancestors, she went right on in, freely entered the bull-roarer's forest. Everywhere spirits were worshiped, the woman entered. "Ha!" the old one exaggerated. Odu fell into disgrace.

Ifa was consulted for her. *"Hen!"* said Ifa, "you will have to calm down."

"Why should I?"

"Because of the power given you," said the diviners, "so people won't begin to understand what that's all about."

"They won't!" said Odu. "Nobody saw Creator give it to me."

"Sacrifice!" said the diviners.

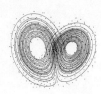

"No!" said Odu. "Nobody will take my power away. They don't know anything about it." Then she put on masquerade cloth and went out. There was nothing she didn't do in those days.

Obatala came to Ifa, saying, *"Hen!* Creator put me in charge of the earth, but this energetic woman is taking over. There's no place she doesn't go."

Ifa consoled Obatala: "No one can wrest the world from your hands. The world won't spoil. You must sacrifice snails, a whip, and eight pieces of money."

When Obatala made the offering, Orunmila said, "Don't worry, adoration will return to you."

Meanwhile, if Odu said, "Don't look!" and people looked at her, they became blind.

"Let's live together," she said to Obatala. "That way you can closely observe everything I do."

Obatala worshiped his head with snails, and when he had finished he drank from the shell. "Would you like some, Odu?"

She drank, and her stomach calmed down. "Oh, I have discovered a wonderful food, snail-water is sweet, snail-water is sweet."

So Obatala provided her with snails whenever she wanted them.

"But how about those things you have? those things you do?"

"I'll share everything with you!" Odu replied. When she went to worship Egungun, though he said he was frightened, Obatala went along too. In the sacred wood she put on the costume but didn't know how to sound like Egungun. Later, Obatala added a net face to the cloth, took up the whip, and spoke with the voice of Egungun.

He went out. *"Hen! Ha!"* people said, "this is truly a presence from the other world. He even frightened Odu. *Hen!* Who entered so rapidly into the costume? Who is speaking with that unrecognizable voice?"

Thus with sagacity, man overcame woman. All over town Obatala rushed in Egungun costume. Seeing he wasn't home, recognizing her costume, Odu stayed where she was and sent her bird to perch on the masquerade's shoulder. From then on, everything Egungun was able to do came about by bird-power. When Obatala did everything in Egungun, he came home, took off the cloth, laid down the whip, and went to greet Odu. Before her he placed all gifts received.

"You can have Egungun," she said; "no longer will woman dare put on the cloth, but the power you will use belongs to us, and when you go out I will dance before you. From now on, only men will take out Egungun. But no one, neither children nor old men, will dare make fun of women. Woman-power is greater. Women give birth, and whatever men

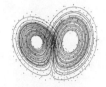

want to do, women must help them or their projects won't come to anything."

So they sang together, and Obatala said that every week everyone must praise women so the world will be peaceful.

Bend your knee, bend your knee before women, for women have brought you into the world; women are intelligence of the earth, women have put us into the world; reverence women.[14]

A deeply troubled woman sits down on the floor of a therapist's studio to draw a series of beaked birds within uterine containers. She has never heard this or any other Yoruba story. Another woman, equally damaged by a judgmental mother, hardly alights before she is off flying all over the place performing everybody's work but her own, that which she lacks sufficient self-esteem to do. Does not the Osa Meji story reflect a common human dilemma, its introverted and extroverted aspects, a dilemma "usually" confronted by women?

In the story, Container, who contains no children, who has no clearly defined job in the world, wants to contain everything. Obatala is ineffectual. She shows him how to inspire awe by adopting a theatrical persona, to which he gives voice. (Logos is always, cross-culturally, the contribution of masculine authority.) The bird she gives him to actualize the masquerade instinctively knows how to peck its way out of oppressive containers. Repressed anger released, paradoxically, by the feminine agency of containment, is here deemed indispensable to the masculine exercise of creativity. More generally, creative impetus springs forth from a holding environment, which it shatters and seeks to re-create in image. The form of the vision captures the corresponding reality. All we ever see of Odu is her container, which eventually became the repository of the wisdom of Ifa. But that is another story.

Sister Crown

The assertion of male political authority as dramatized by royal costume is allied both to cloth embodiment of controlling ancestral consciousness in Egungun masquerades and to the celebration of Orisha (the god) Shango's dynamic presence in the world by his priests when wearing ritual dress in ecstatic possession states. Not only are these three spectacular Selves visually analogous—an *agba* Egungun, a crowned king, and a Shango priest displaying the god's cowrie crown—but the institutions they represent and the conceptions they dramatize are interlocking and mutually supportive. Furthermore, it is a feminine power in each instance who is responsible for the magical efficacy of the transformation. The legendary woman who gave her name and her life over to Shango's crown is Bayanni. In exploring the nature of the god-king's crown, we shall bring the Yoruba stories closer to home by entertaining their protagonists as parts of the inner world shared by expressive personalities across cultural frontiers. It would be a rare woman who has not at sometime or another sat by Bayanni and called her "sister."

In Yoruba culture, the face of a "crowned" person is veiled. Though a chief may be splendidly garbed, we see his face. But a fringed veil of costly beads hides the visage of the sacred wearer of a Yoruba king's crown. This is a metaphor for presence of more than person and signals, beyond status, a transformed state of being. The image is a powerful one, which proliferates itself. For example, a simple version of the royal veil shades the faces of those possessed by the great female Orisha (Oya, Oshun, Yemoja) in Brazilian Candomblé.

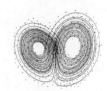

Kings certainly don't rule postcolonial Nigeria, but they continue to preside within limited compass over important Yoruba towns. Selected from among the descendants of a royal lineage founder, the chosen king is the live link in a chain of dead (and unborn) men. His state appearances are ìrọ̀n (see page 76). For when the king puts on the crown, he relinquishes idiosyncratic personality. What his audience beholds, awesomely concealed, is generic royal power of the lineage. Behind the veil one supposes consciousness expanded into the very essence of kingship.

Royal authority, as Robert Farris Thompson has shown in a stunning monograph on Yoruba crowns, is activated by Primal Mother, whose presence is indicated by a beaded bird or birds perched on top of the crown or by a bird motif worked into its surface design.[15] Within the crown, then, as within the Egungun masquerade, ancestral continuity is engendered. Over and over the pattern repeats itself. What is the message? Women come and go. Their bodies are socially useful for a while. Then others replace them. Young bodies harbor a secret that crones are be privy to, for they can abort biological process. Men strive for collective perpetuity through the creation of institutions that won't last unless the adversarial "no" deep in every woman's shadow zone is commandeered. This is "witch control," which involves co-opting the leader or "mother" of witches into the male establishment.

The paradigm of divine kingship among the Yoruba is Shango (see page 60 for the end of his story), who once reigned over the city-state of Oyo by authority of his ancestor, Oranyan. At least, this is one version of his accession; another suggests that Shango was a usurper from a neighboring kingdom; still another, that he was a slave who managed to attain the highest power. It is possible for the "Shango" type of personality to feel at various moments all these situational modes of self-awareness. Grandiosity: My grandfather was a god. Imposture: I am not really a Yoruba, but here I am pretending to rule them. Charisma: At the right moment I charmed them into electing me to deserved office. Alienation: I'm really Nupe/Bariba; I'll never be one of them (even if I am their king). Persecution: I'm debased. They can tell who I once was. Everyone secretly has contempt for me. I'll show them! Further: Things have come to such a pass that with one part of myself I am going to have to kill the part I hate, the

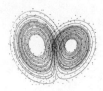

part they hate. Or: Unable to live in this lousy world, I'll enter a state of altered consciousness and merge with the All.

Kingship in West Africa was an inheritance ideally devolving upon the junior rather than the senior brother. Shango was the youngest son/grandson of the Yoruba people's founder, Oranyan, who in turn was youngest offspring of the Creator. The senior brother is apparently problematical. Either he is too aggressive—a threat to the reigning, fatherly king, who in some cultures ritually banishes him—or he's inept, too passive. Orisha Ogun is paradigmatic elder brother of the first type: too adamant, too violent. The would-be king has to be impressive, but a bit weak. It is a self struggling to marshall its forces and succeeding that can attract and unify the disparate members of a group.

Oyo, over which Shango attempted to rule, is the only Yoruba city-state to have expanded its power to imperial proportions. To this day, incumbent kings of other towns must have their authority ratified by the Alafin ("Owner of the Palace") of Oyo, whose own authority is sanctioned by royal ancestors going back to Shango and magically implemented by Orisha Shango's priests at the state shrine in nearby Kòso.

The skirts of Orisha Shango's priests are like miniature Egungun masquerades—the same flaring panels, with their violent red edge. The priests plait their hair like women. Feminine aspects of their appearance, however, are contradicted by an exuberant masculine dance-style: wide stances, deep knee bends, asymmetrical rotations, kicks, striking motions with upraised arms. In trance these priests are capable of carrying burning coals in perforated containers upon their heads. And like Oya's mediums who take the part of fire, Shango's can put flaming substances into their mouths. Even more dramatically demonstrating their god's power of dissociation, whereby anguish of spirit may be transformed into violent show of force, Shango priests play at driving spikes through their lower eyelids or through their tongues with impunity. It is an aggressive entertainment. They force the bystander to confront it, this perforation of the body's boundaries. By contrast, the cowrie vests worn by Shango priests convey a message of prosperity—materialization of the fertility their special god rains upon the earth.

The ceremonial headpieces of Shango's thunder-priests are cowrie-shell casques with snakelike cowrie strands coiling off them partially to cover the face. These casques may be seen as crude forerunners of the delicately beaded crowns of reigning kings. No witch-birds perch upon these casques. They are self-empowering and wholly feminine. They are Bayanni.

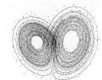

Subsumed into her crown as Bayanni is, reports of her precoronal existence are bound to be confusing, even contradictory, and the reader's patience is begged as ally to that of the investigator whose enthusiasm was fueled by the sense of being the first to empathize with and therefore attempt to piece together a consistent story of the vanishing Bayanni. In Oyo city they will tell you Bayanni is Shango's sister. According to a king list drawn up by Robert Smith when he was teaching at the University of Ibadan, a woman named Bayanni reigned as regent after the abdication of Shango's elder brother, an ineffectual ruler whom tradition describes as being "too mild for the age."[16] This mild, self-exiled brother, known in traditional accounts as Ajaka (who later underwent a personality change and returned after Shango's death to reign as a warrior-magician) is mythologically identified with a minor Orisha called Dada, patron of births and babies, particularly of those born with ringlets. (Shango himself is said to have been born with such a natural crown of cowrie curls on his head.)

In 1950 informants in Meko told William Bascom that Dada was truly elder brother to Shango, but that Shango was stronger. Bayanni is the Orisha, they said, who "owns" Dada, and Bayanni is also the name of the calabash in which the sacred essence of Dada is carried.[17] In Johnson's *History of the Yorubas*, a person by the name of Babayanmi (Father-chose-me, of which Bayanni is a contraction), as a sympathetic act of grief following Shango's flight from Oyo and subsequent hanging at Kòso, commits suicide at Seelè.

Cowrie casques (called Dada) in front of Bayanni shrine, Seelè, Nigeria.

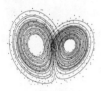

A visit to extant towns in the vicinity of the old Oyo city, not far from the Niger, helped clarify the "history" of Bayanni, but at the same time deepened her mystery. The king of Kishi said she was truly Shango's sister who, wandering distraught in the aftermath of his tragedy, disappeared into the ground not far from where we sat talking: Seelè. A termite mound encircled by a dried strand of palm fringe marks the place of Bayanni's disappearance from the human community. However, the custodian of this forlorn place said that Bayanni wasn't Shango's sister, but rather a neighboring queen allied to (subsumed by) Oyo kingdom who did in fact commit suicide in Shango's suite.

In Seelè town there is a shrine for Bayanni. When a baby is born with ringlets *or* with a caul over its head, the mother brings it immediately to this shrine. The midwife doesn't remove the membrane, for it will fall off at the shrine by direct intercession of Orisha Bayanni, the resident priestess said. Eventually a cowrie casque (called Dada) is made for those who arrive from the other world so strangely coiffed. (The keepers of the shrine would have made one for the inquirer had she not been out of pocket.) Thus are unusual births paired at Bayanni's shrine: the one grows into extroverted richness, earthly authority in the manner of Shango; the other, the caul or veil wearer, follows the inner way of Egungun. Or so I have come personally to understand these prenatal choices, comparable to the (also prenatally chosen) endowments of *àjẹ́* and *emèrè*. With *àjẹ́*'s effectuating power (a magic that can be used for good or ill, again according to prenatal choice) we are already familiar. *Emèrè* is defined by Abraham's dictionary as referring to persons "reborn and having the power to consort with spirits." It is a telepathic receptivity. The powers are not mutually exclusive. A person may come to earth with both abilities, and both are advisably kept hidden.

The confusion between Bayanni and Dada persists in the New World, where a third complicating name/character presents itself. In Cuba, where Lydia Cabrera collected apparently inexhaustible lore among descendants of the Yoruba, Shango's sister is interchangeably called Bayanni, Dada, or Obaneñe ("Little King"). Of this gentle person with three names, Shango, they say, was fond "as of a mother." For of his real mother he was ashamed. Denying the mother, Shango took on "defense of the father," absent or dead. Bringing Obaneñe/Bayanni/Dada along with him, Shango fled his mother's house to set up a *ménage à trois* at Oya's place, where the selfless refugee sister devoted herself to housekeeping. It

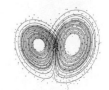

was at this time that Shango was in a state of continual war with Ogun, against whom he sought to protect himself with lightning medicine. Against such a fierce elder brother of an adversary Shango never could have prevailed without the support of women. In the Cuban *lucumi* story, neither Oya nor Shango's sister can resist helping themselves to this lightning medicine, but only Oya urges concerted action against Ogun. Instead, Obaneñe/Bayanni/Dada hides under Shango's sacred palm tree. Yet these three go together like joined stones, said Lydia Cabrera's informant. Where you find one, there you will find the two others.[18]

Throughout the various permutations of Bayanni, self-sacrifice, or at least abnegation, sounds a steady leitmotif. Chosen by the father, Bayanni relinquishes herself to fate. She is Shango's accompanying weakness. As she is hidden, sister crown can save by hiding his uncertain face in resplendent wealth of achievement. For secrecy is also the matrix of authority (*àṣẹ*)—charming, vital power that radiates everywhere.

One night, years after the visit to Seelè, a spontaneous bit of ritual foolery brought the enigma of Bayanni's shifting identity home to me. In the midst of a funeral celebration in Salvador, Bahia, Brazil, there was Shango (as rumored in folklore) actually terrified of ghosts. A Shango priest was playfully behaving like a small boy in the face of Baba Egungun, an aggressive ancestral apparition dancing about the *terreiro*'s performance arena. The possessed Shango priest was actually hiding behind an Oya priestess's skirts. Yet in real life he was the ritual leader of the *terreiro*, ultimate authority of the place.

We suggested earlier that the king's self-mastery magically unifies dissident elements in the kingdom. What happens in European theater is comparable to this. Shango as an earthly king made a mess of it; enemies without and within beset him. Insofar as Dionysos continues to preside over theatrical experience, what continues to attract us there is dismemberment unified. A form is created in fictive space and through a segment of played time that for a long moment holds disparate pieces of society and the self together. If the public, comparable to the real king's subjects or the costumed god's worshipers, be complicit, then the illusion triumphs. But this acting king must first accede to weakness. We must see his body cringe in some way. Then, as he moves beyond mere survival of the pain of existence toward greatness of spirit, the defeated Obaneñe/Dada/Bayanni within each one of us reaches out to crown him with the entirety of our beings. *Kabiesi!* The king is dead but lives again.

"Too little guilt," says Donald Kaplan in his spirited analysis of stage fright, "correlates with the sense that bold alternatives of selfhood are still possible, if only one had the nerve." The darker side of such an uninhibited person will "play to lose."[19] Oya represents the vital side of Shango, the one with "the flare for adventure," as Kaplan puts it. It is behind her skirts that he hides. Bayanni, who plays to lose her identity in "the other," provides the crown that will enable him to confront the father as an equal. Freed from stress and harassments of public and private life, exempt from the menace of war and his own runaway violence, through a corridor provided by women the great Shango has gone over into a state of play, of unlimited erotic options, drumming and dancing. Thus relieved of pressure, divine Shango thunders, or sits down at the kitchen table to eat a hearty meal. And we echo him in our applause.

Brother Palm-Fringe

Elder brother, on the other hand, doesn't have the same options. When the Yoruba imagine the Orisha coming down to earth, it is Ogun who comes first to reconnoiter and clear the way for a softer god (Obatala of the white cloth) and a correspondingly vigorous Mother. Ogun's place is òde ("outside," "the wilds,"), which precludes sustained contact with women and all the ambivalences arising therefrom. Ogun harks back to the beginnings of human endeavor. He invented our survival kit. Such raw energy mobilized for meeting the exigencies of existence is too hot to handle ungloved. When Ogun attempts to enter society, it is in a natural masquerade. Green leaves disguise his violence.

> The day Ogun came down from his hill
> He was clothed in fire and wore a garment of blood;
> Then he borrowed palm fronds from palm trees.
> Attired in fresh palm leaves, he entered Ìré
> And was immediately proclaimed king. [20]

Afterwards, in a fit of pique he inadvertently murdered his male kinsfolk and returned to his natural habitat upon the mountain.

The fringe Ogun puts on in this traditional praise poem is called mariwo. Fashioned from the inner shoots of fronds from the "tree of life,"

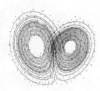

mariwo surrounds Ogun's sacred objects and sites and has also become integral to the worship of Oya, for whom Mariwo is a praise-epithet.

But its use is far more extensive. Everywhere in West Africa one sees this fringe of young palm growth strung out to delineate sacred space and to keep negative energies out of it. *Mariwo* is a magical agency of distancing, a sort of vegetal spell. Only elder brother, the hunter, could have invented this rustic plant-language. Rustling in the wind, *mariwo* borrows Oya's voice. Warning repels threat. An interceptive device of leaves skirts the danger.

Mariwo works both ways. What is vulnerable is protected, and what is painful to behold or frightening is suggestively distanced. When we see a dancing or lurching figure completely covered in shredded fronds, we think "wildness." The bush has come into our midst. What danger is pretended? (To pretend may be thought of as a stretching-out into an environing mental space: the creation of a fictive identity and events to compensate for literal reality's humdrum and ego's felt inadequacy.) Pretending to be cool, Ogun violated the rules of the civilized game. But beyond the pale where he belongs, Ogun is the huddled community's best defense. Out there in the bush, Ogun and his stealthy brethren take death in their own hands: death as knife, machete, rifle. Indeed, so well acquainted with the means of violent death is Ogun that he is often invoked as the unaccommodated thing itself.

Yoruba hunters have their own masquerade tradition, which comes into play at funerals of deceased members of the confraternity Ogun spiritually heads. The name popularly given to the hunters' corporate ancestral force, clothed in *mariwo*, is *l'aiyé wù*, which means "It is pleasing to witches" (they like it so much they forget to attack). Well, strange to relate, Oya liked Ogun's costume so much that she put it on as underwear!

The great mask of Egungun Oya is kept in a shrine supervised by the Onirá, whom one might call the pope of Oya-worship, and tended by women initiates. The mask is dressed in bright silk and satin cloths and wears a headpiece of horns (not buffalo horns, although these are kept in the sanctuary). This is the mask that is performed outside. But it is not the guise in which Egungun-Oya is worshiped inside the shrine house. In preparation for her weekly day of praise-singing, the voluptuous fabrics are removed. Beneath, still horn-coiffed, the goddess of death and regeneration is dressed like a hunter. Only initiates behold this wildness (*òde*). The full name of the entire mask is L'Aiyé Wù, Egungun Ode, Orisha

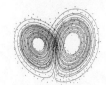

Oya. Implicitly there are three layers to its costume. Two represent marriages of Oya. The external alliance, her second marriage in mythological time, is with Shango, represented by the rich outer segments of cloth. Beneath that luxury we see the image of an austere, forbidding hunter, clothed in powerful amulets: Ogun's persona. The thought of further divesting the image inspires terror.

Hunters are a brotherhood exclusive of women. When the Yoruba religion crossed the Atlantic, certain aspects were necessarily condensed and altered. In Brazil there could be no hunting brotherhood in the African sense, for the wilderness was inhabited by indigenous populations with their own techniques for relating to spirits lodged in plants, animals, waters, and salient features of landscape. Ogun's tools there were otiose. It was through Ogun's brother, the archer Oshossi, that religious contact was made with the Amerindian forest, a contact eventuating in the development of a "Caboclo" strain in Candomblé.

Precariously defined and courageously maintained under dangerous political conditions, the sacred precincts of Candomblé became perforce "cities of women,"[21] the strongest of which centered on the worship of Shango and female divinities associated with him. When the institution of Egungun was revived on Brazilian soil, it became controlled by Ogun worshipers and may be seen as an attempt to preserve male balance through the exclusivity of brotherhood. Thus, one is not surprised to find the following "cloth of contention" story as part of Afro-Brazilian oral tradition.

In the beginning of the world, women intimidated men and controlled them. For this reason Iyansan (Oya) was the first to invent the secret of Egungun. When women wanted to abuse their husbands, they met at a crossroads with Iyansan. Iyansan was already there with a big monkey she had trained. The monkey had been dressed in special clothes. It stood at the trunk of a tree (akòko) and would perform as indicated by Iyansan by means of a switch, known as isan. After a special ceremony, this monkey appeared performing its skills, as dictated by Iyansan, in full sight of the men, who ran away terrified by the apparition.

Finally the men decided to take steps to put an end to the continued shame of living under the thumb of women. So they went to the Ifa oracle to know what they could do to remedy the situation. The oracle sent Ogun to make an offering of roosters, a gown, a sword, and a used hat at the crossroads where the tree stood, before the women arrived. Ogun was there early. He sacrificed the roosters, then put on the

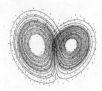

hat and gown and took the sword in hand. Later, when the women came to perform their rite, suddenly before them came an apparition, a spectacle so terrifying that Oya herself was first to flee.

Utilizing the tremendous power Iyansan possessed, she disappeared from the face of the earth forever. From that time on, men have domesticated women and now are masters of the Egungun cult. They forbade and still forbid any woman to penetrate the secret. Only in very rare cases are exceptions made.[22]

Far from its African sources, mythological material has been altered, even distorted in response to situational needs. Yet behind the silly spectacle of Oya and her trained monkey lurks a true totemic affiliation between Egungun and that almost-human primate. It is a link figured forth in a series of etiological tales to be discussed further on. Suffice it here to suggest the ego's need, when threatened by discontinuity and absence, in the face of death to summon up a sense of belonging to a great chain of being. Cut off from continuity of kin, menaced by matriarchal strength developed in response to conditions of slavery, unable to contact the forest (province of Amerindian hunters) where the body moves reassuringly like an animal, certain men went so far as the crossroads to replace Oya's "well-trained" animal instincts with Ogun in drag.

There is another brother of the out-of-doors who hides beneath *mariwo*. This Orisha's euphemistic name is *Babalúaiyé* (Father-concealed-himself-from-the-people-of-the-world). He is not native to Yoruba soil. Babaluaiye is often praised as King of Nupe, meaning "Death." The Nupe origin of certain aspects of his cult does make sense if one thinks of Babaluaiye as an invisible carrier of disease for which he alone is the remedy: that is, as a medicinal power personified (see succeeding chapter) rather than as a legendary person who became a god. However, the cult of Babaluaiye in reality derives less from Nupe practice than from mysteries performed in the region of Save, Republic of Benin.

With this brother, Oya runs parallel in certain ways: both wield purificatory implements, both are involved in sorcery, in transfigurative behavior, and both are profoundly hidden. Babaluaiye's diseases are borne on the wind—not Oya's gales, for they belong to different seasons. Babaluaiye's wind is harmattan, the dry wind from the north that comes clogging the pores with dust and enervating the body with fever. His is the wind of contagious diseases—in the past smallpox, currently AIDS—especially those erupting on the skin; but he also sends nervous com-

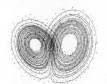

plaints. Both Babaluaiye and Oya are patrons of madness. In Brazil his mediums conceal their god's remedial sufferings beneath a full-length raffia "masquerade" in lieu of palm frond segments. Like Ogun and Oya, Babaluaiye is Death and cannot be seen directly. On January 31, 1983, I was able to attend an Olubaje feast in a Gêgê *terreiro* in Salvador, Bahia.[23] The Orisha who descended to follow the fiber-masked figure of Babaluaiye, being thus honored with a firstfruits feast, were Oya, Ogun, and Nana Buruku.

Behind every ancestor looms a yet more ancient ancestress. Nana Buruku, says Pierre Verger, is the oldest differentiated form of the earth. She can still be anthropomorphically imagined as the mother of Babaluaiye and as the leader of immemorial migrations of her people across the face of the earth. But Nana Buruku in turn is an emanation of the immovable primal mound. The Fon people call the palm fringe *azan* (rather than *mariwo*) and they call the primal mound-mother Ayizan ("Mat of the Earth"), meaning that which was first laid down upon watery beginnings. But piously to encircle chthonic Ayizan with a fresh palm fringe is not a tautological exercise. The fringe protects the nakedness of First Mother.[24]

Azan also protects the vulnerability of the ritually reborn. In Haiti, Fon religious symbolism predominates, and Ayizan's importance cannot be overestimated. Her fringed skirt appears at the edge of the loosely woven brim of the straw hats worn by the newly initiated. The straw-hatted *hounsi* emerge from their seclusion as from the out-of-doors, as if those newly radiant faces glimpsed beneath the harvest veil had been blessed by early morning rain from heaven. The initiation process from beginning to end, so I've been told, takes place under the patronage of ancient earth mother Ayizan.

In Nigeria, Mariwo are fully initiated members of Egungun. In an extended sense, all initiates are "children of the secret" hidden behind the palm fringe, witnesses to an interiority coincident with the "other reality" of mystical experience. The masquerade phenomenon in Yoruba and Yoruba-related cultures may be seen as a dramatizing of surfaces in order to stress the depth of what is thereby concealed. The delighted eye teases the mind to contemplation of the unseen force behind the apparition: that deeper truth being kinesthetically suggested, that engrossment occurring beyond fragmentation of the fringe.

The richness of Egungun fabric endows ancestral essence with prestige in accordance with the Yoruba aesthetic of visualized "impor-

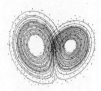

tance." The extended cloth of reputation, devolving from good character, is generationally layered and diachronically segmented to suggest maximal human investment in the swirling art object. The segments shimmer with all the colors of fortune's rainbow. They are red-edged with feminine vitality that apotropaically distances death. Animal skins, particularly that of the python, whose shed skin testifies to renewal within the continuous round of existence, contribute their deeper ancestral strengths to the costume. The simple prototype of this magnificent apparition, a fiber fringe, was borrowed from ancient earth. It is the primal covering of her body.

Masquerading in its most rudimentary form is naturally associated with women, whose bodies lead a cyclical inner life, generative of a private listening and a secret consciousness.

Masquerading by men may be seen as a form of retreat from the world generative of interiority—a housing of the spirit. Men construct masquerades not only to simulate, thus to acquire, the counterpart of women's interiority, but also to give birth to notions of continuity and transcendence exclusive to women. Imaginatively housed within their stupendous artifacts (or metaphysical systems), they dramatize the perpetuation of hegemonic collective values. The surrogate womb in which the conception (of paternal continuity, of transcendence) occurs in the face of death, though borrowed from woman, is protectively dressed in aggression, represented by fibre-shreds from the tree of life, as though to warn us that the peril of wholeness lodges in fragmentation.

Ndako Gboya

Along Oya's river a nearer journey begins

December 13, 1976, Jebba Island. Thanks to the intercession of Jebba's chief, the elders of Muwo, one of the few villages to have retained the ritual, agreed to a special demonstration of Ndako Gboya. Wonderfully, the cloth tubes were not white, as in Nadel's photographs taken in the 1920s; two of them were deep purple and the third mostly yellow. Each accompanied by a male dancer, from crouched positions (like huge mushrooms) in front of the drums at the entrance to the marketplace, one by one the broad cloth cylinders rose, peeled off, and swirled into the open, where they performed as gracefully as medusae in water. But they were in air. They were columns of air rising, bending occasionally in the center to dispel any sense of volume, collapsing periodically until only their flat heads, ringed with streamers (the inevitable fringe), could be seen. Alternately inflated and evacuated by capricious gusts were these cloth creatures, wound and unwound upon the invisible fingers of a storm.

A chorus of women, led by the Ndako Sagi, praised their performance in rhythms accentuated by bead-netted gourds and vigorous shoulder contractions. The colors of the women's wraps, blouses, and headties, all prints, blended under the midday sun into opulent shades of menstrual brown and placental purple. But only men knew the secret.

Afterward, the elders of the compound to which the masks belonged agreed to discuss the event. It is not the mask alone that drives out all the bad things, the sickness, the sterility, they said, but rather the

empowering *ebala*. What's that? Well, for example, they said, if you wished to enter this village and there was an *ebala* against you, forget it. Were *ebala* opposed, you couldn't even arise from that chair.

How do you make *ebala*? An animal or animals must be sacrificed. Which kind? Whichever kind(s) appear to the Maji Dodo (Master of the Terrible) in a dream. This animal comes to him in the night. Then there are drinks. Poured into a calabash? Of course. With water? Of course, that is the most important ingredient. Water from where? From Kunko source, about a quarter of a mile from here. At the source is a small stone, no bigger than the palm of your hand. Where the water flows from beneath the stone is the secret place. . . .

We form a circle, the elders went on. In the center is Maji Dodo. The blood is not poured into the calabash, but runs out upon the ground. We dance around. The masks are there, bending to drink as the *ebala* is spoken. . . .

The good things we get from Ndako Gboya are health, children. The animals kept at home will fatten; farms will prosper. And those that carry Ndako Gboya are always young men? Most often. But sometimes, when there's a witch we can't get to confess, or when there's so much evil we can't handle it, *then we ask a woman to get inside the mask and dance. She will be stronger.*

When these words were said, the spokesman for the masquerade society did not alter his voice, but pronounced them matter-of-factly. It is the listener who underscores their importance. It was an epiphany—as if Oya herself had uttered them.

Ndako Gboya refers both to the type of mask we have just

Ndako Gboya performing in Muwo village, Nigeria, December 1976.

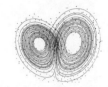

seen and to the ritual of purification it performs. *Ndako* means "very senior" in Nupe. *Gbo* implies great size. *Oya*, of course, is Oya; but the Nupe
have no notion of "Oya" apart from this context. Unlike the neighboring
Yoruba and the Fon, the Nupe have no pantheon of gods. Instead, they
have magical medicines and rituals with which to control evils attributable
to human malevolence. So this is how Oya entered culture in Nupe: as a
swirling windcloth empowered to accomplish good-riddance. No more, no
less. And it is crucial to our understanding of her mode of being as a
goddess.

Although the Nupe have no anthropomorphized memory of Oya,
they do recall a personage named Shango, a legendary ancestor ("the
father who begot us")[25] who produced "medicine" as a substitute for spo-
radic divine intervention on the part of an increasingly otiose creator-god.
Moreover, they say it was this same Shango who for the first time used
magical cloth in purificatory ritual. His was originally the problem for
which Ndako Gboya was the solution: a genesis consonant with what is
said of Shango's shameful mother and of his flight to Oya's house in far-off
Cuba. (See p. 93.) The original Master of the Terrible, then, the one who
learned how to harness Oya's power, was he who mythologically became
her husband!

A certain king, the Nupe say, had trouble with a domineering
mother. His diviner told him to procure a certain number of lengths of
cloth, which the diviner himself sewed into a tube. While medicine was
applied, an incantation (*ebala*) was spoken that enabled the cloth to rise
into the air. There it hovered, spun, and then, like a hawk spotting its
victim, dropped suddenly down upon the offending dowager. Shango's
mother was never seen again, but the ritual, having proved efficacious, was
repeated.[26] It is a story that may be associated with two circumstances
reported in Johnson's *History of the Yorubas*. One is legendary: King
Shango, feeling after many years of neglect the urge to worship at his Nupe
mother's grave, decided to send an emissary to make inquiry and arrangements. He summoned the man, only to discover that he could no longer
remember his mother's name![27] The other is historical fact: Upon their
sons' accessions, the real mothers of Oyo kings were put to death and a
proxy Iya Oba installed to play the part. This practice answered to a
double need: for the sacred king to sever all earthly attachments and at the
same time to retain empowering matriarchal presence. As it happens in
the mind, so in the palace, so in the public square. Oya's ancient Nupe

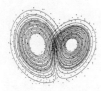

cloth is a remarkable visualization of repression and displacement: devouring mother devoured by proxy.

The historical "reality" reflected in these slivers of legend and event would seem to be that of a dynasty of Oyo kings whose ethnic roots were Nupe rather than Yoruba. The means these intruders used to establish control over possibly dissident subjects was masquerade cloth. Thus the Yoruba religious imagination arranged a marriage between Shango (son of a problematic, vanished mother) and Oya (ritual medicine made of whole cloth), a Nupe princess whose father controlled the river.

But this Nupe dynasty alternated in old Oyo with another, whose pretenders were Bariba (a powerful kingdom to the west) and whose means of social control were lightning, the throwing of thunder-stones, and rain-making. These magical techniques, the property today of Shango priests, are central to the practice of traditional Sonrai-Zarma religion upriver, where the climate is very dry. In this middle zone of the Niger the techniques are "owned" by priests of a divinity locally called Dongo.

And here begins an excursus during the course of which the process of cultural borrowing will veer away from the central theme of "contended cloth" as it illustrates the flow of information and sacred technology along the Niger River, which, Oya-like, couldn't care less about arbitrary national frontiers originally created by colonial powers or even about the exclusivity of ethnic "ownership" of divine forces.

Dongo's priests are Sorko people, who for centuries have controlled all movement along this part of the river. The Sorko too are obtrusive. They came in canoes to dominate the carrying trade and harpoon fishing along the middle Niger, as the Kede control the river below the rapids. These two tribes, or castes of canoemen, are generally thought to be distant kinsmen. The Sorko don't "own" local shoals, deep places, and other topographical features of the river considered by aboriginal fishermen to be the home of water spirits; even the Sorko's access to the Holé, the great spirits of the Sonrai-Zarma possession cult, was acquired—except in the case of Dongo, who seems to have been with the Sorko for a long, long time.

The local water-people, the Do, endogenously connected to the Holé and other spirits who inhabit the river, consider Dongo (rather snobbishly) to be "of questionable origin." The Sorko say that Dongo had a Bariba father and a Bella mother. The Bella, black people of the Sahara, have spent much of their recent history as slaves of nomadic horsemen.

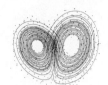

What his genealogy could mean is that rain magic associated with "thunder-stones" (Neolithic celts) and with the gods Dongo and Shango did originate in the Sahara among the Bella. But others acquired the secret—or parts of it, notably the bards of the upper Niger and the Bariba. Weather control is a complex culture-trait, secret yet widely diffused, "questionable" in origin as Dongo and Shango are problematic in origin—a situation reflective of the status of slaves and "casted" groups (like bards) in a highly class-conscious region of Africa.

The power of rainmaking is exemplified by a ritual ax, a common attribute of Dongo and Shango. Its progenitor would logically have been a stone one. But Dongo's now has a metal blade. It is distinguished from similar regional axes by its little crotal bell, affixed to the place where haft joins blade. Shango's dance wand is a double ax made of wood, sometimes with a celt design etched into each "blade." The symbol of power stretches—shifts shape, embodies itself in different matter—to accommodate the personality of the god. The double ax sprouts, like horns. In Yoruba cultural context Shango is a fertility god associated with drumming and with feminine companions, including, as we have seen, the feminine in himself.[28]

A missing link between Dongo and Shango can be seen in an ancient Egungun masquerade lodged in the Ologbin compound just a few yards away from the shrine house of Egungun-Oya. The name of this Dongo-Shango composite is Ologbojo (The-bard-who-controls-rain). Its headpiece consists of five sculpted busts of Shango set in a circle to form the struts of a crown, the hub of which is a carved hairdo of the type worn by Shango priests. Its impersonator brandishes a single-bladed ax like that belonging to Dongo and his Sorko priests along the middle Niger. This is the story of Ologbojo's origin:

At a certain point in Oyo history, the Alapinni, of Nupe lineage and head of the Egungun cult, together with the king's council, of which he has always been an important member, attempted to control the Alafin (king of Oyo) himself by masquerade means. The court at that time was in exile, but the king was determined to resettle old Oyo city, from which Nupe depredations had driven the Yoruba. The Alapinni and the council for their own reasons were opposed. To the abandoned site of the former capital each council member, under the Alapinni's direction, sent a strange apparition (weirdly clothed people with physical anomalies). The king's scouts reported back to him that the place was uninhabitable be-

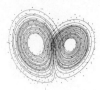

cause haunted. But the king's bard, who knew what theatrical impersonation is all about, asked for permission to visit the site himself and have a look at these "ghosts." His suspicions confirmed, the bard returned to report confidentially to the king and to propose a countermasquerade event that would dramatize a "ghost-catching" king's supremacy over the Alapinni and his henchmen on the council. The Alapinni threatened to break up the initial performance of the play by causing it to rain. But the bard's control over the weather was stronger. The event took place. A masked king chased the ghosts away. Forthwith the council retaliated by poisoning the bard. The aggrieved king prepared an elaborate funeral for his loyal, ingenious entertainer during the course of which the masquerade bearing his praise-name, The-bard-who-controls-rain, appeared for the first time.[29] Today, when Ologbojo and the Alapinni's ancestral mask, called Jenju, meet at times of festival, they stand opposite each other, fists raised in sign of power stalemate. Neither will bow before the other. But all other Egungun except Oya must bow to them.

There is reason to suppose that bardic rainmaking power, lodged in the efficacious Word rather than in specially treated stones, linked to the drum rather than to the ax, was developed along the upper Niger.[30] Just as itinerant bards might well have learned some of their secrets from inhabitants of the Sahara, so they certainly moved downriver with whatever they knew. Evidently the Bariba were particularly hospitable to their talents. In any event, by the time of the legendary Shango (mid-fourteenth century?), this power was locally associated with the Bariba, to which the besieged king of Oyo sent Oya to fetch lightning-medicine and from whom the Sorko "acquired" Dongo.

Thus Oya conveniently serves as intermediary between two aspects of royal authority needed by Shango's people: Bariba mastery of weather and Nupe cloth-medicine ritual. These two magical means of social control are in the oral histories associated with alternating, contending dynasties: one with Nupe roots, the other with Bariba. In a sense Oya still serves Shango as intermediary between these two aspects of his legendary self. Orisha Shango remains on the Bariba "side of life" with its elemental energies: fire, water, and numinous stone projectiles. This is the enabling, fiery Oya. The Nupe "side of death" is mediated through Oya-Egungun. She remains responsible for the shadowy task Ancestor Shango was the first to tap into in Nupe.

To return now to Ndako Gboya: A second story is told of its origin. Being the folkloric equivalent of a grade B movie, this one cannot possibly feature the Ancestor himself. Rather, it is said to have happened "in the time of Shango." Again the usual complaint: women were misbehaving. Always quarrelsome, they had turned insolent. When provoked, they threatened to unleash their destructive, nocturnal powers. As a result of this, "a certain young man" went into the bush, covered his head with his own garment, then charged down upon an especially officious group. All fled in terror save one stalwart old woman, whom a delegation of old men subsequently beat to death with an iron rod for her intransigence.[31]

It is important not to romanticize the other's culture by avoiding nightmarish material like the brutal bludgeoning of this old woman. The strands of fear, envy, and hate are well knotted into Nupe and Yoruba psyches too. What is of interest to the observer from another culture is how institutions have been developed to work through these threatening raw places in the human soul so that men and women can covertly borrow missing qualities from each other in order to achieve or at least attempt to achieve social harmony.

However, it would seem as though in the masquerade/woman-power complex we are studying, men had borrowed more and bestowed less. The access to masquerading is an honor bestowed on relatively few women, and those few women are beyond child-bearing age and therefore able to be ritually classified as men. Having acknowledged a need for instigative feminine energy, for feminine "flow" and feminine "bulk," men have been deaf to the clamor of women for an effective voice in the shaping of ideology and management of political and social affairs. Yet "behind the scenes" women reputedly have had their say—at least until the advent of colonialism. But how much say did they have with regard to the status of women?

It appears to be the case that those who borrowed the masquerade used it to relegate women's activities to various enclosed spaces defined by men. Thus, unable to escape identification with bodily process, unheard women's attempts to subvert the system will be imagined in psychobiological terms as *bad* witchcraft that eats at the vitals (of society, as of the individual person). Furthermore, special psychic power to effectuate desired results, which has nothing constitutionally to do with sex or with inner male-female identifications, will be popularly tainted with potential destructiveness—as are women insofar as gender is socially constructed.

Witchcraft, like masquerading, is a many-layered phenomenon. Rumor and cultural stereotype are the "outer garments" worn by women who resent the system as well as by those who simply give the impression of being especially talented. Masquerading provides the possibility of male spiritual growth by identification with the Ancestor as with (covertly) Woman. Can anything comparable come of the stereotype of evil-design?

Iyalode and Royal Nupe Woman

The world is our market
Heaven is home, O
The world is our market . . .

So in the words of the Ifa oracle sing our Mothers. As a spirit group, witches are invisible, but those who fear them imagine their nocturnal activities to be the counterpart of aggressive games women play in the market. Market is synecdoche for world at its most intense moment, at its most social; and women are in charge of it. Market is expressive of life's transience, but also of life's erotic pulse. It is the place of encounters, seductions, exchanges, transfusions of energy. Oya is "owner of the market." Here we shall be concerned with the worldly power of women in this space they have made for themselves, not without resentment on the part of Nupe men, who (since Islamization anyhow) have tended to view women traders and women who have risen to economic prominence generally as rejects from the child-producing machine—either women of pleasure or the willfully sterile—a slant congruent with their unequivocal dread of witches. Not so, traditionally, the Yoruba.

The impetus to achieve economic independence for herself and her children is strong among African women. It is impressive to see the sense of self that a little commerce on the side can lend mortar-and-pestle drudgery. When it is not her day to cook for the husband she shares, a

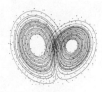

woman may prepare snacks late into the night and walk several kilometers early the following morning to sell them in front of a public place such as a factory. The special strength of Yoruba women in this regard is a function of Yoruba urbanization. For several hundred years the Yoruba have congregated in towns from which paths radiate to distant farms tilled by men. Yoruba women process and sell food. They sell other things too— drinks, cloth, manufactured products—the range of their activities being limited by the ages of their children and by the number of women sharing household chores.[32] As a consequence, toward independent women Yoruba men have developed attitudes of admiration, resignation, ambivalence, but in the best of times certainly not horror.

The chief of the compound in which Oya's great mask is enshrined, for example, is economically dependent upon his five wives—a situation that might well in the beginning elicit from the foreign visitor ethnocentric feelings equivalent to a raised eyebrow. The senior wife, with whom the chief has little personal rapport, runs a tiny general store to whose inventory he has ready access. The second wife sells palm wine, which the chief and his cronies drink lavishly. The third and fourth wives are professional praise-singers, whose lively team performances reflect glory upon himself in attendance and provide cash for *ad hoc* expenditures. The youngest wife, resident in his house, buys kola nuts wholesale and in her free time arranges them attractively on straw trays to be carried about on the heads of her small daughters. The chief does a bit of farming.

The less visible work the chief of Ologbin compound does brings in little income but heals people. It wasn't until I saw him gently and successfully treat an excruciatingly painful hernia by magical-medicinal means that warm respect for the chief rose up in my heart and I understood how the economic system, centered on him as a sort of queen bee, really works. In those twelve hands, though it sometimes may get a bit frayed, the rope of life remains unbroken. For the power he has is double. The chiefly status, which satisfies Yoruba criteria of visible reputation, is only half of it. The other power cannot be overtly acknowledged, but people come to him for treatment because the results of his work indicate that he has it. An effective healer, man or woman, must possess this gift that "answers" the situational need (in the case I witnessed, "hernia"). *Jẹ́* means "is" in a relational sense: "responds to." But it also means "works" as in *Oògùn yìí ń jẹ́:* "This medicine is efficacious." *Àjẹ́* is the noun for it, a three-letter word for "witches," which our Mothers don't appreciate. They would rather be known euphemistically as beautifully feathered birds. And as an occult power, nobody would admit to having it for good or ill. How unlike the situation in our culture, where such gifts, everywhere advertised, are like as not to prove spurious!

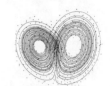

Finally, I would like to add that subjectively experienced, the chief in question has two personalities. One is aggressively "macho." Cock of the roost at Oya Egungun's shrine (actually, one of the women who tends it has gifts of foresight that he doesn't), he can behave arrogantly, without respect for women's feelings. But there is a softness about him as well, a femininity that relaxes his features and that I could not account for until asked to go through that process of hernia-healing with him. Similarly, the leader of his praise-singing team of wives, a tremendously talented woman, under the stimulus of a performance situation, takes the stance of a man to belt out her genealogical histories, which feature *men's* accomplishments.

To return to the situation in general: market women are organized into unions for regulation of their relations *inter se* and also for expression of their views as a public interest group. Among the Yoruba their spokeswoman is called Iyalode. This is a secular title, achieved rather than inherited, bestowed by her sisters in recognition of her skill in articulating issues and also in managing her own commercial enterprises—a sign that she will be able to manipulate those substantial resources needed for the maintenance of chiefly status. The name *Ìyálôde* means "Mother-of-the-outside." As the Iyalode incorporates the mystical power of Our Energetic Ancestress into her being, as she speaks with sharp tongue and incisive mind, as she answers to needs, hers is a constructive, outward-directed charisma that clears the air of resentment. Or so it was in traditional Yoruba society, but times have changed.

Contemporary Nigerian feminism, with its traditional roots in the marketplace, has addressed itself primarily to undoing the damage colonialism and westernization have done to women's political and economic opportunities. The plight of the Iyalode in this regard has been eloquently documented by Bolanle Awe. When she wrote the report from which the following passage is excerpted, Ms. Awe was High Commissioner for Trade and Transportation in Oyo state—the only woman of that status in the local government. Now, while continuing to head the African Studies Center at the University of Ibadan, she has just been appointed Chair of the Woman's Commission, a federal position.

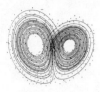

During the period of foreign domination, women seem to have been the most affected. With their western preconceptions of female inferiority, colonial administrators tended to relegate women to the background in their governments. Consequently, many female titles disappeared, while some of their functions became obsolete through lack of opportunity [to exercise them]. . . . With reorganization of local government administration in the Western state, Iyalode is no longer a member of any of the important councils of government. Even the market and therefore the market women have been removed from her jurisdiction and placed under control of new local governments in each town.[33]

For gifts and tribute traditionally accorded the Yoruba chief of women, a salary was substituted that compares unfavorably with that of her male counterparts. Similarly, religious westernization (especially in its predominantly Protestant form) has done much to diminish the Iyalode's mystical importance. And witchcraft in the pejorative, popular sense has correspondingly increased. That is, fear of clandestine female malevolence has become an all-too-ready paranoic response to psychosocial disequilibria attendant upon modernization. The belief in the responsibility of unseen agencies for one's failure to meet current social demands is stressed at the expense of its counterpart, individual accountability, which in traditional Yoruba philosophy is tied to prenatal choice. In choosing a certain type of head-destiny, one chooses most of the good or ill luck that goes with it. However, one's character (ìwà) can compensate.

Those who can't cope with the arduous task of making it in competitive, capitalistic societies blame "the mothers" either through the "witchcraft option" or, as in our society, through the psychological syndrome of the "wounded child." In both cases those apt to accept the charge are those who suffer from the consequences of an "unlived life."

The role of the leader of market women in Nupe society has a rather different history from that of her counterpart among the Yoruba. Her title, before Islamization, was Lelu (or Erelu in Yoruba).[34] At times of crisis, the Lelu was expected to exercise the mystical power of women for the benefit of the whole community. In wartime, it was she who prepared and activated the medicine of invisibility, as did the legendary Princess Oya on Jebba Island. If epidemics struck, causing infants or cattle to die, if crops failed, if a disproportionate number of women remained barren, and if witchcraft in the negative sense was deemed the cause, then by means of her third eye the Lelu was expected to identify the offending witch and exact a confession. Only when the magic of ill will flamed beyond the Lelu's personal means to control it was the Ndako masquerade ritual called for, but the whirling cloth never performed in the capital, where the crowned Nupe king, in conjunction with the Lelu, was apparently capable of coping with the invisible danger.

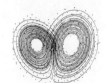

When Oya crossed the river to marry Shango, the Egungun cult replaced that of the crowned king of Nupe in this regard, and the Lelu's role was performed by an official known as Ato, She-of-the-sharp-tongue, a religious title whose eponym was Oya's granddaughter. Much can be learned about Oya's difference from other Yoruba Orisha by visiting her native ground and by gleaning what one can of Nupe history. Some patterns of action brought with her already existed in Yoruba culture, and so an easy graft was formed; but other aspects of Oya that seem odd in Yoruba context make more sense on the other bank of the river. For example, Oshun is also a mythological wife of Shango, but Oya is his queen. One doesn't think of Oshun that way. Queens, royal women, and women of title generally have a different history in Oya's other country, which presumably schooled her imperious disposition.

At the court of ancient Nupe, instead of ordering his mother killed and engaging a substitute, the new king bestowed a title upon her, upon his senior paternal aunt, upon his eldest sister, and even upon his eldest daughter, were she old enough to qualify. The bearers of such titles were required to be "strong women," that is, between the ages of forty and fifty upon accession, and of independent judgment. To make this latter requirement easier to fulfill, the entitled woman's marriage would be formally dissolved. (Though she moved into the king's palace, she continued to see her former husband if she wanted to.) A titled woman participated in the king's council and in time of war was permitted to lead her own army of retainers of battle. (Ms. Awe says that some Iyalode in the past outfitted armies.) Oya's cutlass, then, has seen real action.

At the time of the Fulani jihad and the ensuing conquest of Nupe at the beginning of the nineteenth century, Nupe women of power were rapidly unseated. Only one titled royal woman remains, the Sagi, who has no voice in council and no memories of prominence in battle.[35]

The royal Sagi, queen mother, of Bida [whence the capital was removed from Jebba Island] proved to be a *very* old woman, attended by

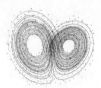

her sister, named Fatima. "It is good," said Daughter-of-the-Prophet, "to talk." I agreed. Sitting on low stools beside the early morning fire kindled directly on the earthen floor of the round sleeping hut, while Fatima massaged the Sagi's skinny, arthritic legs with eucalyptus oil, we spoke of many things. Of colors, for example. "Red is the most important," said Fatima, "for with Allah's power[36] it can turn into anything you like." In the old days, she said, only women of title were permitted to wear red, yet crimson cloth was sold in the evening market because that's when the other *royal people* came to shop. When we came to discuss the elements, Fatima automatically made a moral assessment of them. Earth is always good, she said. If a person is sick, we say "the earth can heal him." Air is always bad, "a destructive thing," she said. There are those who take advantage of strong winds to ride out and accomplish their destructive purposes. Water, in Fatima's view, is "mixed," like people. Water is both good and bad, the quiet and likewise the flowing. For all waters, she said, be they rivers or ponds, are beings, each distinct; and the people who live along the edges of these waters differ accordingly. The Niger is "a devil of a force, very strong. We do not know, and therefore cannot say, if it be man or woman." How about fire? Very good! See—warming us. Fire cooks food. And that "other" fire? Yes, she admitted, there is that fire too, which wicked hearts may possess. You can see it in the night sky.

That evening in the king's market, what woman would have resisted buying a beautiful red woven shawl?

Redolent of the sort of woman-power unacceptable to Islam, the word *Lelu* simply disappeared. The head of the market women in Bida is given a Hausa honorific, Sonya. The Hausa being a trading people, the imported word signals that her activities mustn't swerve from regulation of women's commercial activity. But in out-of-the-way villages and little towns, the market head adopts the royal honorific, Sagi. Since Ndako Gboya appeared to be an all-male cult directed against women, the masquerade continued after the jihad to be publicly performed, until the arrival of the British, at which time it too went underground. The acting Sonya of Bida suggested that "royal women" were particularly active these days in Doko village.

Though "Sagi" was scrawled on the door, the woman who opened it certainly bore another, hidden name. Women, already assembled in her courtyard, were preparing to hold a meeting somewhere in the bush. There was no way I could go with them, so she invited me to come back and spend the following night in Doko. However, when dusk found me there again with my bedroll, the "royal woman" greeted me with a look of horror that still tingles my spine. In the interim, I imagine, she decided that a dangerous foreign witch had come to devour the secret contents of her mind. There was some truth in this. In her eyes one could see, as one rarely sees, the quiver of real evil enmeshed in fright. Such must have been the expression borne by the old woman whom those brutish elders bludgeoned with iron. The door closed. Along the darkening uterine walls of Doko I actually ran to the adjoining village, its lorry park, and the off-chance of a ride.

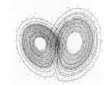

Six years later, not far from Oyo city, someone I knew rather well got that look in her eyes. But it was already dark, too late to flee anywhere, no choice but to ride out the night in an adjoining room. The "attack" began in a dream, or what seemed like a dream. Literally paralyzed in such a situation, one has to summon all available forces to a point. It is a madness, somebody else's, grabbing hold of the victim's matching weakness. The other side of witchcraft's attack is deep-seated lack of *amour-propre*.

Tears give the witch away. If yours be the stronger power, you can make her cry. You can hold a specially treated copper ring before her streaming eyes. Although the power to make things happen for good or ill is a gift one is born with—which like other gifts, second sight, for example, can be cultivated or remain quiescent—still there remains another sense in which all women inwardly answer to the projection (transference) of potential evil design. And we make use of this shadowy aspect of ourselves to claim an enabling power. Surely the moon at crescent knows herself entire, as she has waxed and waned countless times.

Granted, the Lelu was specially endowed from the beginning. She proved her strength and was granted further, visible authority. The woman who confessed to her, though, was powerless. It is not simplistic to speak of such confessions as seizures of self-worthlessness: perverse means of achieving momentary prominence, else socially denied. In Nupe context, one does not find a titled woman thus confessing. On the contrary, the Sagi's sister discreetly conveys the message by means of the color red, which, if you have the power (verbally rerouted through Allah), can be turned into anything you like. So the one who confessed to the Lelu did commit a crime, but not the one for which she was indicted. It is a crime that our sisters, and we ourselves, commit in less spectacular ways all the time.

To acknowledge one's darker—envious, depressed—propensities is worthy of honor. No wonder witches worthy of the name in Nupe were deemed "royal." For they had made a pact with themselves to govern a host of dis-eases and demons of the soul. And they could get it together in the marketplace. No wonder these "royal" women had the right to buy red cloth after sundown by oil-lamp flicker. I did not. It was a sentimental gesture, touristic, a sort of theft that even now is difficult though important not to despise.

Before moving further along this equivocal path to title, it seems appropriate here to essay a divagation downstream in order to tell the Erelu of Itebu's story: a cautionary tale of what happens when the reality of woman-power, particularly that of efficacious speech, is denied. For no matter how legitimately conferred a strong woman's title may be, insufferable difficulties may arise in its maintenance. Thus the exceptional woman is isolated on the verge of madness.

In Benin City, Nigeria, the power of the sea is worshiped as Olokun, a king who brings riches and fertility to women. In many ways Olokun is Shango's watery counterpart. The human kings of Benin City are crowned in Olokun's image. Igbarun is the name of Olokun's dark river wife, and it was in pursuit of this "dark river" theme that I happened late one night to arrive at the far-flung Yoruba enclave of Itebu in Okitipupa Division. Itebu lies at the end of one of those extremely narrow roads that intersect and occasionally parallel lagoon routes leading Niger Delta traders to Lagos. To come upon a Yoruba-speaking town in those watery parts was a great surprise. The king of Itebu is addressed as Kabiesi, an appellation deriving from old Oyo, Shango's own "Hail to the Chief!" But the official cult in Itebu is Olokun's rather than Shango's. There are two titled women in this town, the Erelu, who became my friend, and the Remaowone (Lovely Daughter), whom I never saw. (The Erelu would be comparable to Oya; the Remaowone, her co-wife Oshun.) The Remaowone is of less importance here, said the king of Itebu, because of the present Erelu's strong personality.

It is a personality at odds with the town. In Benin City the Olokun cult's votaries are mainly women; but in Itebu all women are excluded from the one official shrine. The Erelu, whose given name is Emeli, is an

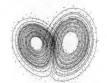

Olokun priestess, initiated in Benin. How, then, does she manage? At dawn, by the waterside, her grizzled hair powdered with sanctifying chalk dust, Emeli conducted her own rites. Stationing two red feathers (from the tail of the chattering gray parrot) in the damp sand, Emeli lifted her white wrap and waded out into the dark stream, calling:

> *Owner of the sea, O*
> *Owner of riches,*
> *King on land is great,*
> *Greater is king in water . . .*

After the simple ceremony was over, the few women in attendance dispersed to their chores; and Olokun's chief priest, who had been watching at a discreet distance, went off to prepare for the king's late-morning worship. As soon as he was out of sight, Emeli, being an old woman, lifted up her underskirt and peed.

Two hundred yards away from the beach, on high ground, the Kabiesi's council of chiefs (which illegally excluded her) began to assemble in the palace. Emeli, the out-of-business Erelu, took my arm and led me into the shade of the king's carport. The royal Bentley had gone off on an errand to Lagos, and in its place two straight-backed chairs awaited outcast feminine dignity. There, for hours, it seemed, while council convened in the palace, sisterly libations were poured: palm gin, lots of it, accompanied by unburdening of talk. Thus does isolated intelligence in a small town anywhere in the world seek confirmation in the romantic aspect of a stranger. And thus, for her part, does the stranger naturally gravitate to the estranged one, capable of such sudden intimacy consequent to much brooding on differences.

That afternoon the Kabiesi made a most hospitable gesture. In the neighboring town of Atigere, he said, elders would be able to tell me "dark river" stories. We would make the journey together, by canoe. The outing was successful. Returning at night along dark meanders of the local stream, the Kabiesi and I fell to talking about all sorts of things—the sound that water-spirit masqueraders make with their *igbirin* pod anklets, how costly his competition for chiefly office had been, and, inevitably, Emeli. She's a drunkard, he said in a mildly contemptuous tone, so there's no governing her tongue. She'll say anything, anytime. But she's so bright, I objected. Even with palm gin skewing her sense of propriety, she is very insightful. Maybe it's just that she hits the mark at the wrong moments? Then truth

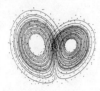

can be embarrassing . . . ? Half the time, the king finally conceded, what the Erelu says is worth my listening. Furious at such condescension, I fell silent. We both fell silent. Nothing could be heard. Not even the boatman's paddle spoke. Though we were going against the sluggish current, the competent old oarsman, moving implacably through corridors formed by papyrus reeds and carpeted with water lettuce, never once broke the surface of the water. Nor could we see anything. Heavy mist from Olokun's ocean obscured the stars, perhaps the moon. Suddenly there was a strange outburst of chatter off the port bow. I started up from my thwart seat. (The king sat behind me in a red leather upholstered chair, its legs precariously wedged against the gunwales.) What's that? A madwoman, he replied. She lives alone on an island over there. Talks to herself. Sometimes she turns up at market . . .

Taking Title

Though a title may be inherited, it still has to be ritually contested for. One day, visiting the Oya shrine within the palace precincts in the town of Ede, I heard the commotion of loud cheers. What was going on? An informal barricade, lined with crowds of people, had been set up next to the corral where the Timi (king) of Ede's white horse was tethered. The Timi, it turned out, was conveying title upon a new group of chiefs of various quarters of the town. As each title came up for bestowal, the candidate literally ran for it: three times forward (a short dash of about fifty feet) and twice back, running backward. The first two dashes culminated in prostration before the Timi and a covering of the head with dust. The third meant victory. The Timi crowned the victor with the *akòko* leaves of chieftancy. Another title was announced. Another youngish man stepped up and ran for it. The white horse whinnied often during the proceedings, reared, tried to tear itself loose from its post and bolt out of the corral. It was a curious juxtaposition of efforts.

At that time I had never seen a Baba Egungun up close. Bob Thompson, a man who knows the ropes, suggested it would be possible to see the layered costume put on. Clairvoyantly, as it appears in hindsight, Thompson had said that when I got to Oyo I should look up the Alapinni and ask to see Jenju. He told me exactly where the Alapinni's compound was.

"It is not the time of festival," said the Alapinni; "therefore, you cannot see Jenju. Even were we to hold a special demonstration, you could not approach the mask. Unthinkable—to be present at the robing of the impersonator. Unless"—the Alapinni paused—"you were to become Ato." *Ato?* I had never heard the word. Well, I considered, whatever that is, why not give it a try? I wondered how Thompson had managed to get in to see Jenju. Well, he was a man, first of all. Second, he knew the ropes. Maybe he dashed the Alapinni. Ato, whatever that meant—and the Alapinni didn't seem to be propositioning me—was my way, so I had better take it. I could always pull out if I got a bad sense of things.

"Ato," I replied, "Why not?"

"Well, then," said the Alapinni, "We'll look it over." By that I knew he was referring to Ifa. "Come back tomorrow morning."

"What does the word *ato* mean?" I asked Mr. Awujola, an elderly gentleman, former Baptist school teacher, and prince of one of the ruling families up north. At that time Mr. Awujola was associated with the African studies program at the University of Ibadan.

"Born with a membrane on the face, I believe, madame," he said.

"Why, so I was, how odd," I exclaimed, and asked if he would be good enough to go back with me to Oyo the following morning. I had begun to be a bit afraid of the Alapinni. There was something about his face, across which the skin was so tightly pulled as to seem grafted. Was he once a professional boxer? I wondered. Victim of a traffic accident? Seated at right angles in his dimly lit audience chamber, we could, now in introspect, have been in Tartarus.

Later that evening a friend told me she thought the word *ato* meant "triplet." Actually, the eponymous Ato was both. Born eldest of triplets, with a caul over her head, this Ato and her brother Amuisan were progeny of the original Egungun, Oya's ninth child. As a result, all triplets are automatically members of the Egungun cult. Those who survive childhood are required to have masks made that represent their own spiritual doubles. These costumes are not worn by the surviving triplets themselves, but by impersonators, so that during the annual festival of the dead, a triplet may have the unique experience of confronting in the street the ancestral component of its own soul.[37]

A third way of becoming an official Ato is by inheritance. What had happened, so we later found out, was that the woman thus serving the Alapinni's masquerade had died without a daughter willing to replace her.

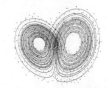

I guess he was waiting for a natural Ato to show up. Maybe, since the American in Yoruba dress had expressed interest, she was the one. There are many Ato—one for each senior mask. The Ato's job is "to wield the sword." The eponymous Ato was Oya's granddaughter.

Once Ifa had seen the caul on the impulsive candidate's face, what was involved on the public level was seemingly endless protocol—an entering into the frame of title-taking as such. Here Mr. Awujola proved a godsend. He got everything clarified as we went along and coached the barbarous American in correct behavior. The religious part of it, what we went through at Oya's shrine over in the Ologbin's compound, was more difficult for him. Despite his profound respect for traditional religion, occasionally on our way back to Ibadan he would sigh, "O madame, I wish my savior could be your savior."

The first thing we had to do was obtain audience with the Alafin (king) of Oyo and beg permission to take title upon the territory he ruled. The king's secretary refused to deliver the carefully composed letter seeking audience. Obviously a heavy bribe was wanted, but this I was in no way prepared to offer. What now, Mr. Awujola? The thing to do was to court the favor of a wily, genial personage called the Kudefu (whose title required he be a eunuch), chief of palace retainers, who in his role as watchdog for the Alafin lives in an apartment along the wall of the huge formal courtyard, which through his little front window may be viewed in entirety. There, dressed in pale blue damask, the Kudefu sat by the hour, and for the better part of three days Mr. Awujola and I joined him, attempting to cultivate an informal conspiratorial relationship that in the end would induce him to exert pressure on the churlish secretary.

At noontime the glaring courtyard, surrounded by low-slung red clay buildings overhung by a continuous corrugated tin scowl, became void of all human traffic. Immediately opposite our dog kennel, a royal wife had set out a flat box containing the ingredients of her liberation: Lifebuoy soap, cigarettes, wooden matches, a few kola nuts. . . . But at noon she too retired. And those petitioners, clad in fashionable imported eyelet lace suits, who had waited to the wilting point outside the king's audience hall, they too departed. Cops stationed along the veranda dozed over dog-eared copies of the *Daily Times*. The uncooperative secretary closed his box of dusty petitions and went home for lunch. May he choke on a chicken bone! Eventually, supervised flattery of the Kudefu reached its saturation point. He gave in. The secretary followed suit. We were admitted to the Alafin, a brisk pharmacist in pretitled life, who seemed

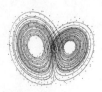

oblivious to all this languid conniving with which access to his spontaneous attention was insulated.

The Alafin arranged a preliminary meeting with Joseph Ologbin, the Onirá, senior priest of Oya, who came to the palace accompanied by a group of old women. Although this wasn't required by the occasion, the old women got to telling stories about Oya. The get-acquainted meeting extended its contours and those of the goddess dominating it, dominating all of us. On the banks of the river, they said, Oya built her house, and on her sacred day of the week she forbade all crossings. As the Nupe, through Kede canoemen, controlled the flow of trade, so this Oya the old women were talking about controls the flow of blood. And a third "husband" of Oya emerged, another *lile* (strong, hard) one who propagated upon her a mysterious brood of nine, who are not Egungun, whose malefic descendants we had sensed wafting through the Alafin's courtyard at high noon. These children of Oya can cause sudden paralysis, miscarriage, madness . . .

From the palace the focus of activity shifted to the Onirá's compound, the shrine house and the great mask, central image of her power. At that stage I was permitted to see only the outer layer, with its luxurious panels of red and pale blue satin, its wild animal skins, its headpiece of spiraling horns. Such a mask, rich and flowing rather than ragged, is known as *àlàpàlà*, "cloth that demarcates (farm) boundaries." During Oya's annual festival, all Egungun in Oyo must come bow before this, their common ancestress. "Oya is Agan," said the Onirá. Hers is the final power. She is even stronger than a *lile* Orisha like Shango or Ogun because she adds the womanly power of enticement. "The culmination of the Oya-Egungun initiatory experience is the wearing of that mask. Or rather, the goddess herself wears it, blotting out the impersonator."[38]

The procedural road led back to the public domain again, where those born with a caul on their heads will always founder without advice. Fortunately Mr. Awujola was there when the time came to return to the Alapinni's compound for a consideration of finances, which would be used in part for buying drinks for the crowd the Alapinni hoped to attract to the installation. Also drummers would have to be well paid, animals slaughtered for Jenju and the other masks that would come out, and various official participants rewarded for their services. Oyo is a populous town. The potential crowd (nervously, I tried to put it out of my mind)

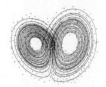

was sizable. A person of some significance in Africa is expected to spend money. If a candidate for title isn't personally wealthy, then relatives help out, for the cloth of reputation includes them in its folds. Because I was alone on a modest grant and had just undergone a heavy ceremony in the Onirá's compound, the Alapinni helped me out, *noblesse oblige*. May these words extend news of his generosity to the four quarters.

My friend Laide Soyinka in Ibadan and her friend Ms. Bolanle Awe were also hearteningly supportive. For them the occasion meant the forming of a link between educated, professional women like themselves and traditional loci of feminism in the marketplace and at the shrines of the Yoruba goddesses. Ms. Awe had been doing research on Oshun, and Laide has roots in the Abeokuta region where the power of Our Mother is very strong. That very week Laide, smartly dressed in the locally woven cloth she advocates (instead of expensive, imported Swiss eyelet), delivered an address at the University of Ife calling upon women to oppose the "restless acquisitiveness," violence, and corruption permeating all levels of Nigerian society. "For who can best appreciate the agony of this situation but women themselves, the mothers from whose bodies all our citizens were produced?"

By ten o'clock in the morning the Alapinni's compound was packed with visitors. There had been no rehearsal. Not even any instructions. We sat side by side dressed in our best. Nearby was Mr. Awujola looking magnificent. A group of women led by the Iya Agan, the Ato's senior in the cult, came forward to sing praises of the Alapinni's Igbori lineage, including the following character sketch of the original Ato, considered an ancestress of his:

> Twin Ogogo, *little Ato who is a sharp and rapid speaker*
> (*abenu jégejége:* "with a tongue like the edge of a masquerade
>   cloth")
> *On the day the current was sweeping Ato away*
> *Sweeping Ato away like calabash placed on a current,*
> *Ato exclaimed pleadingly, Please rescue me, tender indigo shrub.*
> *The indigo stretched its tendril forward and Ato clung on*
> *Which is why Ato is called Òfòrí, "Absent-minded person"*
> *Whom the indigo plant rescued—*
> *Little Ato with tongue sharp as a razor. . . .*[39]

As the praisers were dancing and singing, suddenly out of the crowd four strong women appeared holding up symbols. This was

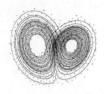

astonishing—like the dumb show in *Macbeth,* or the way it was at the Eleusinian mysteries when basket, sheaf, and who knows what else were shown. The first woman presented and then put on her head a gleaming crown of cowries—the Bayanni, with its tentacled, writhing cowrie fringe. The second woman held up a bronze mask (like Clytemnestra's), which I cannot identify. The third woman, whose title (I learned later) means Mother-of-sellers-of-rats-and-fish, carried Oya's buffalo horns. (Rats and fish, both hidden creatures, comprise the first sacrifice ever made: to the heavens by the earth in behest of rain.) The fourth woman dandled a pair of miniature cowrie vests, worn by images of the Divine Twins (Ibeji), whom Shango protects. These were handed to the new Ato to dance with because they weren't so "heavy" as the other things.

After we had danced awhile together with these *sacra,* the Ala-pinni signaled that the installation procedure would begin. It was the same sort of race run in the town of Ede, but the prize was not *akòko* leaves, rather emblems of office: a looped necklace whose beads were strung in groups of three, a fly whisk (a shank of white and a shank of black horse tail hairs bound together), a broad leather (placental-looking) fan. These any chief might hold an appropriate version of. The last item, a bloody reticule, fist-sized, is the Ato's distinguishing accessory. You won't see it that way, though. Any Ato worthy of the name has it subsequently covered in nice leather, or perhaps embroidered satin. And heaven help the profane person who looks within it. Later, the new Ato was given her *isan* switch of dried, incised wood and shown the avenging sword.

After the presentation of these regalia, it was time to dance the stations of the Alapinni's compound. Side by side, they danced, he in yards of the stiff, woven cloth (maroon with a stripe in it) they call *aşo-lawe,* the "little" Ato (almost a head taller than he) outfitted by Laide Soyinka's seamstress and the night-market sellers of Bida. Slightly inclined to the earth, and with the dignified energy of their middle years, they encircled the tumulus called "heart of the compound," which prevents malefactors from entering. The second station to be danced was a clay mound called the Iya-Maase, uniquely found on the Alapinni's premises. This mound literally smolders with pent-up rage. At our approach, two women poured bucketfuls of water upon Iya-Maase to cool her down, thus recalling the words of the Ifa oracle: "Though rain may extinguish ordinary fire, that of the great anthill cannot be quenched (for it is stronger)." The taboo of any female official of Egungun reflects this rain-repellent magic.

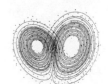

"We burn deep in the earth with an ancient fuel." From the Iya-Maase's mound the route led to Igbale, the sacred backyard forest.

Returning, there suddenly was Jenju, "The one who devours in the bush." No one saw where he came from. It was as though he simply materialized out of the sound of those Bata drums going off like machine guns. All seven feet and countless pounds of the bulk of him came on joyously dancing. Fearsome though he was, with his headpiece of thickly encrusted skulls, with his anonymous mesh face, raucous voice, and abrupt lunges, it was impossible not to be flooded with immediate affection for Jenju, as for the gruff beast of the fairy tales, I suppose. The new Ato ran up and unabashedly embraced him.

Holding his arm to help the beast in his cauled blindness across a small gully eroding the edge of the Alapinni's compound: that memory is very clear. The Alapinni faded out of the picture, presumably went home. No matter, Jenju and the little Ato were partners now. Surrounded by Bata drummers and whip-wielders, they danced through the streets and into neighboring compounds for what, when he came out of it, must have seemed like seconds in the shape of hours to Jenju's sweating carrier, in his green bathing trunks. The Ato's bare feet showed no scratch or blister, swept away as she was by something that seemed a high-noon distillation of a score of Halloweens run up Park and down Madison Avenue with a covey of gaily dressed children, exuberant in the gusty darkness of our latitude.

Stand back! The touch of Jenju's masquerade cloth to the living is fatal. But the wind raised by his gyrations is beneficial. At a certain point another Egungun joined the pair to complete it: Ato and her towering brothers. With passing cars they played trick or treat. Now and again, leaving everyone else to catch up, Jenju would dash off across some yard, up the steps and right into someone's reception parlor. Down the stairwell ten Naira notes would flutter like blessings from the ancestral forces they were intended to solicit. In one house, behind a curtain, two Egungun officials relieved the impersonator of his mask and plied the dazed youth with two liters of beer. Then the costume was carefully re-placed, and Jenju, re-become Jenju, rushed out into all the excitement generated by his appearance. Along the shoulder of the tarred main road came the third mound of the day, a rather nondescript bump that called for a trampling-down dance. Okiti-Jenju, "Jenju's refuse heap," they called it.

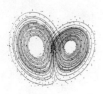

The mound within is to be cooled down, then circled piously around. The mound along the public thoroughfare is to be stomped down. The disciplinary function of Jenju, rendered otiose by the secularization of government, has been reduced to danced gesture. Yet perhaps it was always articulated symbolically, as a warning not to act out anger, not to vulgarize the power-to-accomplish, but to keep it, if one had it, smoldering under cover in the heart of the compound. Inevitably I thought of Athena persuading the Furies to go underground beneath the Acropolis, there to transform themselves into "The Blessed Ones," guardians of the city's fertility. One responds to powerful experiences in forms provided by one's own culture. Different associations would have been drawn from a Yoruba participant.

Of the triplets born to Oya's youngest son, Ato was sole survivor. She hung on to an indigo plant as the current that could have carried her away swept on. The indigo plant produces a deep blue dye, almost black, water's surrogate, which sticks fast to cloth. But with what caustic? *That* is the secret. In the midst of the black flood, the Ato hung on.

Title, too, is a masquerade. How to wear it? How to become it? To play when occasion presents itself a mythological role that somehow fits, even if borrowed from another culture, is not the same thing as naturally exhibiting "chiefly" behavior. Thinking along similar lines, but from a different perspective, Meyer Fortes, the British anthropologist, asked this question: "How [in Africa] does the individual know himself to be the person he is by what amounts, in the last resort, to the combination of unconscious forces of Destiny and the fiat of society?"[40] It is an enigma deepened by radical discrepancy between these two validating agencies. "Unconscious forces of destiny," however one imagines them, are universal, whereas society's fiats, like the languages they are uttered in, are only approximately translatable and trigger already learned behavior. Bolanle Awe and Laide Soyinka, who so marvelously carry what they are, would have no more trouble slipping into a traditional chieftancy than they find it difficult to put on cap and gown. They can clothe themselves in any honor. Their culture has prepared them to assume dignified behavior.

A few days after the ceremony installing an Ato in Oyo city, the Oyadolu family, who "own" the great mask of Oya in Lagos, celebrated its annual festival. The Alagba, head of the Egungun cult in Lagos, extended an invitation by telephone. It was no longer a question of research with notebook, camera, and tape recorder, but of showing up, of responding to the occasion, and therefore of masking very real feelings of imposture, which had always been a problem for the Alapinni's Ato when faced with society's fiat. Which is why, she imagined, those unconscious forces had propelled her toward that vacant slot in the Alapinni's modest repertoire of titles. For a person who has trouble being visible, the cult of the invisible as spectacle provides an ironic "marketplace" reflecting an otherworldly home.

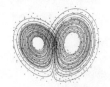

Clutching the little reticule of office, dressed in *aşo-lawe*, the Alapinni's Ato entered the compound at No. 16 Agarawu with trepidations so old they had become second nature. But the welcome, even as it had been long ago in the primary classroom, was hearty. A chair had been waiting then between two children with neatly bobbed hair. A chair was waiting now between the Iya Agan of Lagos and the Oyadolu family's Ato.

The three women in their armchairs dominated the narrow wooden veranda along the raised first floor of the main house in Oyadolu compound. Male Egungun officials sat below in folding chairs set up on the earthen surface of the courtyard. In front of both groups a lavish display of "hot drinks" and "minerals" had been set out on little café tables. In some ways the scene was familiar, especially those aspects of urban life that, patently excluded, nonetheless drifted in: sounds of traffic and radios, the office jobs from which most participants had come and to which, after a shower and a change of clothes, they would sleepily return the following morning. In some ways it was like attending a bembé in the Bronx.

The Bata drumming began with praises of the Oyadolu lineage, followed by praises of Oya, whereupon the Iya Agan, beckoning both Atos to follow, stepped down to join the dancers. The resident Ato gave us a heavy-lidded smile and stayed put. She was overweight. She was not feeling well. She was out of sorts. And besides as later research would disclose, Atos don't really count for much in Lagos. If she resented the visitor, well, that was her problem, coldly reasoned the Alapinni's Ato, who had everything to learn from the charming Mrs. Adunni Awolola about Yoruba dancing. For the Iya Agan of Lagos was tireless, ageless (though chronologically well over fifty). During lulls in the ceremony, when the Bata drums kept on playing. Mrs. Awolola would lead her apprentice out thus to instill gestures comprising the unique introspective fluidity of such dancing.

Since this is not the African dancing one sees on the stage, it is important though difficult to express its special tonality in words. It is a dance with cloth as extension of self, a dance with a loose piece of fabric—a shawl that Yoruba women tie about their hips to emphasize the voluptuousness of that part of the body. Untied, wielded as a kind of invisible partner, it suggests an emanation of soul. Men borrow it from women for the purpose of dancing thus reflectively. Often Mrs. Awolola lent hers during the course of the evening to the most expressively meditative of all male dancers present, the handsome young Oloje of Lagos. Thus, in the simplest way did Yoruba men take cloth from women in order to dance with the feminine in themselves.

The first group of masked spirits to enter the courtyard were the prankish "born-to-die" children. The Iya Agan was busy ushering them in, acting as their custodian, supervising their unrehearsed performance—these miniature Egungun veiled and gloved. The resident Ato had dozed off. What was the visiting Ato's responsibility? "Just remain seated," said the convivial Alagba, who had taken the Iya Agan's place beside her, "and move your fly-whisk from side to side slowly with the music. For it is good for people to observe important behavior." So that was it—the exemplary virtue of a chief. Then and there it was possible to adopt it, that contained, deliberate comportment whose metronomic pulse was embodied in the swaying horse tail switch, which stayed the consciousness of the one who held it like a hemiola played against triplets. Swelled beyond one's ordinary contours by the not quite legitimately pur-

Egungun-Oya of Lagos, February 1977, as she comes out at dawn to conclude an all-night ceremony in her honor.

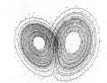

chased red shawl from Bida, it was possible in accordance with this advice and the whisk's ponderous momentum to expand to the exact edges of another culture's expectation. And for an entire occasion then it was possible to sustain it, this matrix of entitlement, to which —even were the circumstances never repeated— it would be possible inwardly to refer in the future. For this gift all verbal acknowledgments to the other culture will seem wanting.

At dawn the great mask of Oya appeared—not the familiar silken gown with the spiraling horns on its head, but a sterner Egungun-Oya with grim, rectangular face and mortarboard head, an Oya created entirely by men, one of whom in a husky voice prophesied from within. By now all participants who serve the ancestral spirits had changed into white cloth, tied over one shoulder in the old-fashioned way (like a simple toga). How like Oya to appear in such a coarse disguise from her tin-roofed "forest" at the very moment when the electric light bulbs strung about overhead were being rendered otiose by a few clear streams of sunlight striking the white percale clothing of her worshipers. As she came lumbering forward, illumination gently wrapped itself about their rejoicing bodies, and it was possible to bracket the representation and be uplifted by the idea, to sing in harmony with the others, to ask of the invisible its blessing.

Masquerade as Monkey Business

If, pressed lightly, a seemingly resistant surface gives way to become a door, then, should one continue on through, a modification of consciousness occurs that permits interpretation of ensuing events as belonging to those "unconscious forces of destiny" that Meyer Fortes saw as partially molding the African personality, if not (on account of British "social fiat") his own. But when, instead, there's a frustrated banging of head against ungiving wall, how is one to take it? As destiny again, or as social fiat? Surely there must be a transferential counterpart to the resounding no as to the gentle yes. One receives what one asks for. And yet again, if one's way of getting to know the subject of one's investigation is (shockingly, no doubt) to become defined by it, then perforce a delineating boundary appears that in good faith one can't step out of. Yet rebellious feelings surface. The free-wheeling investigator wants "out" as well as "in." She would like to play an as-if game with freedom to challenge the rules. What arrogance! She can't do that with impunity in her own society. Which is partially what motivates her, one supposes, to go out of those bounds. But social space is always bounded, and a woman will like as not find herself circumscribed as a woman, or as investigator painted into a corner.

Returning to Oyo after some years meant absorbing more information about Oya in a leisurely way without the task of public notice and necessarily now from a constricted angle. I wanted to live in a Yoruba

household with no access to the English language. I wanted to see what it would be like to begin to think in Yoruba. There was a choice of family. After that everything followed. To stay as close as possible to the shrine of L'Aiye Wu, Egungun Ode, Orisha Oya meant becoming an ex officio member of the Ologbin family rather than of the Alapinni's household. Thus placed, one felt the pull of Yoruba lineage, which is, after all, what the institution of Egungun celebrates; yet pride functioning as exclusivity and possessiveness will be felt as burdensome and will curtail what can be known.

For example, to have studied cowrie-shell divination with Morenike, an elderly priestess who came over to the shrine once a week, would have meant moving bag and baggage into Ajabata compound, a kilometer distant, where Morenike lived. Priorities prevented that. Even occasional visits to Morenike caused friction. "Everything you want to know about Oya is right here," said Joseph Ologbin, the Onirá. "Everything you want to know about cowries, I know." A more extreme case of lineage jealousy was revealed when we tried to visit Oya L'Akesan (Oya of the King's Market), the other major mask of the goddess. Eventually the Onirá was prevailed upon to give this visit a try. The foreigner's desire to "do research" superseded his better social judgment. But once the decision had been made, Ologbin's pride became involved in the project, and he wanted it to succeed. The result was total embarrassment. Even if "our" L'Aiye Wu outranked "their" L'Akesan, and despite Ologbin's considerable status of Onirá, the lineage to which Oya-Iyalode (Head of the Market) as a mask belonged wouldn't give us, the Oya-Egungun people, the time of day. When pressed, they became surly—a demoralizing experience for our group as a whole and an insulting rebuff for the Onirá.

Had the guest in the Ologbin compound been a male expatriate, would this have happened? And would such exercise of masculine professional clout have been any fairer for its success to the people involved? As it was, curiosity had violated the host's feelings. Comeuppance, though, was immediate. The photo of Oya L'Akesan not taken was compensated by the calling in of a professional photographer to snap the Onirá, seated in full regalia, surrounded by five standing wives and the resident Ato, inwardly infuriated to be thus factitiously compromised for posterity. Framed at once and immediately hung in the Ologbin's reception room, that photograph is a reconstruction of reality: a masquerade restorative of entitled potency.

The pinch of lineage contours has been felt socioeconomically and even genetically by us all, and so can be plausibly come to terms with. But like racism, sexism is a more problematic restraint, especially when experienced as a betrayal of its own values by a society that relentless ideological colonization has pushed toward such "progress." Everything Mrs. Bolanle Awe wrote about the plight of the Iyalode in the postcolonial era was registered on the dulled faces of her introverted, theoretically entitled sisters, wilting under an electric fan in the waiting room outside the shrine called Ile Odu (Place of the Containing Mother) on an enervating Sunday afternoon in Lagos. The event requires context.

Lagos is a modern city, of great license, glutted with material goods (cars jamming the streets, cheap manufactured goods from Japan and the United States sold at high prices on the sidewalks), vulnerable to electric power breakdowns and the permanent stench of open sewage, political corruption, and peculiar little fanaticisms erupting like the headlines of tabloids gleefully recording them. "Of Bitches, Witches, and Sweet Mothers" (*Sunday Times*, March 20, 1983), a banner announcing a local matron's forty-minute battle to rescue her youngest from the jaws of a crocodile, could just as well have applied to the revelations of one Olatunji, a trader of No. 1 Akande Street, before the divorce court. "My wife used her powers to render me impotent," declared Olatunji.

"The battle line has been drawn," announced a feature article the ensuing Sunday, "between Nigerian witches and Professor Godspower Oyewole, the metaphysician," who boasted to the reporter of having trained over two hundred people to assist him in halting a world conference of witches slated soon to convene in Benin City, Bendel State, at the behest of an Olokun priest whose name was disconcertingly familiar to this reader.[41] Did the meeting (or the fight) ever take place? No soap operas had ever thus engaged the foreigner's passionate attention. Yet like soaps this sensational journalism featuring invisible female agents of destruction was about deteriorating domestic relationships, and the format in which the episodes were presented suited outrageous Lagos perfectly. The most exciting twist to the ongoing story was that commanding a three-quarter-inch typeset banner across three columns:

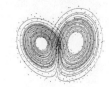

A Big Cobra which miraculously found its way into the Kainji dam power house caused the current nation-wide blackout, the federal Ministry of Mines and Powers has been told. The chief engineer in charge of the power station however said he could not explain how the snake found its way into the apartment [*sic*]. The chief engineer, who was conducting the minister Alhaji Mohammed Hassan and his entourage around the power house, also said that there had been a similar incident when a rat entered the power house.[42]

Arguably, the perceptive context is overdetermining. Had a cobra or a rat managed to get inside a Con Ed power plant, would the reader of the *New York Times* have chuckled to herself, "Aha, the Great Mother's revenge!"?

Not everything gets reported in the tabloids. The truly sinister quirks, tics, warpings within which any social body responds to the pressure of feared disintegration have to be correspondingly sought out of the corner of the eye or overheard at lunch counters. The following incident took place at the UTC cafeteria on Broad Street in downtown Lagos:

> She sits down with fried omelette, a little regression into European diet, and coffee. An African guy comes by with his tray, pauses. A nod, not quite a smile, is exchanged. He sits down. She notices that he has two glasses of water.
>
> "Oh, I think I'll go get some of that. Where's the tap?"
>
> "Here, take some of mine."
>
> To her surprise he gets up and goes for another. To her further surprise he comes back with two more glasses. That makes three in all on his tray, plus the coffee.
>
> "You sure do drink a lot of water."
>
> He mutters something about keeping the body in good condition. He's smoking Marlboro, she Target [the local brand]. She comments on the incongruity. He says American cigarettes are "part of his wealth." She looks quizzical.
>
> "What wealth?"
>
> He has a tobacco factory, or works for one, it isn't clear which. "All over the world . . ." he mutters, then asks:
>
> "What is the meaning of that ring?"
>
> "You wouldn't ask if you didn't know."
>
> "It's for homosexuals and lesbians."
>
> "What? This ring!"

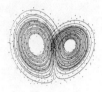

"It's a secret society. They're all lesbians and homosexuals. I know someone . . ."

He trails off, then mutters something about "Islam quenching the scum of the earth." Mixed metaphor. Terribly mixed-up person, she thinks.

"Now look here, you're wrong about Ogboni. People are joining it because it's modern, because it includes women. It's like a reformed church. Anyhow, this is not an Ogboni ring. And how can you, a Nigerian . . . ?"

"I'm not a Nigerian. I'm a German, born in Berlin, the best . . ."

A madman, she thinks, gingerly getting up from the table.

Such were the creatures hatching in the open drains of the popular imagination that spring in Lagos. No wonder the Egungun officials, traditional defenders of ancestral virtue and virility, seemed to be taking obsessively rigid precautions so far as women (and innovation in general) were concerned. But for a long time, apparently, it has been the rule that in Lagos only one woman, the Iya Agan, could enter the Igbale, Oya's Igbale, sacred precinct of the masquerade.

"We are not farmers, you realize," said a local member of the Ologbin clan, meaning: Up-country people like those Ologbin in Oyo let women run wild; we city-dwellers know how to keep them under control. The Araba, chief of Ifa diviners in Lagos, was on my side. According to Ifa, the Ato belonged in the Igbale. This is the text he cited.

Unwittingly, Ato tied me up!
Little Ato with her sharp, sharp mouth
Here's the Wielder-of-the-whip tied up in Agure!
When I didn't give the secret away
Why are you tying my hands like a hostage?
Ato, daughter, of "Sees Death," of "Carries Death"
Daughter of "Sells Death to buy cornmeal"
Daughter of "We have seen Death and want to sell it in the market"
Daughter of "Though I took the corpse to market, nobody bought it
So I had to pick it up again and start on home"
Death is a river
Ato, daughter of "I sold Death because I was hungry"
Ato, daughter of "I sold the world in order to celebrate in the
Igbale"[43]

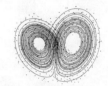

The last line is ambiguous. Either "I cleaned up my act [stopped working with the left hand] in order to enter the Igbale," or "I bartered my gift of witchcraft for admittance to the Igbale."

It was not that the Ato mistakenly tied up her cult-brother. Actually, he had been selected to carry the sacrificed chicken in the funeral procession. The chicken, like the cock Socrates wanted his friends to give to Asclepius, opens the way for the dead man's soul. The acolytes selected to carry these chickens are bound because along the way they become possessed by the newly released spirit of the dead person and the bonds help control their motions.[44] So the brother who complained about the ropes didn't know them. Or pretended not to.

It seemed astonishing to the naive Ato from up-country that Ifa wasn't gospel to the Egungun fraternity of Lagos. "Custom," to which there can be no rational rejoinder, was invoked instead, like parental fiat: "Because I say so," which must have been why she struggled with such infantile tenacity to gain admittance to the Igbale. Oya's shrine in the Oyadolu compound, at first, then the inner sanctum Oya shares with Odu were the restricted areas she tried to take by verbal storm. The mood in Lagos was obviously not conducive to the task. Yet it but acted as a goad to the Ato's feminism. The Araba gave avuncular advice from the seclusion to which a severe stroke had banished him from public view. Reason itself seemed to have been thus crippled. Under his guidance the proper offerings were made to open the door, alas stuck closed.

Frustration peaked that Sunday afternoon at the communal grove, Ile Odu, where all Egungun officialdom periodically gathers to worship ancestral spirits dogmatically watching over the chaotic town of Lagos. The chants accompanying the libations were broadcast by loudspeaker to the few "important" women assembled on straight chairs in a small anteroom made of poured concrete and painted an awful yellow. On the wall above the women's heads was a crude mural, done in the style of local sign painters for barbershops, depicting an Egungun masquerade chasing after a woman with a club. Among the real women present was the Iya-Monde of Lagos, before whose titular ancestress the Alafin of Oyo used to kneel as before no one else in the kingdom.

NEPA (Nigerian Electric Power Administration) had managed to get the current going strong again after the cobra episode. Over the loudspeaker boomed the voices of the male celebrants. Now and again the voice of the Iya Agan could be heard. Hers alone. Oya's fan whirred on a cumbersome stand in the corner opposite the loudspeaker. Her strong women, sumptuously dressed in imported fabrics, wore invisible overshawls of boredom. They tuned out, as though beneath cauls. It was impossible to imagine why they were there.

To return to the text cited by the Araba as justification for the Ato's (theoretical) presence in the Igbale, the "world" she "sold" in order to celebrate the mysteries taking place in the sacred forest is necromantic. It is the business of those who harness catabolic energy of decomposition to accomplish negative magical purposes. You don't have to go into the graveyard and dig up a corpse for a bone or two and a lock of its hair. In the outdoor market such things are sold, along with other potent ingredients like pulverized dried fish, dried rat, and the red tailfeather of the gray parrot. For a price, if so inclined, you can even buy a human skull entire from one of the Ato's former congeners.

The proverbial family to which the Ato of the text belongs— those named Sees-Death, Carries-Death, and so on—corresponds in life to the Ologbin family, whose compound accommodates both L'Aiye Wu, Egungun Ode, Orisha Oya, Oya's great mask and Ologbojo, mask of the rain-controlling bard. To this day, it is a family of entertainers (recall the Onirá's pair of praise-singing wives) whose mythic founder was the first corpse to have an Egungun mask substituted for him in funereal ritual. But this is only a titular affiliation for Ato. Genealogically (though this, too, is a fiction) she belongs to the Igbori family of Nupe provenance whose forebears instructed the Ologbin in Egungun ritual and upon whose descendants the office of Alapinni, owner of Jenju, devolves. According to Ifa, into whose text on the origins of Egungun practice oral histories of both Ologbin and Igbori families have been incorporated, this is how the first performance came about[45]

There was a family of hunchbacks. The father died. The eldest son saw the corpse and fled. The second son shrouded it, but neglected to make other funeral arrangements. The third son took up the corpse and attempted to sell it in the market to the makers of magical medicines. But those traders rejected it, so the third son started home as encumbered as ever. On the way, weariness grabbed him. He abandoned the corpse in the bush. Outraged at such neglect, the dead man's spirit consulted the Ifa oracle.

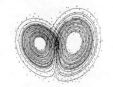

Meanwhile, the king of Oyo gave the eldest son, who had inherited his father's position as royal bard and entertainer, a wife named Iya-Máàsè (The-woman-is-continuously-cooking). Years went by. Childless, Iya-Maase consulted a diviner, named Amuisan, who foretold a son, but not until her husband had conducted appropriate funeral rites for his father.

One day Iya-Maase went to a certain stream[46] to draw water. There in the bush a monkey jumped out upon her. As soon as she realized she was pregnant, Iya-Maase took refuge among her own people, in a place called Ọpọndà (Tray of creation), populated by monkeys.[47] Shortly after her hybrid son was born, she abandoned it on a rubbish heap in the bush and returned to her husband in town.

Meanwhile, the child on the dunghill was happened upon by a woman named Ato, who brought it home and adopted it as her own. Ato's husband, whose name was Ogogo, of the Igbori lineage, did not object to having his wife care for the child; but he conscientiously reported the event in town.

Now Iya-Maase confessed to her husband that the abandoned child was hers. Should he, of the Ologbin family, acknowledge the bastard? The oracle priest said, Yes, such was the will of Ifa, but not until the bones of his father had been brought back to his compound and a funeral ceremony conducted as follows: The cortège should begin in the bush (thereafter called Igbale, sacred forest, precinct of Egungun). Offerings both to the Dead and to Witches were to be brought. The dead father's second son was to provide the masquerade cloth. The youngest son was to carve a wooden likeness of his father's face. Ato's husband, Ogogo of Igbori, designated impersonator, was to strap the half-and-half child upon his back in order to create, under the cloth, an illusion of the congenital lump. The eldest son, stepfather of the apparition, was to go before, proclaiming to the townsfolk that at last he was bringing his father home.

Everything was performed in accordance with Ifa's specifications. When the people saw the red-gowned, hunchbacked apparition, they cried: "See how well set are the dead man's bones!" (Egungun gún!—thus providing a popular etymology for the cult.) The procession halted in the private backyard of the deceased's house. There, in a special room constructed for the purpose, both costume and half-and-half child were hidden away from public view. Inside the room the child's name, Agan, was pronounced for the first time. Ato, who continued in residence to tend it, became known as Iya-Agan, even though she was only its foster mother. (Iya-Maase disappears from the story.) Ato's husband took the title of Mariwo, and every time the masquerade went forth, the diviner who had predicted and engineered all wielded the sacred switch named for him, Amuisan.

GENEALOGY OF A MYSTERY

"Real Parents"	Angry, childless mound-woman	Bard is hunchbacked (Neglected Ancestor) Violent monkey
	Gift from the King of Oyo, a continues-to-cook woman	Replacing neglectful, deformed, and sterile eldest son and husband
Foster Parents	ATO	OGOGO
Titular "Parents"	IYA AGAN	Impersonator

(a hybrid child) AGAN (an unseen power)

SUPERNATURAL REFLECTING MIRROR IMAGE

Buffalo is humpbacked	OYA	SHANGO
Alternative 1	Uses anthill as Fertility charm	Gets rid of Mother Replaces her with substitute
Alternative 2	Divorces Ogun Reverts to animal	Regresses her to primordial anthill
Alternative 3	Is "raped" by an Orisha of violence	Displaces himself by committing suicide at "the place of tying the umbilical," homeland of monkeys
		Becomes father of twins, closely tied to monkeys

The first eight of the litter are mute

1 2 3 4 5 6 7 8   9

(Anthill Mother) IYA AGAN = EGUNGUN (Monkey-voiced/defaced)

caul ⟨ATO⟩ — AGAN — ⟨AMUISAN⟩ caul

Sole survivor ⟨voice⟩

This scenario of the genesis of a deception enveloping a real mystery illustrates the mediating genius of the Ifa oracle as productive of ambiguous texts whose human authors have disappeared in the service of an authoritative, transpersonal ordering of human affairs. Postmodernist literary critics might well stand in awe of Ifa! It is interesting to observe

how levels of the story's implication are gently shaded in, without loss of narrative impetus, through names given to the characters in their shifting roles. One wants to follow the plot to the end, even if, as though it were a verbal masquerade, one can't see through the scrim. This particular story is reconciliatory of rival families. Three lineage claimants to the "invention" of Egungun masquerades are given their due.

Shango's descendants, represented by the Oba (king) of Oyo, provide the political context for the innovation. More intimately, it is the Oba who provides the sterile eldest son with the essential woman, Iya-Maase. We have met the Iya-Maase before—in the Alapinni's compound—being encircled as women cool her down with bucketfuls of water. In psychological terms, as ritualized by ancient political practice, she is the mother who is gotten rid of so that the king has space to reign over himself, thence over the kingdom. Her alter ego in the story is the anthill/refuse heap in the bush upon which the corpse of the father and the body of the monkey-child are abandoned. In her dowager-womb the bizarre transformation takes place.

The Ologbin's claim to precedence of masquerade performance is confirmed by the staging of the drama in the entertainers' compound, by its being an Ologbin family affair. Theirs are the three neglectful sons with their various strategies of denial: looking the other way (first son), "shrouding" (second son), and the third, more active procedure of disowning. The traders in magical medicines refuse to buy the corpse (tipped off by the Ato?) because it is destined for the sacred grove. The third son cannot be quits until he carves an image of the old man.

Although the show eventually "belongs" to the Ologbin clan, it is stage-managed by the representatives of the Igbori lineage—first as surrogate parents (the Ato and Ogogo, her husband), then as cult officials and impersonators. There is an interesting contradiction embedded here. Ogogo, all diviners would agree, is the first ancestor to return to life, the first bona fide Egungun. But this is the impersonator's name in the story. The corpse is a presupposition made on behalf of the performance of the rite as of the text, whose meaning remains equivocal. The "rite," which is the right way of doing things, reverts to the Alapinni's ancestors. It is a procedure rooted in Nupe culture. The bardic convention, as exercised by the Ologbin, has a different provenance. (See pp. 108–109.)

It is the monkey, totemic animal of Egungun, who accomplishes the miraculous insemination. In another version of this story, a widowed woman (out fetching firewood rather than water) is raped and impregnated by a monkey. Their child becomes king. This king of simian origin gets married, but his wives are unable to bear children until the bones of his embarrassing progenitor are brought from the bush into town in Egungun procession.[48] Whether testosterone from monkey balls has ever been used as a magical cure for male sterility in Egungun cult practice would certainly never be divulged to a stranger-Ato. But one imagines there must be a symbolic means of transferring potency from our animal ancestor to the impotent—who are often capable of having sexual relations with a resistant woman or with a socially inferior woman powerless to resist their advances. Such behavior implies an unresolved and incapacitating bond with an emotionally demanding mother as well as a self-hatred projected upon "worthless" womankind. This I take to be the problematic of these monkey stories.

The medicinal secret of feminine fertility resides not in the trees but on the ground. It is from termite mounds or anthills that fertility charms are taken. Sometimes the queen ant herself is used. Or the charm is concocted of the earth substance already worked through by insects. The latter is suggestive of the "working through" of resistance to childbearing. Thus Iya-Maase and Monkey have within the context of this "likely story" merged their respective potencies to produce a child that is half-mound, a shape preserved in the hunchback costumes that elevate what one imagines to have been congenital deformity in the Igbori lineage to the status of sacred characteristic.

The lineage just-so story is repeated on the mythological level of discourse with Oya as protagonist. (Oya's buffalo also carries a humped load on its back).[49] Anthropomorphized, Oya is supposed to have had difficulty in bearing children. According to Ifa recited in Nigeria, her brood of nine ancestral spirit-children were produced with the help of termite-mound magic. (Soldier ants defaced Egungun, the youngest of those "born on an anthill", so he had to go about veiled.[50] According to Ifa as recited in Brazil, Oya was barren until "raped" by Shango, "a man of violence." The first eight of the litter thus produced were mute. The ninth, after Oya had performed the proper sacrifices, spoke with the eerie voice of a monkey.[51]

Because these stories are products of a masculinist ethos, it is tempting to second-guess them so far as the sexual and reproductive themes are concerned. Thus, whether by mound magic (revering the nat-

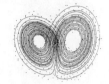

ural fecundity of women and vicariously enacting the Oedipal dream) or by simian violence (fearing the hegemony of women and imagining rape as the cure for impotence: "Shango's" problem projected upon "Oya" as frigidity or barrenness), Egungun, divine prototype of Ogogo, is conceived by the mind as having a veiled face and an unusual voice. And this is the way in performance Egungun appears.

By way of summary now, it takes a doing of violence to the norm in order to bring the Ancestor back to life. And this is metaphorically accomplished by a symbolic raid across the zoological frontier in order to capture lecherous potency and humming fertility sufficient to give birth (out of classificatory chaos) to the Yoruba's dancing star. A mating of mad termite queens and monkeys in the sacred forest puts the very concept of Egungun beyond the ideational bounds of a society whose center of gravity stays in town and never goes beyond the pale—except in the company of hunters or witches. It is a forest in which the vitality of animals and women merges wildly in mounds beneath trees.

Egungun, divine prototype of Ogogo (both corpse and impersonator), is the mythical sire of those titular triplets of the cult: Ato, the only one to have physically survived; Agan, the voice in the night; Amuisan, whip and rod of authority. Both Ato and Amuisan were born with cauls. Agan was so far out he didn't need one. In the world of Egungun, unusual birth is a metaphor for survival after death, as if anomalous arrivals to this world were natural ambassadors to the next. A triplet who makes it into adulthood is obviously a survivor—of many lives. How about the becauled? Born insulated from life, they may be imagined to see beyond the veil of appearances. Yet there is a more somber dimension to their plight. Those who experience what our culture diagnoses as schizophrenic isolation may depict their condition as being encased in a bubble. The literal reality of being born with a caul does not preclude such an interpretation. On the contrary. In Yoruba context physical irregularities are relentlessly significant.

The Ologbin lineage-founders (that vanished father and his three denying sons) are humpbacked, a physical deformity cross-culturally suggestive of introversion and artistic creation, of sexual energy blocked and transformed into *gnosis*. Rejects from ordinary social life, hunchbacks have access to both male and female sources of psychic power. They think, as it were, with their spines. Their backs bulge with fertility. According to European folk belief, to rub the hump of a hunchback will bring sexual

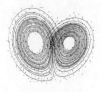

good luck, increase prowess.[52] In sum, distortion magnifies the potential but cripples the lot of these characters, all of whom would seem to belong to the same breed.

Like Oya, the characters in the Egungun genealogies are elusive. There are no fixed identities. In this world of miraculous transformations, all players get replaced by stand-ins and these in turn by other substitutes. Furthermore, Oya's eight mute children cannot say who they are to another person, and the ninth is a ventriloquist. One is tempted to suggest that when delving into Egungun, eventually one reaches something analogous to the psychotic core of the human world, which it is the genius of Yoruba diviners thus to have elaborated in fictional form to account for mysteries behind mysteries behind death's mesh veil. Yet it must be stressed here that no matter how difficult to verbalize the mechanisms, to the traditional Yoruba philosopher, reincarnation is a certainty.

"It is the agitated in mind who dance to Egungun music," is a telling line in one of the Egungun lineage praises.[53] The invisible crazies, our affines in the other world, dance right along with us, we with our hunchbacks, our protective membranes, our powers in triplicate (one for the witch, one for the seer, one for the ordinary person).[54] And the same drums are playing for Oya and Shango.

Wishing to visit the place where it all began, I asked a university archaeologist for directions. When I finally arrived at the site of old Oyo in eerie dusk, along the ridge (the famous ghost-hill haunted by the Alapinni's gang of physical deformities dressed in strange garments, see page 108), naught was to be seen but a menacing silhouette of monkeys. The rainmaking bard was neither right nor wrong. He was only kidding. What a shame they killed him. But then, if they hadn't, there would have been no masquerade.

Tree of Ribbons, Whirl of Rhododendrons

The corporate power of lineage upon which Egungun organization depends, broken in the holds and scattered to the winds of the disastrous Atlantic crossing, could not be pulled together again among its survivors. In Brazil, to which Africans were sent well into the nineteenth century, Egungun was eventually revived as a masquerade cult. In Cuba this was not possible. A different secret masquerade society, with another African provenance, grew up in place of Egungun. However, the ancestral spirits are summoned with the aid of an ancestral staff, bedecked (as it would not be in Africa) with Oya's multicolored streamers of life; and Egungun songs are sung. In the New World, the cult-house "family" of Orisha worshipers has come to substitute for blood lineage. And the head of this group is likely to be a woman. It would seem that no important symbolic config-uration ever completely disappears. As Derrida would say, the erasure leaves traces—even more moving to behold than the entire panoply.

And so it was that a faithful remnant of her broken house gathered upon a piny knoll in Central Park to "feed the hole" down which she can be imagined to have disappeared upon her death two years ago in Puerto Rico. A stick called Igi ("tree" in Yoruba) was dressed to represent the collective of which she remains spiritual head. Each of us contributed a scrap of bright fabric or ribbons to which bells had been attached. Thus every family member, according to Johnson, was required to contribute a length of cloth; and so each person affiliated with an Egungun mask

must contribute a pelt or panel for its refurbishing during the annual festival.

When all had been knotted upon the ancestor stick, the whole was dusted with chalk and rubbed with palm oil. Then everyone present blew cigar smoke and sprayed white rum upon it. And the little Ato ran around sprinkling cornmeal.

At a storefront memorial ceremony the following day in Harlem, this Igi with its ribbons, bells, and scraps of fabric was pounded on the floor by the lead singer, a Cuban. Upon a dais at the back of the store the appropriate nine candles, glasses of water, hot drinks, tobacco, and foods had been set out to placate the dead Madrina's spirit. Nothing was remarkable in this. What was astounding was the picture of her, blown up poster-size and so draped with many-colored scarves as to form a benevolent Egungun "face" too real for inquiry into the mystery behind it.

Luckily the singer had an all-absorbing task in mind. Taking a swathe of rhododendron leaves off the dais, "Dance with this," he said in Spanish, "while I sing the praises of Oya." It wasn't "important behavior" in the Alagba's sense that he wanted, holding firm to the Igi pole as to motley scepter. No, this was America. Action was wanted, cleansing action, the blessing of windblown rhododendron branches swirling about the room to Bata-drum rhythms played for the nonce upon a pair of congas. So that's what the *akpón* got. The rest of the picture is blotted out. There are only the storm-tossed rhododendrons spiraling around the *akoko* tree of many colors.

Oya de-e mariwo
Omi sa loro, yo koro.

Oya arrives, sang the voice, *mariwo.* With brother palm fringe she hides them and shields us so they won't come too close, Oya's ghosts. She sweeps that we may not be swept away upon her tumultuous dark river. Thus we keep custom.

Notes

Part epigraph is from "La loi de genre," an address given at New York University, November 7, 1979.

1. John Picton, "Masks and the Igbarra," *African Arts* 7, no. 2 (Winter 1974): 38.

2. "We have extremely restricted access now to that world-frame constituted by ancient Greek women but we have every good reason to suppose that it could be characterized as an enclosing vision rather than an imprisoned one. . . . Behind the facade of public docility women had lives of their own and, arguably, a more comprehensive understanding of men than men had of women"

(John Winkler, "The Laughter of the Oppressed," in *The Constraints of Desire* [New York: Routledge, Chapman & Hall, 1990], p. 209).

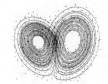

3. Ria M. Coyne, op-ed page, *New York Times*, January 15, 1984. Coyne was responding to the issues of fertility drugs and artificial insemination, which had in her opinion received sexist coverage in a previous issue of the *Times*.

4. Compare Simon Pembroke, "Women in Charge: The Function of Alternatives in Early Greek Tradition and the Ancient Idea of Matriarchy," *Journal of the Warburg and Courtauld Institutes* 30 (1967): 1–35; Joan Bamberger, "The Myth of Matriarchy: Why Men Rule in Primitive Society," in *Woman, Culture and Society*, ed. Rosaldo and Lamphere (Palo Alto, CA: Stanford Univ. Press), pp. 263–380; Froma I. Zeitlin, "The Dynamics of Misogyny: Myth and Mythmaking in the Oresteia," *Arethusa* 11, no. 1–2 (1978): 149–84.

5. Cited in Henry Drewel and Margaret Drewel, *Gẹlẹdẹ, Art and Female Power Among the Yoruba* (Bloomington: Indiana Univ. Press, 1983), p. 1.

6. Drewel and Drewel talk about the generational and the performative as analogous aspects of *ìrọn* in their initial chapter. "A generation is the worldly manifestation of a permanent otherworldly reality. Like spectacle, a generation is temporary, transitory, and cyclical" (p. 2). Compare Froma I. Zeitlin, "Playing the Other: Theatre, Theatricality, and the Feminine in Greek Drama," *Representations* 11 (Summer 1985): 62–93.

7. Conversation with the Araba of Lagos, February 2, 1976. The myth is imitated in ritual. Agan's clothless, voiced presence initiates Egungun festivals. He arrives, as his praise-song says, like various kinds of sudden rain in the night. This rain fecundates the earth. The rain that clothless Agan arrives like is a trope for the generative power of male ancestors. But rain is also linked to the mystery of Oya-Egungun. It is her secret, that which women who are members of Egungun "avoid."

8. Pierre Verger, "Odu Having to Do with Various Orisha," unpublished manuscript. xxi a.

9. Ibid. (Fagbemi Ajanaku, personal communication.)

10. The Reverend Samuel Johnson, *The History of the Yorubas* (1897) (Lagos: CMS, 1921), pp. 137–39.

11. Henry Drewel, in "More Powerful Than Each Other: An Egbado Classification of Egungun," *African Arts* 11, no. 3 (Spring 1978), note 9, p. 98, speaks of the leaf of this tree as being part of the Egungun symbol-magic system. The bright patches of red on yellow-and-green leaves are associated with the patchwork of the costume, and actual leaves are placed inside the masquerade as a charm of invisibility. The leaf (as opposed to the wooden branch) is associated with Babaluaiye, whose relation to the Egungun phenomenon will be discussed later. The staff of male inheritance, therefore, in sum, is under the tutelage of one strong male Orisha, and the medicinal leaf is the gift of another. The cloth is Oya's. The empowerment of the costume is collaborative.

12. Similarly, stories are always told at night in Africa. The spirits to be summoned by them draw near. The storyteller's voice elicits images in the mind's eye. As she begins to dramatize voices and gestures of the characters thus emerging, so our imaginations work to fill them out into "whole cloth."

13. E. Bolaji Idowu, Olódumarè: *God in Yoruba Belief* (New York: Praeger, 1963), pp. 154–57 *passim*.

14. Pierre Verger, "Grandeur et décadence du culte de Ìyámi Òsòróngà," *Journal de la Société des Africanistes* 35, no. 1 (1965): 201–19. English version slightly abridged.

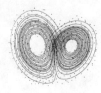

15. Robert Farris Thompson, "The Sign of the Divine King," *African Arts* 3, no. 3 (1970).

16. Johnson, *History*, p. 148.

17. William Bascom, Meko, November 1950. Thanks John Turpin for sharing this information with me.

18. Lydia Cabrera, *El Monte*, pp. 247–48.

19. Donald M. Kaplan, "On Stage Fright," *Drama Review* 14, no. 1 (T45) (1969): 78.

20. Traditional. I first heard the praise from John O. Ogundipe c. 1970.

21. *City of Women* (New York: Macmillan, 1947) is the title of an early impressionistic study of Candomblé by Ruth Landes.

22. Adapted from material in Juana Elbein Dos Santos and Deoscoredes M. Dos Santos, "Ancestor Worship in Bahia: The Egun-Cult," *Journal de la Société des Americanistes* 58 (1969): 88–89.

23. An important epithet of Babaluaiye is Olùbàjé—"He who destroys (or spoils) things"—which is what, ironically, thanks to a pun on the word, his Brazilian worshipers call the firstfruits festival in his honor: Olubaje, "Honoring the Master by eating communally." The festival occurs on the feast day of "Saint" Lazarus, with whom Babaluaiye is syncretized. The information on the name of the feast came from Claude Lepine's "Glossario," in *Bandeira de Alairá* (Saõ Paulo: Nobel, 1982), p. 66.

24. Supportive of a sense of diffusion of ritual custom all along the Niger is a strikingly parallel "fiber" syndrome in Dogon thought, act, and funereal masquerading. See, e.g., the chapter entitled "The First Word and the Fibre Skirt" (likening the covering of the nudity of the mound-mother to masquerading "against death") in Marcel Griaule, *Conversations with Ogotemmeli* (London: Oxford Univ. Press, 1965), pp. 16–29.

25. S. F. Nadel, *Nupe Religion* (London: Routledge & Kegan Paul, 1954), p. 18.

26. Nadel, *Nupe Religion*, pp. 172–73.

27. Johnson, *History*, p. 149.

28. That Shango's dance wand is a double ax does not, in my opinion, imply a Mediterranean origin for Yoruba culture, as Frobenius enthusiastically thought, but rather an independent elaboration of a natural feminine symbol. The Great Mother of Crete's ax is slim; that of Shango is full—whatever its permutations.

29. Johnson, *History*, pp. 164–66. Johnson says the king had the body of Ologbojo buried in an ass's skin. According to the Onirá (Joseph Ologbin), it was an Egungun that was made. The physical anomalies of the masquerades at the site of old Oyo can link this event with the Obatala priesthood of Ile Ife. However, I shall suggest another likely significance in a later section of this essay.

30. Germaine Dieterlin, "The Mande Creation Myth," *Africa* 27, no. 2 (1957): 128.

31. Nadel, *Nupe Religion*, p. 173.

32. Niara Sudarkasa, *Where Women Work: A Study of Yoruba Women in the Marketplace and in the Home*, Anthropological Papers No. 53, Univ. of Michigan, 1973, p. 157.

33. From a paper delivered at a conference on Women and Development, Wellesley College, June 1976. My thanks to Ms. Awe for letting me read her typed draft.

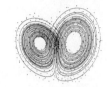

34. The title Erelu is conferred upon exceptional women in Ogboni cult context. The Ogboni is devoted to the juridical power of the earth.

35. The information on official status and titles of Nupe women is from S. F. Nadel, *A Black Byzantium* (Oxford, 1942, 1947–49), confirmed by the present Sagi's sister, Fatima.

36. Under similar circumstances Yoruba would also invoke an acceptable divinity as authorizing conduit for magical transformative powers: "There are some people, called àjẹ́, who are supernatural. But whenever they do any supernatural thing, if you were to ask them how it is possible . . . they would attribute it to the power of Ọlọ́run (the supreme deity). Ọlọ́run is just something under which persons hide to apply all our powers" (quoted in Barry Hallen and J. O. Sodipo, *Knowledge, Belief and Witchcraft* [London: Ethnographica, 1986], p. 105). Thus Fatima's use of Allah as a screen behind which to convey her understanding of "redness," which in turn is a metaphor for the power itself.

37. Ulli Beier, *Sacred Wood Carvings from One Small Yoruba Town*, a special publication of *Nigeria* magazine, 1959, p. 28.

38. "The situation of man between individual being and another Protean being which assumes every shape is made visible in the mask. Hence the participating ecstasy which the mask calls forth and disseminates. It is a true magic implement, which enables man at any moment to apprehend that situation and find the road into a broader, more spiritual world, without departing from the world of natural existence. If anyone were to wear a mask permanently, he would be a dead man or a monster" (Carl Kerenyi, "Man and Mask," in *Papers from the Eranos Year Books* [Princeton: Bollingen Series, 30, 5], p. 167).

39. S. O. Babayemi, *Egungun Among the Oyo Yoruba* (Ibadan, Nigeria: Oyo State Council for Arts and Culture, 1980), pp. 36–71 *passim*. This pamphlet includes important praises of the Egungun lineages.

40. Meyer Fortes, "On the Concept of the Person Among the Talensi," in *La Notion de personne en Afrique noire* (Paris: CNRS, 1973), p. 311.

41. By a curious coincidence, this gentleman, encountered at a celebration of Nigerian independence in New York in 1978, was the son of the woman who generously shared information about Olokun and his dark river wife when I was staying in Benin City. He said he was returning to Benin City via Oyo, so I asked him if he would be good enough to take a python skin to the Alapinni for me to give Jenju. Alas, he kept the skin for himself.

42. *Daily Times*, Friday, March 11, 1983.

43. Fela Sowande and Fagbemi Ajanaku (The Araba), *Oruko Amutorunwa* (Ibadan, Nigeria: Oxford Univ. Press, 1969), pp. 59–60.

44. Babayemi, *Egungun*, p. 49.

45. The story from Ifa ("Ọ̀wọ́nrin Ọsẹ́") is recounted by J. A. Adedeji, "The Origin of the Yoruba Masque Theatre," in *African Notes* 6, no. 1 (1970): 71–73. This simplified prose version is not in the Ifa format.

46. The Aasa River, Babayemi, *Egungun*, p. 59. The Egungun forest is always by a stream. In this case the river might be a homonym of her name: the Moshe River, an important affluent of Oya's Niger. Mound of anger and River of transformation are the natural polarities in Egungun myths of origin. They represent the extremities of the human condition—sterility and dissolution—with which Egungun attempts to cope.

47. Hunters' praise of Ijimere (brown monkey): "Child of a dog who lives in the rain! Citizen of Ọ̀pọ̀ndà! Pimply one, progeny of wild animals who makes vows with the hunter!" (R. C. Abraham, *Dictionary of Modern Yoruba* [London:

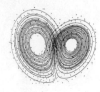

Hodder & Stoughton, 1958], p. 293). The "Tray of Creation" is another way of looking at the "load" worn by the senior Egungun.

48. Babayemi, *Egungun*, p. 6.

49. The Ogbin lineage praise *distinguishes* the hump on its ancestral masquerade from that on Oya's buffalo (Babayemi, *Egungun*, p. 95).

50. Babayemi, *Egungun*, p. 10.

51. Dos Santos and Dos Santos, "Ancestor Worship in Bahia," p. 88.

52. Personal communication, James Hillman. My thanks also to Doris Albrecht for her input on hunchbacks.

53. Babayemi, *Egungun*, p. 61.

54. Hallen and Sodipo, *Knowledge, Belief and Witchcraft*, p. 114, text no.

55. "Anyone who is both *àjẹ́* and *emèrè* has three powers—the power of *àjẹ́*, the power of *emèrè*, and the power of *eniyan* (the ordinary person)."

part three

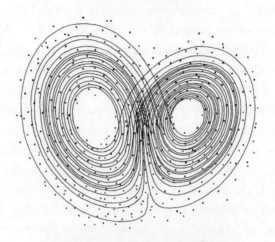

buffalo-woman
and the hunters

And the Moon, which presides over origins, was also called "the bee"
because Taurus is its exaltation and bees are born
from ruminants.
—Porphyry

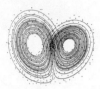

A third environment within which Oya commonly manifests herself is the "bush" or forest. Again, uniquely among the Yoruba Orisha, she takes the form of an animal in that wild place. The African buffalo, her avatar, embodies many characteristics we already associate with Oya, and in this guise the goddess acquires instinctual depth, moral weight, and a fierce commitment to her own kind. The centerpiece of this section, "Buffalo Woman Becomes Oya," is devoted to exploration of a remarkable story from the repertoire of the Ifa oracle that details two transformations: from buffalo to human woman and thence to Orisha.

Borrowed and elaborated upon by the diviners as a therapeutic text, the core story belongs to a genre of hunters' tales, a couple of which will be preliminarily investigated for the light they shed on the problematic of hunters' desire to be alone in the presence of elusive animals.

Apart from the necessity for sustained periods of solitude, two other aspects of the venatic way of life coincide with aspects of Oya's complex persona. These are witchcraft (usually translated "sorcery" in the literature of hunting) and fatality. Goddess of the hunt and goddess of death are identical in the forest, where Oya's concern (like that of Artemis in the Greek tradition) is with regulating the kills and preserving newly born animal life. In the civilized township, where Oya appears as goddess of death in masquerade form, she is in turn preoccupied with ancestral continuity and reincarnative process. These aspects of the "great round" with which the Great Mother cross-culturally is identified are seen in African thought to be alternating currents. In the bush, animal renewal negates human continuity. Indeed, hunters are socially dead and therefore theoretically without progeny. Or so one learns in Mali.

Hunters stray across boundaries. They belong to an interregional fraternity, like scholars. If you are a hunter and you find yourself in a place so far away that nobody speaks your language, a local hunter will share his campfire with you; together in the evening you will set off in pursuit of whatever game's about. And so in this section we will be traveling from Mali to Nigeria to Mali again.

Although hunters' myths and sacred rituals are elaborated within a cultural context, their ethos is everywhere the same (if they are professionals who follow the tradition developed long before commercialization of the hunt), and the psychology of their calling as well as its metaphysics will be roughly equivalent. Further afield, medieval hunting stories and philosophical discourse on the art of hunting will have a similar resonance even though there's a world of cultural difference between marvels of the European forest and sorcerous activity in the African—for the latter is an occult science.

The first chapter of this section is "literary," in that it sets the tone of the hunting venture as any romantic from the outside might imagine it and gives an overview of its mythology and historical practice in Africa, particularly in Yoruba-speaking Nigeria. The second chapter, "Night Hunting," takes place among Bambara speakers in Mali and is experiential. Following the central chapter on Oya's buffalo avatar, there's a short, grim, cryptic chapter on myths and stories having to do with the mystical patrons of the hunt in Mali, Sanene, and Kontron, that those readers specifically interested in Yoruba material may find boring but that psychologists of the feminine and folklorists will, I hope, find suggestive. Although the Sanene-Kontron material, so far as I know, is here being newly compiled and subjected to comparative scrutiny, the buffalo-woman of the final chapter is well known to amateurs of Malian epic, most of whom will probably never have heard of Oya. I have tried to make visible the link I've always sensed was there. Were they not borne on the same wind and swept along the same river? It is a story I fantasize as having begun with the woman of Laussel.

Conceiving Animals

Beneath the colorful silken coverings of Oya's great mask at Ira in Oyo city stands the facsimile of a larger-than-life-sized hunter. We have glimpsed it before, as in a dream, this formidable image: dark, rough tunic embellished with leather sachets containing occult medicines. Now at our approach it disappears. The shrine room vanishes. We are standing before a dense thicket. The brush quivers. Is there a magic word whose utterance will elicit a parting of the twigs through which we may slip unnoticed? There is. The goddess whispers it on the wind. Unscratched, soundlessly we penetrate the hitherto forbidden forest, beyond the outermost boundary of common sense where trees remain rooted and animals have hidebound reactions to things. Where we have come to is a situation highly charged with experience—our own and that of our surroundings, nocturnally perceived as indeterminate and sentient.[1] So in her hunter's guise, Oya, relentless goddess, pulls putative initiates into her obscure wilderness just as powerful contractions of the uterus once forced them out of it.

To be born a human being is to enter culture. We aren't aware of this in the beginning, of course. All eagerness to explore where we are, though the shoe doesn't fit too well we proudly put it on. Though what is expected of us may now and again do violence to our feelings, we value approval more and strive for competence as cure for disaffection. Gradually learning to live "in reconcilement with our stinted powers," as Wordsworth put it, we find ourselves become shoemakers for a new generation of barefoots. Yet civilization does provide gaps through which its endemic discontents can slip. Thus, stay-at-homes may vicariously live unrealized parts of themselves through travelers, poets, visionaries, naturalists—all of whom indirectly serve society by keeping it from stifling, all of whom in a metaphorical sense could be called "hunters" because theirs is an alertness alluring to the "prey."

Hunting is a primal form of human experience. We haven't entirely forgotten it. Long after the ritualized livelihood slipped to an occasional pastime in Europe, the hunting urge became an imaginative pattern of pursuit within a wondrous environment of what can only be recognized in a wild animal. It may be seen allegorically as an aspect of the hunter-hero to be overcome: the beast. Or it may, like implacable destiny, overcome him. It may be envisaged as a spiritual power to be attained. More compellingly for some, this imagined hunting bears a name bestowed by the goddess of love. Such a latter-day practitioner of the venatic art is D. H. Lawrence's gamekeeper, custodian of a foxy sexuality suppressed by the ruling classes, upon whose fleshly territory he poaches. A medieval practitioner, Manerius, hears the sounding of the horn. Magically his virile strength revives, and simultaneously a trembling "foreign" princess rises up: sudden surrogate for the wild hart he had been exhaustedly pursuing. A passionate embrace replaces the impossible kill as together Manerius and his princess traverse "the outmost boundary of love."[2]

But the venatic art contradicts itself. Hunting is a way for men to flee into the forest away from such tangling embraces. Think of Hippolytus. A classic Greek hunter may prefer the company of the hunting goddess to that of real women. But he mustn't presume to put himself on a par with her. Think of Orion. Nor must he make the awful mistake of seeing her naked. Then Artemis either will turn him into an animal to be hunted by his own hounds or in animal form herself will gore him. Think of Actaeon and Meleander.

There are African parallels. Whatever the literary conventions of his time and place, the mind of the poet as he traces these imagined patterns of pursuit runs like the harried stag close to its rejuvenating sources, with the result that hunting myths and stories, no matter how seemingly mannered, allegorical, or far-fetched, remarkably reflect the real thing. The scene of the hunt in European literature is saturated with enchantment, endowed with a restless "interiority" of its own that the mind of the questing hunter must be open to, in effect coincide with or

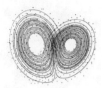

forfeit the object of his pursuit. And yet it would be dangerous to our survival to think of this responsive, permutative place exclusively as projected psychic wilderness.

"Hunting is not those heads on the wall," as Amiri Baraka put it.[3] Or, as the Hausa hunters sing it:

> It is not for the meat
> But for the sake of the game
> That we hunt.
> If you think meat's our aim
> We will go back!
> Meat's to be found at home
> Or at the butcher's.[4]

Trophies and communal feasting are but desirable bonuses. True hunters everywhere pursue the art for its own sake. In West Africa nowadays hunting is a type of deep play that provides a certain temperament with the opportunity to lead a roving life apart from the routines and responsibilities of the agricultural and trading communities. Though again this is not his primary goal, the hunter may acquire a certain heroic status impossible to the judicious farmer. Exploits that qualify hunters for heroic status are celebrated by specialized bards who know what both hunting and exaggeration are all about. In certain African societies hunting has given rise to its own literary genre, which, expanded, becomes epic. Unlike European literature about hunting, African oral recitations include praise-songs of animals actually uttered by their trackers. Furthermore, hunting gives rise to theater in Africa. When the hunter returns to the village, in the course of celebrating himself (perhaps in collaboration with a praise-singer), he enacts the stalking, sighting, and taking of the animal, which may be impersonated by a young boy.

The life of the hunter recalls an earlier phase of human history, chosen in preference to lax, confused conditions of the present. For hierarchical political and social life requiring obedience to collective norms and deference to elders, hunters substitute the libertarian bonding of brotherhood. Even across tribal frontiers, all hunters are brothers. They are a subculture with their own set of values, beginning with personal loyalty. Because they are constantly exposed to danger, they have what to nonhunters seems an exaggerated concern with purity. Before entering the bush they must be in a condition acceptable to the spirits who rule it;

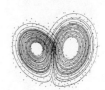

otherwise they will not be given a sight. And even though luck falls their way, great care must be taken afterward to placate the potentially vengeful spirit-double of the fallen animal.

Like artistic creation, the hunt begins with an amorphous openness to whatever traces may randomly present themselves, a getting of the lay of the land before following up promising leads. Then the tracking begins. A sight of the animal itself intensifies the commitment, which might be thought of as a dance with an unseen partner, whose tantalizing elusiveness is matched by the hunter's stealth. When conditions present a fortuitous moment, the hunter's keen eye desires to immobilize the animal as his hand releases the power of annihilation. It is not an enemy's life he takes. In watching and stalking, all patience, his imagination has become its friend. He takes it as he would take a woman. In killing the animal he sacrifices something in himself. The pain released belongs to both of them.

But we anticipate. Already we have gone out of our depth. It would be a mistake prematurely to narrow the implications of a complex activity to a single moment of truth that may not even occur. For hunting, like a vacation, is the better for not being too structured. That one never knows what may happen is the essential pleasure and risk. Nor are all hunters up to the sacred task allotted to them by the goddess—be she Artemis, Oya, or Nyalé. Not all are carefully inoculated carriers of the charge of death. Not all are capable of *askesis* (the discipline of purity) undertaken for the sake of carnal vision. Simple venatic longings are legion. There's the case of the Sunday hunter.

What most of us can easily identify with—nostalgia for solitude in natural surroundings—is not limited to Europeans brought up on Wordsworth, Rousseau, and the American Transcendentalists. Sophisticated Nigerians, who like as not have read all the above-mentioned, express this urge in the African vernacular as "having a fondness for bush meat," in pursuit of which teacher, barrister, or businessman will take off for a few days to his natal village. He does not, be it emphasized, take off to meditate in the midst of a landscape. One is always made reassuringly aware of embodiment of spirit in Africa. No, plunging into what Merleau-Ponty called "the flesh of the world," he takes off after "bush meat," with its undeniable overtones of "good sex." His predecessor may be glimpsed in the following !Kung story about Pishiboro's younger brother and Elephant-woman.

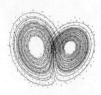

Pishiboro is one of the names of god, one of whose wives was an elephant. One night Elephant-woman, while Pishiboro and his younger brother were sleeping, took them both up and rolled them between her thighs. Disconcerted, Pishiboro's younger brother said, "Let's get away from here while it's still dark. This wife of yours may want to kill us with her attentions." Next day, the younger brother returned alone to camp. By a ruse he managed to kill Elephant-woman. He pricked the heart of her. Well, then, the first thing he did was to cut off one of her breasts and roast it.

Already he was sitting high up on her body eating his fill when Pishiboro spied him in the distance. Angrily the god advanced, thinking, "Ah, can it be that my younger brother has killed my wife and is sitting proudly atop her body?" The culprit handed him down a piece of roast breast.

When Pishiboro had eaten thereof, the brother looked scornfully down at him and said, "Oh, you fool, you lazy man. You were married to meat and you thought it was a wife." Seeing the truth in this, Pishiboro sharpened his knife and helped skin her.[5]

Thus inadvertently again we are plunged into the deeper drama of the hunt, which concludes with the sacrifice of a recognized need, followed by a "distanced" dismemberment whose subjective equivalent the hunter survives intact. Somewhere out in the bush a new animal, imbued with the released soul of the dead one, is born to replace it. There will always be an Elephant-woman.

But though an atonement would seem to have been made, there is a shady side to these goings-on in Pishiboro's encampment. The younger brother's prick, in performing its forbidden act, denied the wifeliness of the animal, reducing "bush meat" to "dead flesh." What had been a nourishing breast, as though in the acting out of an aggressive, infantile fantasy, was cannibalized. But not directly. Here's where culture comes in. First it was cut off (we would say "suppressed"), then transformed by fire into food. A lousy deed has been cooked up, and god himself by partaking is taken in. The Oedipal and the culinary triangles as diagrammed by Lévi-Strauss are seen to overlap.[6] This !Kung Bushman story is breathtaking in its acumen. Here concisely as in a dream (which may well have been its origin) appears endemic malaise between the sexes. How better to depict grown men relating sexually to women "in ways that seem rooted in the mother-child bond"[7] than by the sight of enormous Elephant-wife rolling fearsomely about. The worry an infant might experience over being crushed as he clings to a sleeping mother is linked to the anxiety of vast sexual demands being made by a wakeful, unsatisfied spouse.

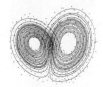

The difference between men and animals is being calculated here before our very eyes. Animals camouflage themselves. They know how to fade into their surroundings so as not to be caught by their natural enemies. However, they cannot be said to deceive themselves. Early programmed responses having grown into obsessive fantasies, men perform that camouflaging right inside their own brains. In the course of hunting, disguises fall away.

Turning one's back on city, town, or village, one branches onto a path that leads past the plowed fields through dense overgrowth toward inviolate meadows and mud wallows. Beginning to sweat, one loosens the collar of acculturation. The terrain takes over. Impossible not to notice what's going on. The greater part of one's mind sinks to knees and feet. Rocks, soggy patches of ground, winding streambeds pose their own requirements. So do plants, some thorny, some ropily rooted and coiling across the path, some with twigs poised to catch at the corner of the eye.

Whatever their tribal origins, the forest's human guests respond in accordance with what's there. Unspoken fellowship develops after only a few hours. So far it's only a hike, but suppose one's purpose in entering the wilderness be hunting. Then, after an indefinite preamble, a deeper transformation of character occurs. It isn't simply that, danger being always imminent, the senses are correspondingly sharpened, which would be true if the environment were rumored to include poisonous snakes. In hunting, man enters into a curious relationship imposed by the Other.[8]

The sport, or dance, requires that man be as much on a par with the animal stalked as possible, acquiring its habits and characteristics to the point of empathetically inheriting its own natural enemies. Thus the hunter enables himself to imagine where the next break into the open might take place. And all the while he must, as we have said, attempt to become and remain invisible. If the surface markings of an animal symbolize its "inwardness"—that which the animal uniquely is, in contrast to other species[9]—what man must correspondingly convey to whatever watches him in the forest is denial of uniqueness, denial that he's human, denial, if possible, that he's even there. Melting into the environment, the hunter perforce establishes a remarkable relationship with its green inhabitants.

Perhaps now what professional African hunters recount of their qualifications may seem less bizarre to the reader. For example: "There are two types of hunters," said the Ancient of Bandougou. "There are the sorcerers, who transform themselves, and then you have the herbalists, who understand the language of plants. The first are to the manner born. The second undergo instruction. If you do not fall into one of these two groups and think yourself a hunter, forget it!" This peremptory Ancient is a living relic of the hunter's passion: a blind man who walks everywhere attended only by his own faithful walking stick, a deaf man who carries an ear trumpet into which his interlocutor must shout above the ghostly report of ancient Dane guns. Though he lost his sight suddenly in an explosion of caustic gunpowder, his hearing deteriorated gradually with the roar of repeated firings. This ancient Bambara's typology of huntsmanship, together with his mutilations, recalls the link Yoruba traditions have forged between hunters, herbalists, and diviners—close allies in the war against entropy and extinction. Thus the thunderous voice of the Ancient, already almost an ancestor, leads us well beyond popular conceptions of hunting as despoiling and desecration to its preservative ethos, which goes back as far as the mind can imagine a distinction ever having been made between ourselves and the other species.

Although Ogun, patron of Yoruba hunters, clears the way into the bush, its therapeutic secrets are in the care of a little creature quick as a bird, furled as a leaf, elusive as a whistle, a sprite we humans (unless we happen to be highly qualified hunters) can glimpse only askance, as he turns correspondingly sideways. Catching the elusive Master of Herbalism, whose name is Osanyin, in the partially accomplished act of transformation, the Yoruba imagination depicts him with but one eye and one leg, thus heightening his accidental quality. Votaries of Osanyin make miniature images of their medicinal genius, which they manipulate like puppets and by ventriloquism cause to speak in a squeaky voice (which may be how plants speak to him).[10] The active virtues of medicinal leaves are envisaged as birdlike. Plants answer to the needs of the body as "witchcraft" responds to situational exigency. On the wrought-iron ritual staffs of diviner-healers the motifs of leaf, of witch-bird with prominent beak, and of bell are almost interchangeable. (There is a type of Yoruba bell-gong actually shaped like a curled leaf.) Bells suggest the realization of vibrations as sound and are metaphors, I think, for the animating chants said over herbal preparations.

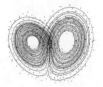

Whatever their local variations, magical methods of bringing game into view and of soliciting therapeutic (and venomous) information from plants cannot have changed much over the millennia. Nor have practical hunting techniques and equipment, as a modern translator of Xenophon's manual on the subject was pleased to discover.[11] Snares, traps, and nets are everywhere set pretty much as they always were. Dogs remain prized extensions of the human hunter's attenuated sense of smell as of his cloddish feet. Dainty iron arrowheads dipped in poison aren't much different from those originally made of bone or flint and continue to be manufactured. Guns are the exception. Like the transistor radios of today, these icons of European technology were irresistible. But they have made a slow and very complicated difference in traditional hunting milieux. For example, iron arrowheads are still used for ritual lion hunting in Mali, where guns are legion.

We are not talking about increasingly lethal weapons brought in by obtrusive European big-game hunters and the African poachers (many of them ex-gunbearers, porters, and guides of the white men) who follow after them into the game reserves, who decimate herds for the sake of ivory. Nor are we talking about Sunday hunters from Bamako and Lagos who depend upon up-to-date equipment. These are ruining the hunt, just as modern industries like lumbering and commercial cocoa plantations are shrinking the bush. The connection between hunting prowess and sexual potency, crucial subtext of the venatic activity, is made a mockery of when the animal hasn't a chance. A "kill" can symbolize attainment of manhood by youths undergoing initiation or can be a substitute for what a grown man with ambivalent feelings is required to perform on a heavy polygamous schedule. The difference between treating animals like expendable commodities and valuing them as awesome equals is paramount.

A short digression on red-neck hunting in the good old U.S.A. seems unavoidable. For just as students in a beginning course on African religions invariably wince at slides depicting animal sacrifice, so any discussion of deep hunting inevitably raises specters of lumber-jacketed types lugging "pieces" and six-packs into what remains of our wilderness. The young outdoorsman who hits the Appalachian trail with a copy of Thoreau

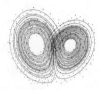

in his back pocket can't possibly hunt here, not now. The birds he identifies, the edible plants he stalks, the streambeds he traces to their sources will "place" him for encounters with spiritual forces comparable to those met with in the African hunters' forest. But he cannot engage in the lethal dance, not in our cultural context.

When traditional African hunters took guns into their woods, they adjusted their mythologies to accommodate them. They endowed guns with a talismanic virtue "answering" to the horns upon the heads of the animals they would aim to kill. African blacksmiths quickly learned to copy the flintlocks brought in by slave hunters, and these by-now-anachronistic specimens of European technology are not only *de rigueur* but in their own way sacred. Imported rifles of later make are relatively scarce among a diminishing contingent of hunters—perhaps two percent of the male population in Mali, one percent in Nigeria. These men do not have hard cash to spend on imported rifles, which *can* undergo a process of sacralization. Perhaps overall only one hunter in ten may aspire to such stylish safety.

The old-fashioned, locally made guns carry a heavy symbolic charge. They are sacrificed upon like altars. In some areas they have become foci of cult practice, thereby splitting hunters into two groups or splitting the male hunting divinity into brothers: one agile and delicate, like an arrow; the other cruder and more aggressive, like a gun. Oshossi and Ogun in Nigeria reflect this bifurcation. Among the Ndembu of Zambia, hunting remains a religious activity undertaken by adepts of two distinct cults, one centering on the mystique and mastery of the gun as an extension of self, the other involved with the propitiation of ancestral shades inhabiting the bush.[12] In a way, these two directions of hunting in Zambia reflect the Ancient of Bandougou's classification scheme. The hunter with the gun is a solitary piercer of obscurities who transforms himself. The earlier ancestral cult, with its diverse tool kit, is concerned with the diagnosis and healing of various illnesses attributable to disharmonies in the human community, most of which can be traced to neglect of the shades of dead hunters. Those attracted to this hunting cult are like "herbalists."

Yet weapons kill. There is a profound contradiction between war and the hunt that tears at the breast of the violent Yoruba god Ogun, whose fate it is to attempt to encompass both. And the two gun-carrying activities often get mixed up. For example, in time of war, hunters are employed as scouts and sharpshooters. Metaphors of hunting are used in epic accounts of war, and epics of the hunt often describe their heroes battling with betusked or behorned adversaries. An inspired killer in war or on the city streets has the hunter's knack of intuiting his potential victim's every move. But hunting is not a collective assault on enemy "others," nor is it a vendetta undertaken alone. It has nothing to do with defense or acquisition of territory. Yet weapons kill; and it was Ogun who first forged them.

Before iron was smelted there were stones to be thrown. Ogun's hand was the first to close about a stone, the first to chip away and form a hand ax, to tip a spear. The god is adamant. This is his sacred image in Yoruba religion—a solitary stone from which the iron ore is extracted by his blacksmith votaries. Iron implements are also icons of Ogun's power: knife, machete, hoe, and gun. It is a tool kit that has evolved over the centuries since he led the Orisha down to earth. The number of its canonical items has expanded from seven to twenty-one. Thus the god's power has tripled. With the introduction of European technology, Ogun has co-opted its more dangerous aspects. Not only the gun has added itself to his repertoire of lethal devices. From the narrow footpath hacked through the underbrush, Ogun has advanced out upon Nigeria's treacherous two-lane highways as patron of careening, *dagga*-smoking lorry drivers well aware of his odds. The Yoruba god of iron has lived with steel too long to stop now. Of ships he became the pilot, as Yoruba praise-poetry advises us, of planes both pilot and bombardier. Meanwhile his mythological brother Oshossi and various regional divinities of the hunt have kept flexible bow and elegant arrow as icons of venatic consciousness and purity of line.[13]

As a rule, women are not allowed in the forest. They remain in the compound, they take the paths to the farms, along the main road they may travel to a neighboring market; even gathering medicinal herbs or fruits from the shea tree, women don't go deep into the forest. And yet . . .

It's the real men who go beyond the outermost boundary of entangling love. If you're an effeminate womanizer who lolls about on various mats and think you're a hunter, forget it! jibes the hunters' bard.[14] And if you plan to go hunting tomorrow, custom forbids your having sex with your wife, any wife, tonight. And yet . . .

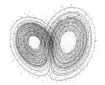

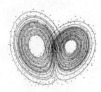

A good kill in the bush will bring increased fertility to the village. "Presenting" animals in a clearing and women's fetuses presenting themselves at the dilated exit from the womb are comparable. So are wounded animals and menstruating women. Among the Ndembu, menorrhagia, intuited as infertility caused by a woman's rejecting her role as breeder, can be cured by rituals that include such abreactive play as the patient's dressing as a hunter and doing a hunter's dance.[15]

Such striking prohibitions and connections—variants of the core Pishiboro-Elephant story—"make visible" what many feel to be the fundamental cause of tension between men and women. They want us fertile, but not too sexy. They want us competent, but compliant. They tend to confuse us with their mothers or compare us adversely with them. That aspect which men cannot quite succeed in domesticating either in their mates or in themselves can be unequivocally encountered in the forest.

Or so one might be led to suppose. But in passing through Oya's dense thicket, we shall be leaving gender issues and sexual politics behind; only upon occasional returns to the village will they perforce resurface, the point being that where we are going is into the perceptual field of hunters, as their guests, by special dispensation of their ruling spirits. And in so doing we shall be able to share in their vision of an alternative world intimately connected to "nature," as opposed to that constructed by those in charge back home. If homo sapiens European-style became grossly insensitive to the world every other species lives in and mass murderer of his own, he also became perverter of the free nature of his feminine counterpart,[16] and it is that counterpart who now calls upon the hunting goddess to take her into the bush to see if things might not be different there.

Although Oya has been said to roam the bush as huntress in the company of a brotherly Oshossi,[17] and although she discloses herself as Death got up in Ogun's rough amuleted outfit within the privacy of her shrine, her profoundest relationship to the discipline of hunting eludes philogenetic systems of classification. As a hunter learns to play the part of the animal, so the goddess of transformation may either play the part of the hunter or become the hunted. Slipping unseen from one molecular structure to another, Oya is sorcery of the strongest kind. Hunters learned it from her. She is partial to hunters. She breathes easily in the forest beneath the canopied trees, beneath the ribs of the sleeping animal.

Night Hunting

Late in the afternoon Moussa Traoré and I took a stroll in the woods. Everybody else was still asleep, but he and I felt energetic, a bit restless; besides, we had not yet had a chance for a private talk, and both welcomed the opportunity.

Moussa Traoré is a young man, in his late twenties, who was then working in Bouraba (southern Mali) as a paramedical officer. It is a district whose inhabitants suffer from black-fly blindness. Now, so I'm told, Moussa is in Paris on a fellowship in tropical medicine. He came along with us to Baru's hunting camp near Bouraba because sorcery runs in his family and herbal remedies are his passionate study. I couldn't have given such an appraisal of his motives then, but there was something about Moussa Traoré that intrigued me. He and Baru, the master hunter, had this something going between them. A spark of playful rivalry (with something not so playful beneath it) animated their behavior together. The afternoon we arrived in camp, Moussa uncovered a scorpion beneath a log that Baru was using as a headrest. He popped the scorpion into his mouth, kept it there awhile, then laughingly threw it to the chickens. Baru gave him "the look"—a mockingly wary, conspiratorial widening of the eye that mutually acknowledged sorcerers and witches exchange in Africa. I had seen "the look" before.

"If you knew the correct incantations," Moussa said somewhat pedantically in the course of our walk, "and if equipped with the proper

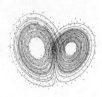

amulets, you could put your hand on any tree—like this—and it would speak to you of what it's good for—all parts of it, leaves, bark, roots."

"And if it speaks deep Bambara, how will I understand it?"

"If I gave you the correct incantations, you could translate them into your own language, even into French [which we were speaking], and the tree would respond in the same language you invoked it in. This goes for all plants."

I believe him. Not a few African healers have said so. But the gap remains between them and someone to whom the plant world remains tantalizingly silent. The most I hear from the tropicals in my window back home is something limp or crisp about the leaf in the morning sunshine. Is this the beginning of our conversation? Moodily, with Moussa I wanted to change the topic. He wanted to vary it. He began to tell me about a magical coil he had that, again with the proper incantations, could turn into a lively snake. Unfortunately he had lent it to a cousin in Bamako who wanted to impress certain people. Did I believe him now?

"Eh, Moussa," I kidded, "all this stuff you do—the snake, that business with the scorpion—what's the point of it?"

"One does these things to show people what one *can* do, the kind of power you have, the *man* you are," he answered with affecting solemnity.

"Yes, Moussa." I had never thought of it that way.

Two days earlier an old hunter named Ouana Togola, hearing that his blood brother Baru Doumbia had brought an unusual apprentice into the bush, gallantly walked thirty kilometers in order to present her with an amulet of obscurity called *dibi koro*. Beneath the windings of *dibi koro*'s dark threads lies the power of becoming invisible to the most formidable dangers. "Circumstances don't change," Ouana Togola explained. "It is the person who must alter. A fierce animal could be there—a lion or a rhino—but fail to charge because it would no longer see you." And so it appeared that, vulgar opinion to the contrary, wearing such an amulet does not automatically take care of the danger, over which we can have no control and which may assume any form at any time; rather, *dibi koro* is a reminder of one's own responsibility in the matter. A winding up of the dark threads in one's own heart makes the medicine of invisibility work. It is a self-mastery achieved in solitude. Ouana Togola did not accompany us hunting that night. When we returned, having slept his fill, Ouana had already started back to his own camp.

There is a sequel to this story. Six years later, a manuscript kindly sent from a Malian friend in Paris contained surprising reference to *dibi koro*. It was the Malian Buffalo-woman, the legendary Do Kamissa, whose story will later be told, who presented its precursor to a pair of famous hunters from the Traoré clan—Moussa's ancestors.

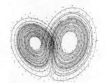

> When I shall be on the point of overtaking you [says the Buffalo-woman], you must throw behind you those three pieces of charcoal I've given you. They will immediately transform themselves into three huge zones of obscurity, separating us. The third and last zone of obscurity will stretch as far as the base of a Cailcedra tree behind whose trunk you must conceal yourselves. When I pass beneath that tree, the term of my life will have come full cycle.

An aside from the bard reciting this, his version of the well-known story connects her instructions with Ouana Togola's amulet.

> If you hear of certain hunters who possess the *dibi* "fetish" that permits them to disappear from the sight of animals, you can say to yourself: This "fetish" originated in these three obscurities emanating from DoKamissa [the sorcerous Buffalo-woman].[18]

It would have been reassuring to have had this intelligence then, for I was but going on hunches.

Besides the *dibi koro* I was also equipped with a prophylactic "snake belt" of which Baru had put together the powdery contents after our first hunt together in the fall of 1976. It was now summertime, 1980. My status had changed. I had come back to be initiated into the hunters' cult of Sanene-Kontron and to venture into the bush in a more committed spirit. I had not yet seen the esoteric image of Oya dressed in hunting clothes hundreds of miles away, though I knew the story of Oya in buffalo skin and horns. The hunch I was going on was that somehow the way of Sanene-Kontron, divine hunting pair of the Bambara, and Oya's way would come to coincide. But my original contact with the Malian hunters was rather fortuitous and had nothing apparently to do with Oya or with buffalo.

In the fall of 1976 in Bamako I became rather discouraged. My purpose, written up as an enabling grant proposal, had been to travel for several months alongside the river Niger looking out for signs of traditional water rites. Clearly this was impossible for the stranger in Bamako. The waterfront wasn't too safe to camp along. Even the kora player I knew once in Bamako was out of town, so assuaging the heart with water-songs

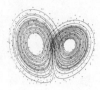

was out of the question. Better turn inland. I remembered an article I had read called "Notes sur les sociétés des chasseurs Malinké," in which its author had maintained that despite the deliberate Islamization of culture in Mali, the hunters' fraternity continued strenuously committed to pagan values and beliefs.[19]

Ironically, my only contact then in Bamako was a European named Heinz Macher, who during the French occupation and even during the early years of independence had served as head of Eaux et Forêts (Department of the Interior) in Mali. Though a famous alligator hunter at one time during his complicated career, Heinz perforce changed sides when appointed to Eaux et Forêts, whose object is to preserve natural resources. Thus Heinz became the sworn enemy of intransigent, traditional hunters whose ethos he forbore to understand. Nor did he have much good to say of women, African or European. However, because he had in his own way a profound love for the Malian countryside, Heinz was always very kind to strangers who shared this affinity. He invited me to stay in his house and introduced me to the Malian administrator who had replaced him. In turn, Eaux et Forêts sent me to another civil servant, head of the housing administration, who as an amateur of the hunt served as liaison between the reclusive professionals of the local hunters' fraternity (donsonton) and the general public.

His office was easy to find, behind the big post office. He was wearing a light blue boubou, as I remember. Taking up the question, ill defined though it may have been, with dignified enthusiasm, this man, Thiemoko Diakité, thought the best course would be to address the donsonton at their next meeting, scheduled to take place that very night. Thus, basing my appeal on what I remembered of the article, praising the assembled hunters for stalwart maintenance of the old ways of belief, I would ask them to sketch out some kind of a research program.

Hunters—who could ever forget that first sight of them, thirty or more wizened veterans, seated on mats, smoking their pipes, dressed each in his own version of the exotic attire characteristic of their calling. The prospect of attempting to touch the hearts of such a group weakened resolve, but there we were; it had to be done. Diakité introduced the visitor with that easy poise of his and molded the gawky rhetoric of her French address into a sinuous flow of spoken Bambara. As we spoke by turns I continued to peer into the dim light of the barrack at those inscrutable faces, at those incredible outfits.

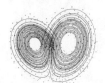

Hunters are not like other men. They are not of this world, and their clothing reflects this special social and metaphysical status. All are clad in earthy, homespun "mud cloth" (*bokolanfini*) dyed in leaves and barks that produce shades ranging from burnt sienna to red ocher to cinnamon or maroon. Upon this reddish background elaborate designs may be painted with pond-bottom mud, for which the herbal preparations mentioned above serve as caustic. (The process produces an effect of light linear configurations against a dark background). As suggested earlier, the association between women's blood and blood shed in the course of the hunt is a pervasive theme in African thought and ritual practice. The "mud cloth" being described here is ceremonially worn by Bambara women at the following crucial times in their lives: just after excision of the clitoris[20] and throughout the ensuing seclusion while the wound heals, immediately prior to the consummation of marriage, immediately following the birthing of children, and *ad lib* by postmenopausal women.[21] Therefore, it might be said, using Bettelheim's phrase, that Malian hunters carry "symbolic wounds" upon them.[22]

Hunters' shirts are further emblazoned with little blackened leather sachets containing magical substances (like the *dibi koro*.) Their trousers, baggy at the seat for comfort and skintight to the calf so they won't catch on briars, accentuate the gaunt wearer's angular appearance. Their hats, made of the same earthy cloth, are rakish and fanciful. The simplest are pillbox style. Others are dog-eared and tassled. A few, worn by those of superior accomplishment (like Baru), are leather crowns—wreathed leather bristling with lion claws and miniature antelope horns, interspersed with small mirrors, from which depend a veil of leather thongs. A Malian hunter will tell you these thongs are to keep insects off his face. But I suspect they are also intended to confer upon the wearer an ennobling and magical invisibility of face and feature.[23] And of course hunters never travel without their whistles, whisks, pouches, knives, and long-barreled, locally manufactured guns. Who would not quail before such a formidable assembly?

The petitioner retired while the hunters mooted the question. Called back an hour or so later, she was with great courtesy informed that the elders of the group had decided to delegate Baru Doumbia to be her guide into the bush. Fifty-year-old Baru is not only a master hunter but a famous one whose feats, real and imaginary, are lengthily sung by professional bards (*donson djeli*) at hunters' funerals and other get-togethers. At

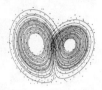

least this was his status before the drought; and hopefully it will be so once again. Here follows a condensed account of Baru's introductory course in daytime hunting.

We had spent the better part of two days tracking a kob antelope, off season [and illegally in a game reserve not far from Bamako], through grasses so high that Baru had to climb up on an anthill occasionally to see what was what. As he stood poised on one leg, with his other foot in its ragged canvas shoe resting on the calf muscles of the supporting leg, the smoke from his pipe said which way the wind was carrying our scent. But our truest compass was time, which showed us, through the degrees of yellowing, sometimes verging into brownish, on the ragged tip of a grass blade, how long ago a set of teeth had grazed there. Perhaps, if we were lucky, the depth of a molar-shaped hoofprint would confirm that the kob had passed by in the early morning dampness. At midday, to clear our vision and cool our heads, the hunter found an open space, and, begging permission of a certain small plant, he began to strip one stem of its leaves, all the while extolling their properties. Subsequently we chafed the leaves between our hands, sloshed with canteen water. Yet, cool, clear-eyed, and oriented though we thus were, we never caught up with the antelope. Not that this mattered. It was the engrossing artistry.

Now we were back in Baru's compound at Maghanbougou listening to the rain beat on the tin roof over our heads. There was to be a party. Baru had sent word to all the hunters in the neighborhood, including his special crony, Sedou Camara. One by one the guests stomped in, dressed in their traditional outfits and wearing formal leather boots rather than the serviceable Keds most of them hunt in. Sedou Camara was there already. When the room began to fill, he exchanged his slouch hat for the ceremonial peaked cap—dog-eared, studded with cowries—of his trade. Soon the harp and its accompaniment drowned out the sound of the rain.

O Baru, killer of lions
O Baru, he is a sorcerer
Who turns into a vulture
Flying high above the forest
Spotting game, O Baru, Baru
Master of hunting . . .

And with a knowing grin, wielding his antique rifle like a baton, in his crown of lion claws with its leather fringe, Baru danced to his praises. High-stepping, suddenly crouching, pirouetting to take aim at a distant phantasmal creature, Baru acted out past and future expeditions, created a stylish choreography of directional weight-shifts as graceful as

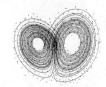

the capricious play of wind about an isolated sapling. In appreciation, everyone shot off blanks to the resounding tin roof. The room filled with smoke. Most of us fled to the porch. We were choking. But the bard kept on playing. Staring intently nowhere because the genius of music had taken him, Camara continued to sing the praises of his friend, "O master of hunting, O Baru, vanquisher of lions . . ."[24]

Now in retrospect the images of that trip seem light-struck. I remember how, as we plunged off the road into the bush, the tall yellow grass, manes of it, came advancing toward the narrow windshield in huge waves, successively breaking over the hood of the Rover. That was when, only a couple of kilometers from the road, we sighted the kob. There was this quick bulk of roan-colored flesh blotting everything out. What was that? Was it real? "Stop!" Baru jumped out of the car and, on the left, direction of that massive apparition, bent down to "tie the bush." I got out almost as fast to watch him literally knot several strands of its flaxen hair.

Now that the Rover had stopped roaring (we left it right where it was for two days), all was suddenly dust of pollen and buzz of thousands of tiny insects, further thickening the air. Impossible to brush them away. An almost hysterical excitement caught at my throat, spun my head. The power of the bush was overwhelming in the dense, fractured glare of infinite, vibrant grasses, spawning the pollen, spawning the insects, as though light itself had been seeded in that place and left unharvested for centuries. *Antilope du soleil*[25]—we never saw the kob again.

Yet all that mad prolixity and dazzle are but shadows on the wall of the cave when compared to the nocturnal landscape of "real" hunting. Were our furry ancestors night hunters also? Or did this practice begin in answer to the agricultural threat—intrusive commotion of slash, burn, till, cut, and thresh? In Mali, where ennobled wild grains have been sown for three thousand years,[26] the imagery of creation myths and the seminal axes of the world classification system are germinative; hunters, animals, and women belong to uncultivated regions of existence. As they go forth to encounter cattle-shy wild creatures at nocturnal watering places, hunters slide past the boundary of reason. Venatic hide-and-seek and sorcerous shape-shifting are correlates. The hunter's famous keen eye turns clairvoyant; phantasms freely materialize in the forest; and telltale signs merge with the ominous.

Being to the manner born is one thing, but becoming a nocturnal prowler on short notice is a shock to the system. Years of backpacking had prepared Baru's putative apprentice to follow his lead the first time; he was counting on that stamina to resurface again. But could he have had any idea of the extreme somatic trauma, especially the perceptual dissociation going on inside his apprentice during those forays out of the hunting camp near Bouraba? Probably he assumed she knew what any aspiring hunter could be reasonably expected to know; but odd as it may seem, not until it actually happened did she have the slightest premonition of real hunting's being a nighttime activity!

July 7, 1980. Arrived yesterday at Baru's little camp, about a kilometer from the Baoulé River (affluent of the Niger). A long, sluggish afternoon. Moussa Traoré found a scorpion. . . . We set off at midnight, four of us: Baru, Bafi (Baru's hunting companion from way back), Diabité (the obsequious gun-bearer), and myself. (Diabité carries Baru's heavy gun of foreign make—Czechoslovakian, I think. Bafi carries his own local musket.) The young people, Maadu (Baru's twelve-year-old son) and Moussa Touré (Baru's *ad hoc* mechanic and jeep-driver), led by Moussa Traoré, the *infirmier,* went off in another direction. They had huge flashlights, each containing five batteries, strapped to their heads with rubber inner tubing. These give off a light that can transfix a deer at two hundred meters, Moussa Traoré says. But fully initiated hunters can't carry lights. Nor do pride and custom permit Baru to shoot deer. Only the kob is permissible in this category. Otherwise, the big animals—elephant, buffalo, rhino, hippo, and the predatory cats—are his designated game. We did see some elephant tracks, but they're too old to consider seriously. It took a lot of concentration to follow first Bafi and then, at my request, Baru, who has a much more predictable way of moving through the thicket. With Bafi, in fact, I wasn't getting the hang of it at all and was stumbling continually. No more than a dancer looks at her feet can the nocturnal hunting apprentice. There simply isn't time. We were traveling swiftly. After a while I found myself shadowing Baru's every motion, miming the slightest muscular gesture of torso or shoulder, and so miraculously didn't trip on roots anymore or on uneven patches of terrain. It was like dream-running.

July 8, 11:30 A.M. Back from another nocturnal ramble. We left camp at exactly six in the evening, crossed a branch of the river, which winds everywhere about us like a snake. It was beautiful, that stretch of river in the sunset, but too dark to photograph. So why carry a camera? Absurdly, out of habit. This is the last time! We were tramping after hippo whose fresh tracks we had seen. At night the hippo come out of

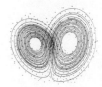

the river to browse. Stretches of chalk flats rise up, perpendicular, as if to smack you in the face. Coming to a meadow—the land settles down again. So many optical illusions! I guess I'm the only one who pays them any notice. At one point we plunged with no apparent warning down a steep ravine to drink, like many another little group of animals during the course of the night, I imagine. Baru took some leaves from a special bush, together with some random dry twigs, and lit a partially smothered fire. The smoke on our faces was not intended to drive away mosquitoes, which are legion, but rather to help our eyes *see* the browsing hippos, wherever they may be. . . .

Mostly, it's sultry. You sweat under long sleeves—imperative on account of scratchy twigs and mosquitoes. Then along comes a breeze, and you push up (or open out, if you're wearing a traditional hunting shirt) the sleeves to cool the skin. Animals can't do this.

Hunting is all about wind direction. It's the only thing that seems to have any direction. Otherwise, there's this incredible randomness. We don't seem to be able to anticipate the hippo-scheme. How could we when for them it must be simply green patch now, green patch now, green patch now?

By 2:00 A.M. I am ready to give in to exhaustion. I don't say anything, of course, but Baru senses it immediately and, as though it were his whim, suggests we all sleep awhile on these cool, wide leaves we begin stripping from little trees along the margin of the mud flats. Tremendous relief. The body acknowledges what pride cannot admit.

Only now, after a bowl of rice and a strong cup of coffee, do I feel my real strength coming back, but now's not the time. The entire camp is asleep. How difficult to dehabituate oneself from solar habits and slip easily into the hunting schedule. Which isn't really a schedule, of course. Lots of factors go into the decision as to when we'll start off, and the decision means "now." Like being on call in night hospital. Huge meals eaten in the heat, then, in the cool of the evening when my appetite naturally picks up, we're suddenly on the go again, me famished as a predator.

July 10. This time, unpredictably, we set out at high noon. By five o'clock we have reached a sandy Somono fishing camp behind the river. I fix coffee, into which we dunk dried bread. Boiled eggs for Maadu (who went along with us this time) and myself. The others don't want any. Our party splits up. Baru, Diabité, and I go back to the place where we had seen the tracks. We settle down—midnight, by now—to wait. It turns out to be a four-hour vigil, during most of which Baru sleeps on those wonderful cool leaves, which also make good mosquito whisks. Diabité stands sentry duty, literally stands so he won't fall asleep. I lie there swatting mosquitoes and listening to the stillness. . . .

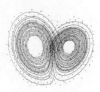

On the way back to camp a storm pursued us. Baru seized a *samana* branch (a type of locust) and waved it vigorously in front of our path to keep the storm from advancing too fast. It didn't. We just made it. . . .

Clearly Bafi is the nexus of whatever ill luck has been dogging our heels, and this despite all proper ritual procedures followed. Bafi, excellent woodsman though he be, seems of a weak, envious, and therefore ill-omened character. Where is he? It's now 3:00 P.M., and he still hasn't shown up.

July 11. Confusion and frustration darken the common mood. Repressed anger (Baru) and deviousness (Bafi) seem to be keeping away the big game—the only ones senior hunters are allowed to go after. Moussa Traoré killed an antelope last night, his second. He went out alone with his five-battery torch. At 3:00 A.M. I woke up to pee. Saw a red-rimmed torch in the distance. It was Baru with my borrowed flashlight. He had been to the river, he later said, the direction we took the first night. He heard hippos, he said, but the wind was against him. Why had he taken the torch with him, even a dinky one? I slunk back in. Shortly afterward, Diabité popped by the hut to say that Baru was going out with the little (locally manufactured) gun for a look around. Would I like to come along? Five kilometers only, and back. We spent those two hours desultorily. It was slippery underfoot. Maybe the hippos had taken off for a swim. I was sleepy. When I woke up at eight, Maadu was in camp, but both Moussas and Diabité had gone off to get the antelope. The young men were delighted to be returning with those bloody chunks on their heads.

We waited all day yesterday for Bafi to return. It turned out he had spent the night in a nearby village. Or, rather, it was the rainy morning and afternoon he spent there, sleeping in. Baru controls his rage; but he gave the returning Bafi a look that could kill a less tough old geezer.

So what had begun with such keen excitement foundered in muddy disarray. Such is human nature. The animals in the neighborhood gave their elder counterparts among men wide berth. Bafi, though a questionable type, cannot be blamed for everything. Anyhow, he's dead now, they say, so let him hope for better luck in life next time. Before we left Bouraba village for camp, the local hunters' diviner, or "reason-seeker," named Bouakorè, had consulted the bush by throwing cowries and making appropriate tracks in the sand poured out on the floor of his hut for this purpose. Bouakorè said that in general the bush was good, would yield to us, but that Baru had to make a preliminary sacrifice of three white kolas and some millet meal. I assume Baru made that offering.

How, then, to account for what happened? Was my presence a factor? The day before we went out on the hunting trip, very early in the morning, all the hunters of the village had gathered at the shrine-mound of Sanene-Kontron to perform the proper rites, including domestic animal sacrifice, which Sanene-Kontron accepted, accepted me. I don't doubt this. I saw it. But there are other ways Baru may have offended the ancient hunting gods besides his choice of apprentices. There are those who say he stepped out of line by acquiring that fancy foreign gun—gift of a white hunter whom he used to accompany regularly on big-game hunts in the upper Ivory Coast. There are those who disapprove of his dealing in contraband cartridges, though it was Baru (framed, in all likelihood) who spent time in jail while the profiteering soldiers and hunter-friends to whom the cartridges were distributed got off scot-free. Baru, whatever he does, is highly visible and therefore controversial. He's a graceful tracker and fearless hunter when the game presents itself. Just look at those horns and claws on the wall of his little house in Maghanbougou.

Baru feels bad that the two times we've been out we've been "unsuccessful." I try to explain that I don't feel that way at all, but because he does, the next time, whenever money can be found to fix up his old jeep (now on blocks in a dusty lot), we'll go out again in style. Meanwhile, during times of drought and dearth in Mali, Baru has begun to see

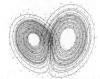

Portrait of Mariko of Bougouni, philosopher of earth and the night, March 1983.

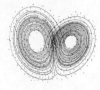

clients. To judge from the numbers lined up in the shade of the mud wall of his modest compound, already he's acquiring a good reputation as an herbalist.

"It is not essential to the hunt that it be successful," says Ortega y Gasset. The spirits of the bush (not Ortega's way of putting it) keep the eventualities balanced. The animals have to have a chance to elude their human pursuers, just as the truth lurking within that segment of night-hunting will, I suppose, continue to elude the inquirer. For it's a truth that can't be shot with a twenty-two. "The beauty of hunting lies in the fact that it is always problematic."[27] Since I don't carry a gun, which Ortega would scornfully take to mean that I have only a platonic affair with the hunt rather than a true passion for it, I see things differently than Baru does. The person who sees things the way I would like to see them is old Mariko of Bougouni, whom, shortly after the events recounted above, I asked to talk to me of amulets of invisibility, of hunters and the night. Old Mariko's face is as beautiful as his words. He is of the blacksmith caste, whose mythic ancestor is Ndomadyri, spokesman for the fourth cardinal element: solid earth.

> The power of belief is intrinsic [old Mariko said], beginning with first principles as a frame for subsequent discourse. It is in the person; that's what causes the miracle. The act is not dependent upon the amulet so much as upon the powerful persuasion of the user. If you know that uttering a certain incantation will have a certain effect, then you yourself, your desire, will create it. It is a question of confidence. If I give you "the word" and you don't believe it, not really, then that word will have no cutting edge. These days, lots of hunters pretend they accomplish miracles; but actually, for the most part they cannot, for the above reason. . . .
> The ancients used to swear by the sun when it came up. "Sun," they would say, "just as no man can prevent your rising nor stall your course across the sky, so may no man prevail against me. May all plots and conspiracies against me be discovered, as you sun, up there, see everything that's going on." Night, on the other hand, is a time of confusion and uncertainty. Man in the night knows only what he himself does. At night, a person could bathe at that tap over there, and someone sitting as we are right here would not be aware of it. It is the Great Obscurity. No one can fully penetrate the world of night. No human consciousness can pierce that secrecy. Only the earth knows. Which is why, ultimately, one must swear by the earth; because everything happens to us upon earth and only the earth is aware of the secrets men harbor within themselves upon it. Even the pilot up there in his plane must take

off from earth and come down to earth again. I have confidence in some, but there is no man, not even you, my old friend [Diakité], to whom I would hand a knife and say, "Shave my head."

To be a hunter is to hold to your word, to be impeccable in your honesty, in the directness of your thought and speech. That is the way of the hunter. Unfortunately, the universe demanded things of man he didn't live up to . . .[28]

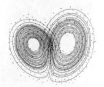

Buffalo-Woman Becomes Oya

After sunset, no pounding is heard in the small village on the margins of the forest—unless it be the permissible *thud, thud, thump* of brash young hunters pulverizing saltpeter with which to fill their cartridges. Here and there in the darkening courtyards ringed with round mud houses and granaries, shadowy women's forms bend straight-backed from the hip over cast-iron cooking pots balanced upon stone hearths. The glow of their cooking fires brindles salient contours of the women's smooth, dark faces and, catching the loose ends of head-ties, discloses snatches of their bright patterns. It is a playful dialogue.

Upon the cool serenity of outstretched straw mats, men converse in that intimate, disembodied proximity only darkness can give. For it is the voice defined by the inner contours of a man's bodily experience that ingenuously proposes itself then, and one's ear at once absorbs it, him, his characteristic way of conveying what wants to become shared event or mutual quandary, in turn eliciting remembered analogues, alternatives humorous or tendentious.

Out in the forest, night's more elusive truth begins its operations. Rustle of leaf, snap of twig, the grinding of hidden molars on grass stems, the startled cry of a bird, perhaps already the report of a rifle, articulate the heavily suspect silence. As the night wears on, tendrils of wind shoot forth to inform wary nostrils of what's afoot—over here, over there, capriciously dissolving or veering about, dispatching scents, withholding crucial evidence, now encouraging concealment, now invisibly disrobing it: wind, active agent of an obscure fatality involving all creatures, caressing them, drying their sweat, only to turn and sustain the leap that will destroy them.

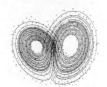

Paths leading out from village into forest branch into cleared areas where resisting soil is worked, worked again, eventually left to revert to scrabble bush and eager softwoods. It is an in-between area attractive to insects, snakes, birds, and rodents, and stealthily visited by larger animals. Comparable to penumbral areas of consciousness, these fallow gardens are the locus of fables in which observed characteristics of animals intermesh with the projected social behavior, desirable and undesirable, of human beings. Plots of such stories, traditionally told only in the evening darkness, are likely to be variations on the theme of outwitting followed by comeuppance. European collectors call the protagonists of these tales "tricksters." Hunters venture further. Sprung from experiences deeper in the forest, involving creatures farmers haven't observed, their fables turn fabulous, pitting a human hero against shape-shifting demonic forces. Or perhaps the hunter-hero is led to embrace a strange woman whom he chances to spy shedding her animal skin and to whose animal identity she will revert when her lover inevitably betrays her. (Similarly, fishermen's tales lead underwater in pursuit of and eventual capture by Mamy Wata, as the fish-tailed Siren is popularly called in Africa.)

Though the fantasy of kill as embrace would seem to lodge in all hunters' psyches, the observed physical and social traits of the animal infatuating the hero are not irrelevant. On the contrary, they are constitutive of his vision. Fleeing the forest fire depicted by a Renaissance painter, onto a universal canvas of dreams appear "the man-faced roe and his gentle mate; the wild boar too turns a gentle face." No terror upon these visages, glosses a twentieth-century poet; rather, a "philosophic sorrow" animates them.[29] So, too, in Africa it is usually the fleet deer with whom the pursuant soul would mate. Yet occasionally it is the profounder sorrow beneath the hide of a rampaging beast, the buffalo, which speaks to the heart of the hunter.

To begin with ritual traces of the more likely pattern: among the !Kung, girls, from the time they are seven or eight, are scarified little by little over the years before marriage in imitation of the gemsbok, "stately, gray antelope with spectacular black markings."[30] Stripes like the gemsbok's are made on a girl's legs, thighs, buttocks, cheeks, and forehead, not only for beauty but as denotations of fertility.

According to Yoruba myth, from duiker antelope was made the medicinal charm that caused earth to spread over the primordial waters.[31] Accordingly, the hunter-bards of the Yoruba begin their animal-praise sequences with tributes to this delicate creature of beginnings, whose meat is prized for its tenderness and whose lovely skin serves a variety of decorative and ritual purposes. Though duiker lives in the forest, she emerges alone (Olúkòjò, One-who-doesn't-assemble) to browse in fallow farm plots. It is the solitary animal who touches the heart of the lonely hunter.

> O duiker whose coat shimmers like a freshly ironed garment
> Olukojo the loner, whose white cloth enhances her dress
> Sleeping on a white cloth spread out in her little meadow
> Strutting in the disused farm, rustling the elephant grass
> Beautiful as a tray of brass, smooth, polished, and shining
> Whose feet appear brass-coated in the dry season
> Whose forelegs in the rainy season immerse themselves in softened
>   soil
> Highly sexed female
> Cleaning her private parts with her tail-whisk
> In the presence of a man.[32]

In Mali, hunter-bards sing of Donson (Hunter) Makan, who fell in love with Maje, a horse antelope. It is the story of a gifted young hunter of great physical beauty who, to his mother's despair, refuses to have anything to do with available village girls. He has a passion only for the hunt. Then one day, on the way to market to buy some powder for his cartridges, Donson Makan encounters a beautiful antelope. He follows her. She transforms herself into a beautiful young woman, whom he marries. She makes him promise not to reveal her identity. The jealous marriageable women of the village arrange to dupe him into revealing that identity by getting Donson Makan drunk on fermented honey-wine. He betrays her. She flees. But because of her love for her children, she lingers in the neighborhood. Furious at her desertion of him, Donsan Makan shoots Maje in her antelope-form.[33]

The tragic tale of Makan and Maje runs illuminatingly parallel to that soon to be told of the goddess Oya in buffalo form, whom Ogun the hunter entices into marriage. Distinctions between animals blur at the edges of dispersal. In Brazil, the Yoruba buffalo story, probably syncretized with the Malian, depicts Oya uncharacteristically as an antelope and wildly substitutes Shango for Ogun as her hunter-lover,[34] thus creating a metaphysical muddle that Oya, for all her shape-shifting, refuses to wallow in. No, she's not an antelope. Yes, she's a buffalo. And this is no way an arbitrary distinction.

> When buffalo roars in the forest
>   village-child runs to the nearest tree and climbs it
> When buffalo dies in the forest
>   head of household is hiding in the rafters
> When hunter meets buffalo
>   he promises never to hunt again.[35]

Though antelopes are shy, they may be coaxed into staying where they are. With luck and a certain coy stealth a hunter may approach one. The game is to arrest their flight, not his. Buffalo exacts a paradoxical oath from hunter. It is he who must first disarm. To phrase this in psychological language: the buffalo of the above poem demands withdrawal of a hostile projection, while her sister duiker consents to be mesmerized by a favorable. The "supreme instinct" of the animal being to make itself invisible,[36] it is no wonder that of the Yoruba divinities, all of whom have emblematic animal familiars, it is only Oya, the wind, who actually arises out of and returns to the animal. This ancestral animal linkage, the ritual programs over which Oya presides, will be discussed at length in a subsequent chapter. Here it is the theriophany itself that will concern us.

"If you want a good hunting dog, pick a pup that can run." Or "If you are curious about comings and goings, ask the doorsill."[37] Sound tracking advice from the hunters' bards requires preliminary acquaintance with the real animal before entertaining the imaginary. The varieties of antelope are legion; African buffaloes are all one species.[38] From the Sahel through the forest onto vast plains of the veldt, the species adapts body bulk and color, length and pitch of horns, to requirements and possibilities of the environment. And yet no two animals have their horns set in exactly the same way. Each is unique. The West African buffalo we shall be talking about weighs close to seven hundred pounds, and its horns measure not much more than two feet from tip to tip. But in other regions, where there aren't many trees to get in the way, the arc of the horns may expand to five feet and the avoirdupois to more than a ton. Yet withal the

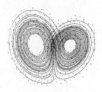

animal can keep a steady thirty-mile-an-hour pace on the flat ground and, if need be, climb rocky steeps as daintily as a mountain goat. Deftly, despite wide girth and broad horns (curved inward for the purpose), a forest-dweller can insinuate itself into seemingly impenetrable thickets without breaking more twigs than a rodent would.

Courageous, intelligent, a buffalo facing deep water, will swim across. Trapped by brushfire, it will neither panic nor resign itself to the worst, but make a break for it. Facing man, a buffalo will confidently look him right in the eye, then take decisive action: flight or fight. If the former, it's effective; if the latter, there's a terrifying attack. Buffalo cows will charge hyenas who threaten their young. Even heifers two years old are capable of fending off entire packs of these foul predators. Which is why, as the hunting-bard says, "Great buffalo fighting doesn't appeal to the cowardly." Loyal to the last, the herd protects its own against lions and human hunting parties. Yet, if undisturbed by violence, except during the short mating season just before the onset of the rains (Oya's tornado time), the life of a buffalo is essentially ruminative.

In the dry season, buffalo come out from hiding at night to browse upon new grass growing up from the burned straw residue of the human agricultural cycle. The venturesome shoots are succulent. River fog protects the animals from importunate discovery. Stray hunters, losing the scent, circle futilely upon distant ridges. Then, at daybreak, the buffalo reassemble and, single-file, an old female in the lead, vigorous bulls in the rear, heifers between, they regain wooded cover: stream margins or inviolate muddy clearings where they may drink, sleep, and ruminate until darkness once again frees them to forage at their ease.[39]

The adult males of such communities ("herds" of from ten to twenty in restricted environmental conditions) are very dark brown, or black from a distance. The females are reddish. ("Reddish" women are often praised by African men, and African women use red camwood as a cosmetic.) On their broad hips and shoulders, perhaps on their bossy foreheads, African artists who cast bronze statuettes of such moon-horned creatures place little birds of unknown natural species. Witches' familiars, spirits of preternatural intelligence, these are Buffalo-woman's messengers: cardinal points of her redoubtable orientation. This gift the living herd relies upon. For although elderly bulls of the species, who no longer wish to pit boss against boss in the thunderous mating game, retire away from the herd in small groups lazily to forage for moist grass and to loll in

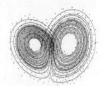

uncontested mud wallows, senior cows remain to contribute their experience. It is one of these grandmothers who becomes leader of the young-bull-dominated herd, which, following her example, slips through occult openings in the thicket and disappears.

It would be on the edge of day, edge of the forest, then, that a fated encounter between Buffalo-woman and Hunter might take place—she already assuming human form, he lingering in forest dreamtime wherein strange configurations take place. Suppose Hunter, bored and discomfited by the chatter of ordinary village women, hopes against hope to bring a piece of the forest back with him. Suppose she, rather than winding her sleepy way from intrusive "forest farms" (*oko igbó*) to the densely forested, hilly reserves (*òkè igbó*),[40] decides to take the path toward the marketplace, where already her human sisters are setting up their stalls. By the sacred anthill their paths cross. Again Oya is constellated in human consciousness.

This English version of the story follows the oracular format in which it was originally recited by the Yoruba diviner Awotunde Aworinde in June 1970 in Oshogbo.

how buffalo was taken in by hunter

1 Greetings! Now we want to praise Osa Ogunda
    a sign explaining the birth of Oya.
    "Osa-Ogun can fight" is the name of a medicine
    that will enable you to overcome your enemies.
    Eeeeee! Do you see the road Ifa took to be so called?
2 Little Whirlwind (the herbalist) sat down like thatch—
    What Moonshine! was the name of the diviner
    Who cast Ifa for Chief of the Hunters
    on the day he set forth in search of a wife
    to shine brightly for him.
3 If you are on the lookout, sacrifice,
    the diviner said, the following items:
    yams that sprout
    a small pot of guinea-corn wine
    four hens, four pigeons
    and four bags of cowries.

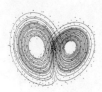

4 Sacrifice completed, he went on his evening hunt,
   stayed out all night, but sighted nothing,
   just lay on his platform up in the trees, waiting.
 Dawn came, and the hunter decided to wait a bit longer
   until it was light enough.
   to make his way back home easily.
5 Then all of a sudden he saw a bush cow approaching.
   She looked to the right
   she looked to the left
   saw nobody
   and strode along the path majestically.
 When she came to the base of a termite mound,
 to the hunter's great surprise she began to remove
 her own skin—
   arm strips
   leg strips
   and the hide of the head.
 He watched her make a bundle of all this
 and stuff it inside the anthill. Then,
   she looked to the right
   she looked to the left
   saw nobody
   and changed herself into a beautiful woman.
6 Up on his lookout platform the hunter just sat there,
   watching.
7 When she was dressed in human clothes
 This beautiful woman went back to the termite hill
   took up her container of locust-bean seeds
   and proceeded toward the market.
8 The hunter waited until she was out of sight
   then slipped down from his perch
   sneaked over to the place where she had hidden her skin
   took up the bundle, and made off home with it.
9 Then Hunter went to market to buy
   locust-seed spice.
 Irú, three shillings' worth, please,
   he said to the woman.
 I can't pay you now
   but surely you won't mind
   stopping by on the way home
   to collect your money.

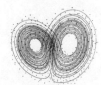

10 When it was evening, she strolled down the street
    where the hunter lived, calling:
        Irú, irú, did anyone here
        buy *irú* from me in the market?
Hunter came to the door and said it was he.

11 I have come to collect my money, she said.
    Very well, but won't you come in for a moment?
    Here, he continued, Have something to eat before your journey.
        And he offered her some of the yam
        And he offered her some of the drink
        which he had sacrificed to Ifa.

12 Having eaten yam, having drunk some wine
    the beautiful woman felt very tired, and sleepy.
    By the time she woke up, it was dark enough
        for her to leave without comment (of busybodies).

13 When she reached the place she had hidden her skins,
    the beautiful woman found them missing.
        Ai! Ai! What sort of a thing is this?
    I looked to the right
    I looked to the left
    saw nobody.
    Who, then, could have taken them?
    It must have been the man
    who bought my locust-seed spice
    without paying. Better go back
    and have a word with him!

14 When she reached Hunter's house, she pleaded:
    Please return those things removed
    from such-and-such location (not wanting to name it).
    I didn't see anything of yours.
    You did! Please, I beg you.
        Have pity on me, I implore you!
    Marry me, then! said the hunter.
    I will, said the beautiful woman,
        but you must promise
        to observe my taboos.
        Never mention to your other wives
        where you found me nor what it was
        you took from me.
    Is that all? Well, then, I promise,
        said the hunter.

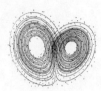

15 So that was it. Time flowed on
          carrying them with it.
     She had her first child,
          then her second, three, four . . .
     Time flowed on, until one day
          Hunter saw his red beans
          ripening on the farm
          and asked his women to come out
          and pick them.

16 Now, his elder wives
          had never stopped asking
          where *that woman* had come from.
     No relatives had arrived,
          not one, not once
          to visit her, nor
          had she been sent for, ever.
     What sort of a thing is this?
     Hunter persistently refused to tell them.

17 However, one evening,
          they plied him with food
          they plied him with drink
          until he was no longer able
          to contain himself.
     Master, esteemed husband, father
          of the household, you
          owe it to us. It's
          only proper that we should know
          the sort of character with whom
          we are forced to associate.
     We are from good families
          (apparently she is not)
          but whatever her lineage
          we deserve to know it.
     Don't you think it about time you told us?

18 Can't you leave that poor woman alone?
     What's she to you? he roared in his drunkenness
     Washn't she that bushhh cow of a woman
          I saw taking off her clothes out in the forest
          that day I bought *irú* from her
          and she came to collect her money?

That's why I married such a buffalo
    someone to confide in
    someone to shine for me
What do you skinny women know
    of the wonders of the forest?
Why shouldn't a hunter marry an animal?
Now, does that satisfy you?
Get off my back, I'm tired.

19 E-heh, they gloated; it's a good thing
    You told us now, isn't it?

20 When the time was ripe for harvesting beans
Hunter went out to spend the night on the farms.
    The women, he said, were to join him
    the following morning.
As soon as Hunter's wives arose
    they stopped by her door.
Are you ready?
Not quite, she replied, for she was busy with her children.
Hurry up! goaded the wives. Sunup already.
    It's going to be a hot day.
Please be patient, she coaxed, I'll be ready in a moment.
Reddy, Reddy, come when you're ready, they taunted.
We'll go on ahead
    take your own time, Reddy
    just keep on chewing your cud.
    Your hide's in safekeeping
    up in the rafters
    so count yourself fortunate,
    Red woman!

21 *Ai! Ai!* Her stomach hit her back
    with the suddenness of it.
As soon as her co-wives were out of sight,
    she sent her children out of the house
    put her hands on a bag made of giant pouched rat
    then went to fetch water.
Now she climbed up to the storage place under the roof
    seized the bundle containing her hide
    and began to soak it.
Pulling it on, bit by bit
    over the calf
    over the thigh
    over the arm

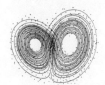

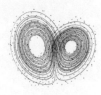

Now! She jumped down and ran through the town
    without touching or harming anyone
She ran straight to the farms.

22 Running into the first wife,
    killed her,
Running into the second wife,
    killed her,
    also the third.
Then she saw her children coming along the path.
Seeing the buffalo, they began to run.
Please don't! See . . .
    (*Pulling the hide away from her cheek*)
I'm your mother!
No, you're not, you're a buffalo,
    cried the children. Leave us alone!
Won't you please go back to the forest.

23 Of course, it must be so,
    I am going, but first
    (*Breaking off a little piece of horn from her head*)
    let me give you this.
Whenever you want me to do something for you
    just ask this.
Call it properly, call Ọya
    for that is my name
    and I will always answer to it.
Should anyone act with malice toward you
    just let me know;
Should you want anything—
    money, wives, children—
Just call on me, call Ọya, Ọya.
Farewell!

24 So saying, she pulled the hide back over her face
    and set off in the direction of her husband.
He saw her coming. That buffalo in the distance—
    instinctively he knew.
Ai! Ai! My wives have ruined my life!

25 She would have killed him at once,
    but he began praising her.

26 Noble Buffalo
Nothing stops you
You make your own road through the thicket.
No undergrowth is too dense for you.

Fighter, please don't kill the hunter
   simply for the sake of killing.
It was he who fed you bone-yam
It was he who gave you guinea-corn wine to drink.
Please spare the hunter who hosted you.
Fighting bush-cow!
27 And she was moved to pity.
This day I'll have gone for good
   but I have left a horn with my children
You too may call
   if you need me
   if you know how
Know that I am
   This sound—Ọya!
   This form—Buffalo!
   This power—
Whereupon she vanished.
28 Which is why diviners call this road of Ifa
   Ọsa 'gun le jà
   Meaning, "He used magical medicine to achieve his purpose"
   Meaning, "Buffalo-leaf, be victorious"
Medicine-can-fight
   child of bush-cow
   child of Oya
Here is the explanation.
Greetings for the sacrifice prescribed and accomplished.[41]

When a person consults the Ifa oracle he has a "presenting problem," which the diviner, without initially knowing what the problem is, will assist him in solving in four stages, which can be envisaged as four levels of treatment. First there is the casting of the lots (palm nuts or a chain of pod-shaped tokens), which, by putting the isolated client's case into generic situational context, brings preliminary relief. Ifa, the oracle, says: Of the 256 possible windows looking out onto Being, this is the one before which you now stand with an affliction endemic to this "place" and under scrutiny of or attack by certain invisible forces, which will have to be placated according to their own requirements. This spiritual diagnosis, resulting in the inscription of a graphic sign and in pronouncing its name, as illustrated here—

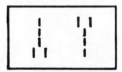

The manner in which OSA-OGUNDA is drawn on the diviner's board. Finger marks in the sacred wood-dust are reproduced as pen marks on paper.

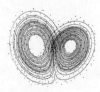

is immediately followed by praising the configuration in order to activate it. Encomia include the singing of special chants and the recitation of stories that, whatever their folk roots, are now considered part of Ifa's sacred canon. As the diviner recites stories appropriate to the configuration that has been turned up on the divining board, it is up to the client to choose the one most applicable to his (yet unspecified) problem. Ifa stories are always presented in an imaginary divinatory context in order to make the identification easier. Having recognized an analogous case, the client then opens his heart to the diviner, who, guided by remedial specifications built into the story itself, prescribes a sacrifice or offerings to be made and a medicine, which he will prepare only after the client has performed his obligation to the spiritual forces worrying him.

The sacrificial ingredients are symbolic of resistances clogging the flow between inner self, behavioral self, and invisible world. In this instance, seed yams and guinea-corn wine (stanza 3), fertile and fermenting food substances, are offerings traditionally given to Egungun—male ancestral energies concerned with the perpetuation of clan "species." The hens and pigeons—brooders—are designed to placate restless feminine energies, primal mother, Odù. The cowries rev up the client's libidinal forces by paying Elegba, divine trickster and intermediary, to get things going.

The designated medicine, praised, concocted, and dispensed, will enable the client to triumph over his enemies within and without. It is a fighting charm (stanza 1) whose principal ingredient is "buffalo leaf," the chant for the activation of which praises its "big horns." Also herbally associated with Osa Ogunda is a plant variously called "draw semen" and "eldest son," which has the dual virtue of stimulating virile power and soothing fretful crying in children.[42] Already the lineaments of a complex are being herbally suggested. A person fitting into this part of the Osa Ogunda picture feels impinged upon and ineffectual. The sexual corollary of this condition is impotence. The client goes around with a crying child inside him. This vulnerability, once the cooperation of male and female ancestral forces has been secured, calls for collaborative action by Oya in her buffalo form and by Ogun the hunter. In developing a hunterly relation to the animal-goddess, the client will presumably acquire a more solid sense of self. Applying "fighting medicine" to his body is only the beginning. Hopefully the story will linger in his mind, calling him back to issues deeper than manifest symptoms. It all depends on his capacity for inner growth.

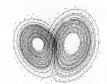

The slow-working part of the cure, the story, is as ambiguous as life itself. Like an epigraph, the fictional diviner's name (stanza 2) sets the mood for what's to follow. *Àjà fídí balè ni l'òsùpà* literally means "The ceiling plopped down on the ground is what (we) call the moon." But, if you lengthen the vowel of the first word, retaining its tonal qualities, you have *Àája*, a little whirlwind or mini-Oya who whisks people into the bush to instruct them in herbal remedies. But *àjà* as a gerund means "fighting," consonant with the herbal remedy associated with Osa Ogunda. Further, there's a joke implied in the phrase—a lunacy, something impossible. "Little Whirlwind sat down like thatch—what moonshine!" is an attempt to recapture some of these puns in English. The meanings of the diviner's name are refracted upon other surfaces of the poem. The hunter wants a wife "to shine brightly for him"—a full-moon wife whose horns are hidden in the storage rafters under the ceiling of the house. With careful artistry the diviner-poet constructs a parallel vantage point for the hunter (stanza 4), his sighting platform upon which he spends the night and from which, like a moon, he looks down upon the buffalo turning into a woman. And since such lunar dreams can't work out over the long run, Hunter's house does collapse over his head. "Ai! Ai! My wives have ruined my life!" (stanza 24).

Yet he precipitated his own ruin. First he betrayed Buffalo-woman's secret. His jealous wives operate in accordance with collective values. Marriage means lineage connections. The newcomer doesn't seem to have any. They get him drunk, and he discloses her breed, as previously Buffalo-woman, drunk on sacrificial guinea-corn wine, gave herself to him. Yet already the situation was perilous. And what did Hunter do but go off to his bean field. Red beans are "witch food," the harvesting of which symbolically coincides with the jealous wives' fatal (because now in-formed) provocation of the intruder.

Hunter, hostile to ordinary village women, distances himself from the entire situation (created by himself), thereby forfeiting control of the household. A successful polygamist has to know how to negotiate with women and how to mediate their quarrels. Simply to throw up his hands and walk away invites moral chaos. Yet how could he have got away with such an affront to common sense as to bring an exotic "reddish" woman into the compound, especially should she (predictably) prove astonishingly fertile? The fires of witchcraft flame. ("It's going to be a hot day," stanza 20.) But of course the wives' cruelty will redound upon them with the

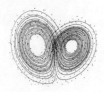

vengeance of a provoked (once would-be sisterly) animal. By means of her own vastly superior witchcraft, suggestively located in her pouched rat-skin bag (stanza 21), Buffalo-woman reverts to her savage state, destroys her enemies, and on her way out of this world reveals a now numinously compassionate nature to her initially terrified children.

This is an extraordinary depiction of how the goddess emerges from childhood experience. The caring mother, who had put her children's needs ahead of co-wifely (communal, social, economic) duties, suddenly splits. At first this is terrifying. Mother seems alien and very fierce. But as she makes off, the seed of another relation to the feminine takes root. Perhaps it was when mother seemed "beside herself" that an early intimation of the goddess slipped in.

"Pulling the hide away from her cheek" (stanza 22) is a descriptive phrase of poignant delicacy and restraint, which precisely represents the shared intimacy possible between human being and tutelary divinity. Thus disclosed, Buffalo-woman's secret vulnerability—the way in which she's "human"—allows us to be intelligibly linked to rather than rampantly possessed by the goddess. Her children have been privileged to glimpse that inner integument of sorrow in which the divine animal is contained and which, constraining her wildness, engenders her compassion. Then the hide falls back into place. Toward the forest she continues on her way. But the way toward us remains open. We can communicate our needs through the token she has bequeathed.

The crescent horn Buffalo-woman breaks off (just a little piece of her power) is the self-surrendered trophy of a hunt whose meaning is turning out to be the reverse of what it originally seemed. The horn is a token of recognition. Holding it in our hands, we grasp something of the goddess's intention. With Hunter as intermediary (as a priest able to "tame" a part of that natural force Buffalo-woman represents), she takes up residence for a while in the human community. But her presence "in person" is only an intermediate stage. In the beginning, the story is told from Hunter's vantage point, so we aren't privy to her motives; but wasn't this her intention all along: establishment of a nucleus of her worshipers, or "children?" At the moment of separation, an important distinction is made. It is to us, the children of Oya, that she first articulates her sacred name and to us that the piece of horn is given as a "transitional object" of meditative attention. And being a Great Mother Witch, she will "answer to" our situational needs. Hunters may also call her, but theirs will be a different relationship.

It is interesting to note that the *irú* (locust bean seeds, fried, mashed, and sold as a delicacy) that Buffalo-woman carried to market are Ifa's own favorite offering food.[43] So it would seem that Buffalo-woman had consulted the oracle in the forest to know whether or not her problematic sojourn in the human community would be successful! The pods of the locust, which when shaken sound like the wind, are sacred to Oya, and we often use their music to call her. The Ifa oracle delights in that which is opened up and processed. One imagines that she made that sacrifice (of *irú*) to Ifa on the way out of the forest to a new quality of being inclusive of our human consciousness.

Unworshiped, the gods disappear to an elsewhere beyond our ken. European sociologists of their post-mortem then turn around and speak of god-making as part of the process of legalizing the way those in charge run things. As the locus of earthly power shifts, say the sociologists, so does the mythological charter. But people don't "make" Orisha, they recognize, negotiate with, and serve them in order that their natural power may enhance the lives of the devotional community. Thus to recognize and intuitively to "name" gods makes dialogue with the "tamable" part possible; but control of such forces writ large will always remain an illusory human boast that no Yoruba in his right mind would make.

"Nature as Demon" was the headline of the lead editorial in the *New York Times* (August 29, 1986) following the eruption of poisonous gas from a lake bottom in Cameroon. The editors took this event as an occasion to remind us that "natural" can be lethal and that man-made pollution is the lesser of two evils.

> Science has tamed nature. . . . A world without technology
> would be prey to something worse: the impersonal ruthlessness of
> the natural order, in which the health of a species depends on
> relentless sacrifice of the weak.

The editors conclude by invoking the strenuous words of T. H. Huxley, to whom man's task was conceived as a "constant struggle . . . in opposition to the State of Nature" to develop a worthy civilization. See, we told you so, the neo-Victorian editors of the *Times* are saying, with no conception of themselves as part of the problematic process of nature. Is there not in the highlands of all being the potential for drastic overturning like

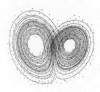

that which befell "psychotic lake"? To create cultural forms expressive of various natural forces that have succeeded in calling attention to themselves is neither to invent nor, be it repeated, ultimately to control them. It is to lend them perceptual religious shape.

Into each cultural space the gods arrive differently.[44] Yoruba society recognizes character and affirms charisma (ìwà and àṣẹ) in a person capable of attracting followers and maintaining them by generous, supportive behavior. Such a person will prove worthy of allegiance by his luck in overcoming enemies (including those that debilitate the flesh) and by his skill in handling situations (natural disasters and social messes, including those caused by pathological behavior) once they have occurred. Stepping into such a society, the gods of Yoruba similarly solicit encomia, feasts, and a body of loyal followers.

They desire great reputation, yet not as in monotheistic societies, to the exclusion of others. Family pride in one's Orisha is kept in place by the understanding that different people dance to different drums and by deference to the regulative agency of Ifa. Supportive alliances are formed like that between Ogun and Oya in the story under discussion here. It is acknowledged presence in the human community that Orisha seek in order to fulfill their own obscure purposes. They begin by making themselves known to human beings within susceptible range. Well fed, drummed for along the correct acoustical channels, verbally praised and danced, their taboos heeded, in turn these gods will release healing power through appropriate plant substances. Yet even well-worshiped Orisha remain unpredictable. Finding a flaw in the fabric we can't see, Oya can suddenly decide to rip it. A placated lake in Cameroon can turn upside down and kill off entire villages with poison gases. To live with the gods is to live dangerously; but when they are dead to us, we put life itself in jeopardy, *pace* the *New York Times* and T. H. Huxley.

Hunter and animal share a way of being illustrative of human-divine relationship. In the above story, the adversative direction hunters take from cultural norms—their advocacy of solitude, their exasperation with laws and hierarchies—is explored as a religious path. "Whoever takes to buffalo hunting has the custom of stocking medicinal charms for invisibility" is a Yoruba hunters' proverb.[45] But as we know, circumstances don't change; it is the person wearing the amulet who must alter. Upon this complex notion of invisibility Ifa priests (whose debt to the hunters goes beyond the borrowing of an occasional story) elaborate their programs

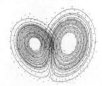

of treatment. Catching a final glimpse of Hunter standing as upon the doorsill of dreams with Oya's name on his lips, the diviners' client must wonder. The client is clutching a medicinal preparation that "can fight" and that can "draw semen" even as it quiets the sobbing child. But at what price, he must be thinking in some deeper place, the cure?

For Hunter, whose story is the most essential part of the client's cure (being a slow-working symbolic medicine that can eventually provide transformative healing rather than temporary relief of symptoms), has lost his human wives, who, crabby, jealous, and cruel though they appear in the story, are nonetheless vehicles of everyday social reality and must be taken seriously. Like Psyche's sisters in Apuleius's tale, they recognize the lunacy into which their husband has fallen, and like Psyche's sisters, through betrayal of the demonic identity of the lover, they instigate the sacrifice of an illusion: that it is possible to bring such a beguiling creature into ordinary domestic space.[46] In the Yoruba story the wives in turn are sacrificed (gored by the extraordinary beast) and with them Hunter's inflated supposition (with its attendant passivity) that he can have everything. What he can now have is a relation to (rather than an erotic merging with) the goddess Oya. If he wants a conjugal soulmate, he'll have to start searching all over again. He may remain solitary. Hunters and polygamy don't jibe. When it comes to monogamous relations in traditional African societies they have always been the cutting edge.

Like a lunatic, Hunter stands there with a message for client having to do with being both "proudly self-sufficient" (like all hunters) and needy as a baby—libidinally regressed.[47] Ironically, even his career is undergoing transformation. No need for Yoruba hunters anymore as scouts, nor as marksmen. Now that standing armies are maintained, hunters are hired by municipalities (where theft is rife) to serve as night watchmen. And though buffalo, grown scarce, have retreated to òkè igbó forever, still the moon rises, reaches a perfect fullness, then begins to decline. The conjunction on Osa Ogunda could happen again. To any one of us.

Sanene-Kontron

To begin with the crossroads. It is important to visualize this. Coming out of a village settlement along a worn path, the feet face a bifurcation posing alternatives: either to the farms or into the bush; either the way to the river or a shortcut to a neighboring village.

The path that divides has the look of fate. At such a confluence of the ways Oedipus, "child of chance," encountered Laius, the father he unknowingly killed in response to an arrogant gesture from the old man. "Listen, my wife, this is the truth," Oedipus says. "When I came to the place where three roads join . . ." From this place of prediction, you can go "home" either to Corinth or to Thebes. Convergent roads also have the look of fate. It was at the juncture of sperm and egg that began the path our lives are taking.

At such intersections Malian hunters' communal, mound-shaped altars are established. And it is at similar three-pronged forkings of trails in the bush that their portable individual altars are taken out of their leather bags and set upon improvised sacred surfaces of green leaves when they wish to communicate with their tutelary divinities, Sanene-and-Kontron. The leaves serve as a temporary plate upon which to serve Sanene-and-Kontron with water, fine millet meal, and red kola.

Both the altars and the crossroads upon which they are seated are called *dankun*—a Malinké word suggesting the summit of a limit. The

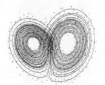

divinities themselves are a convergence rather than a parting of the ways. Where you find the one, there you will always find the other, hunters say. Their names, pronounced as a continuum, are said to be condensations of a proverb: "We have tasted of death and returned to life." The proverb, in turn, serves as epigraph for a terrifying Soninké story purporting to account for the origin of *dankun*, but without ostensibly involving Sanene-Kontron as characters. This is not surprising, given the pair's forest habitat, where traces and disappearances are the rules of the game.

The story, presently to be deciphered at some length, was with concerned urgency given me to read by its collector, Madame Germaine Dieterlen, on the eve of my departure in late spring of 1980 to do fieldwork upon which this chapter is based. Previously we had sympathetically conversed on the topic of women dignitaries in men's masquerade cults. But this current project she regarded as token womanism gone too far. "Ah," she exclaimed, "as a woman I could never have anything to do with hunters, never deeply so; for hunters destroy the feminine and can have relation only with the goddess." Whereupon she produced a typescript, which had to be read then and there.[48]

All qualms, I took it up, together with my notebook. Suppose Madame Dieterlen, doyenne of Africanists, was right? She's a woman of awesome intelligence and with far more field experience than I can ever aspire to. I thought of the tragedy of Hippolytus, the woman-hater, whose one-sided passion for Artemis brought on a compensatory surge from the sea to entangle him in his horses' reins. What was I getting into? Phaedra's fate? There is a wonderful passage at the beginning of the play where Phaedra raves of going to the mountains, of unleashing the hounds, of poising in her own hand a Thessalian spear. Was this, inappropriately, what I was envisaging? Though Madame Dieterlen's Soninké story did not deflect me from the path toward *dankun*, it sure gave me pause, always a good thing, even though subsequently I have come to evaluate it differently than she.

The story tells of a terrible encounter between two hunters coming up from the lush, forested "south" and a woman with her baby who are refugees from the desiccated northern city of Wagadu (ancient Ghana). The woman carries water in a gourd sufficient to last herself and her newborn seven days. Midjourney she meets these hunters, each accompanied by a dog, who beg her for drink. She refuses—a gesture *outré* among travelers. The men seize the container, whereupon she

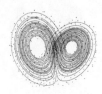

curses their progenitors, in turn provoking them to lay murderous hands on her offspring.

We have reached the limit of permissible human behavior and rapidly gone past it. The famished dogs make short work of the dead child until only its right toe remains. This the dogs fight over until the death of one of them, whose furious master kills the victor. Now the other man kills his dog's murderer. Having broken the fraternal bond between hunters, the man remorsefully commits suicide. There stands the woman alone amid carnage. Now the Creator steps out of hiding and asks the woman, "Are not four souls sufficient exchange for your dead child?" Vengeful as Hecuba, the woman shouts, "No! Never!" Whereupon the Creator restores both men and dogs to life.

The story itself ends here. Now follows an account of the constituents of the first *dankun*. The correlation to be made between elements of the story and components of the altar is derived from comments Madame Dieterlen's informants made to her, upon which I have elaborated. The sources of the elaborations are talks with various hunters, notably the Ancient of Bandougou, and comparative material, as cited.

Both man and beast shit as they die. The first hunters' altar-mound had buried within it the four pieces of excrement expelled by the four dying creatures of violence on the fourth day of the woman's journey south from Wagadu. Their counterparts today are bullets. Each hunter participating in the establishment of a communal *dankun* contributes one piece of iron-shit.

At this juncture a host of implications having to do with the privative semantics of huntsmanship are buried with pieces of iron-shit. In

Altar (*dankun*) to Sanene-Kontron outside Bouraba, Mali. This is a communal altar formed by the *donsonton* (hunting fraternity).

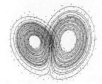

principle, a productive hunter may beget no children. Once upon a time, said the Ancient of Bandougou, and only once, the hunting god Kontron's aim went awry. He hit a balimbo tree, which henceforth always had a dried-up part. With the tree's partial sterility are associated exclusive male bonding, a focus upon penis and anus with no attention to vagina, and catabolic process.

In his discussion of Ndembu color classification, Victor Turner notes that when a sterile person dies, a black charcoal line is drawn from the naval of the deceased downward to the groin as a sign of "dying forever" in opposition to "returning to life" (via descendants), which would be represented by a white clay marking.[49] Burned-out fire. Charcoal represents the Yoruba Orisha Ogun in the sacred container of Ifa divination. Charcoal symbolizes "brotherhood," under the patronage of Ogun. Brotherhood is what one might call a horizontal as opposed to a vertical axis of affiliation. One never hears of Ogun's children. When a man takes the oath of loyalty to Sanene-Kontron, he steps out of the vertical axis and onto the horizontal. All hunters are brothers, are children of Sanene-Kontron. Semantically, the hunters of the Soninké story are goners, but the Creator/Creatrix revives them, and together they institute a cult.

Three items belonging to the woman went into that first *dankun*: a shard from her broken water container, her food ladle, and her winnowing fan (the last two not mentioned in the story, only in the commentary). Water withheld becomes water released. A birth has taken place. Or so it would seem, for these items (food ladle and winnowing fan) are replicated in real altars of today by the placenta of a pregnant antelope sacrificed so that the game will be plentiful. Malian hunters distinguish two sides of the placenta. *Mankongoba* is the part adhering to the uterus. *Nangoloko* adheres to the fetus. *Mankongoba* "winnows"—acts as a protective screen. *Nangoloko* nourishes, hence the ladle. The former mystically represents Sanene, the latter Kontron—not actually mother and son, but in the same relation. As the entire placenta is thought to be the "double" or twin of the embryo, so the divine pair who rule the hunt protect and nourish (provide game for) each hunter initiated as offspring of the dual divinity.

The child's presence in the altar is indicated by a symbol of its big toe, the only part not destroyed by the hunting dogs. Throughout Africa one's big toe is taken to be locus of one's ancestral guardian spirit. It is the site of warnings. If, upon leaving the house, one stubs it, then business abroad is postponed until a more propitious moment. The Ancient of Bandougou told us that although most people think Sanene-Kontron had no children, they did in fact have one, a daughter, Komifolo, whose name means "the big toe," "the first little thing," or, even more abstractly, "the essential." It was this Komifolo, he said, who taught men to hunt. All initiations into the hunting fraternity (*donsonton*) began with her, the first to be shown the art. And they still do.

The elusive mystery of that big toe, "essential" because it represents a condensation of life's vertical dimension (ancestor come back to life in the child), is always present along the trail the hunter follows. To follow the hunter one must become, therefore, sleuth of hoofprints. The double-toed mark of ungulates like buffalo and antelope is all that you see. What's missing isn't actually a toe, it's more like a heel. In truth it's an ankle. Talus bone or astragalus—the terms are interchangeable. Baru said that this missing bone is Kontron's sign, whereas Sanene prints herself double-toed, like the moon in opposite phases. However, I tend to accept the Ancient of Bandougou's threesome. There are further complications.

In Paris, Solange de Ganay and Dominique Zahan happened to show me a ritual "twins vase," of which I made a schematic drawing because of its resemblance to the receptacle used for offerings to the divine twins in Haiti. At the time I had no idea it could possibly have anything to do with hunting. The single cup of the trefoil illustrates the child born after twins, they said, and is called "the dominant." (Ubiquitously, the child born after twins is very powerful.) Esoterically, the vase represents the three primary Bambara

Figurations of Sanene-Kontron as Crossroads, Hoofprints, and Twins. A third element is always necessary to compete the picture. On the left, "Separations of the Paths," which is the occult sign for twins. On the right, schematic drawing of ritual Twins Vase, which includes a third bowl for the child born after twins, "the dominant."

gods. The twin on the right side is Faro, androgynous water spirit. On the left is Ndomadyri, solid earth, patron of blacksmiths. Nyalé, the fiery feminine principle is in the "dominant" position. The asterisk incised on the handle of the vase, oriented eastward, is the divine spark of the Creator, which Nyalé herself embodied when the cosmos came into being.[50] Thus Nyalé appears twice on the twins vase along a vertical axis.

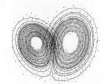

Translating this model back into the Soninké story, the two hunters may be seen as twins, the woman as "the dominant," and the "spark" as the creative power that brings those who "have tasted of death" back to life. Where is the child?

The child was not revived. Its permanent sacrifice for the sake of a different social order in the forest haunts every hoofprint traced by ungulates and tracked by hunters.

As if to compound the enigma, when I took the notion of the hoofprint with its invisible astragalus to Youssouf Cissé, the Malian scholar whose article on hunters had sent me along this path in the first place, he took a stick and drew on the ground the Komo society's graphic sign for twins. This figure, called "separation of the paths," represents both the crossroads with which we began this discussion and an ungulate hoofprint. The hind part of the hoof, which never gets printed on the path, is the "dominant," said Cissé rather cryptically. But what he said makes sense. Lined up with the twins vase, it is going west—the direction of sorcery, of woman, of the wind. If the paths are diverging, then the "dominant" is heading back where we came from. As an ancestral principle, the big toe does just that. The child whom the woman in the story carries is the reincarnation of a feminine principle that "died" or was suppressed.

The domain of the hunt is the domain of death. "When the hunter takes up his gun," roared the disabled Ancient of Bandougou, "one says he is already a cadaver; for his weapon, which he carries loaded, at any moment can kill him. We also consider the gun itself to be a dead thing. (Sterile?) And the third dead part of the hunt is the animal, whom the hunter entices by saying, 'Come to me. How can I kill you when all three of us (man, weapon, game) are dead already?'" On the magical level of operations, this ghostly status of all players in the drama ensures the invulnerability of the hunter, the accuracy of his weapon, and perpetuity of the animal species. The seemingly unique ungulate is dead, pregnant with unseen congeners. It is to this bizarre propagation that the dark hunter, wearing the cloth of wounded women (see page 169), dedicates his

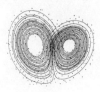

desire. This is why, in theory, he can propagate no children of his own species. He cannot have it both ways.

Is not "to destroy the feminine and have relation only with a goddess" too stern a reduction? Following the hunters' path leads us into myth, and, as Santayana says, "What the soul desires is not arbitrary. Life is not objectless dreams. Everything that satisfies at all, even if partially and for an instant, justifies aspiration and rewards it."[51] Before turning to various hunters' accounts of Sanene-Kontron, which may provide a way to rephrase Madame Dieterlen's statement, an essential missing feature of the *dankun* story—its antecedent—should be sketched in. This Soninké tale, familiar to any Malian, is also known to students of American literature for the use Ezra Pound (through Frobenius) made of it in his *Cantos*. The woman is a refugee from Wagadu, ancient kingdom of Ghana, which fell, they say, because of a great impiety that was committed. A gift was refused because a sacrifice was not made. Yet, from the hero's point of view, a dangerous monster had been defeated.[52]

The city of Wagadu on the edge of the desert had been fabulously wealthy in gold owing to its situation at the intersection of trade routes leading across the Sahara and down into Guinea, where the gold was mined. This prosperity was maintained by placation of the great Python of Bida, lodged at the bottom of the city's principal well. Every year the serpent required the sacrifice of a young woman. (Either clans rotated in their contribution, or the woman was identified by divination.) At a certain moment in time, which was the beginning of linear history for the Soninké, a young man objected to having his fiancée fed to the serpent. He hid at the edge of the well. When the tutelary spirit uncoiled itself and rose to the lip to take her, the young man stepped forth and slew the creature. Forthwith the city was cursed with drought. The lively gold fled from the hands of its merchants. Caravans began to avoid the place on their way south to pass by Tombouctou instead. The hero found himself leader of a great dispersion of his people. And the fertile crossroads at which Wagadu once stood was banished into the bush to become a hunters' altar.

The story can be interpreted at various levels. Sociologically it refers to the Islamization of the Soninké—a defiance of their cosmic rootedness. Into a social structure based on consensual primacy of the group, the possibility of an overriding individual will manifests itself. Catastrophic displacement results. The people of Wagadu became wandering marabouts and merchants. The deepest manifestation of the goddess has been destroyed for the sake of relation to the individual woman—the reverse of Madame Dieterlen's proposition. And look what happens. Furious, the great goddess, possessing the liberated woman, flees Wagadu. Like the great well in miniature, the angry woman (wraith of the goddess) denies the wandering hunters drink. It is a retaliatory version of the very ethos (each for himself) that negated Python's claim to the virgin.

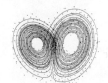

In uroboric guise the goddess presides over a cyclical natural process. It is flow that, ebbing, requires periodic renewal, but that is never quantified nor rationed. The woman the hunters meet is operating on an abstract seven-day schedule rather than on "demand feeding." Yet who would deny the woman's right to protect her baby at the expense of strangers? It is a terrible dilemma.

The story would seem to be situated between two ways of conceiving time: the vernacular and the international.[53] The meeting between the woman and the hunters takes place on the fourth day of her seven. How does she know how long her journey will take? Of course literally she doesn't. The seven-day week she symbolically envisages was introduced into Africa by Islam and reinforced centuries later by the imposition of colonial time clocks.[54] It doesn't take emergencies into account. It abstractly overrules contingencies. It is a parceling of time, which runs out at the end, so there's a day of grace to catch up in.

The traditional week in Africa has nothing to do with the seven planets, but reflects social rhythms of exchange: marketing patterns of villages loosely associated for the purpose. Market-weeks, composed of days named after the places where local markets are held, cyclically repeat themselves without the intrusion of a preferential Sabbath. Markets have to be topographically within range of people visiting them on foot and occur frequently enough to satisfy local buyers and sellers busy with other activities in between. Four rotating markets seem just about right. African market-weeks are customarily four days long.

Upon a day, two thirsty hunters from the pagan south meet a withholding woman in flight from the converted north. A disruption has occurred, followed by a regaining of balance through alliance with the hunting fraternity. Remaining resolutely pagan, the fraternity will in an adversative way continue to support and be supported by the feminine principle within uncultivated nature. The bush where hunters roam is "sterile" only from the point of view of seed-sowers. Actually, it is a

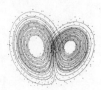

harkening back to a before-the-fall fecundity symbolized in legend by Wagadu and its well and in Sudanese cosmology by twin ancestor births. Islam strengthened a patriarchal denigration of women and banishment of the goddess begun long before the fall of Wagadu, which dramatized these issues in mercantile context. If biological sterility be the curse following hunters into the bush, imaginative fertility awaits them there where her bounty hides and leaps. Literally, hunters do have wives back in the village (usually only one each), and sons do grow up to follow in their footsteps. But, as we have said, it is for the things of the forest that they feel the deepest affinities.

There is considerable difference of opinion about the relationship between Sanene-Kontron and a variety of folktales illustrative of forms a common dream may take. At the core of them all there's a haunting sense of a profounder companionship between men and women than life outside the dreamtime of the forest is likely to offer. Here are four versions—one for each market-day of the week.

1

The place where two roads meet
Is where hunters "support" Sanene and Kontron.
Sanene was a huntress.
Her husband Kontron was a hunter
Who did incredible things.
He could take game without using a gun.
Sanene was a woman afraid of nothing.
She swore by the great pond always to be true to Kontron.
Their union grew stronger and stronger.
Where the two roads meet—that is their union, always.
Both are buried at the crossroads.
Who wishes to worship Kontron, must always worship Sanene.
Kontron was a great hunter; Sanene also.
　　　—Boukoné of Tièndugu. He sang this to the hunters' harp
　　　July 22, 1980, in Baru's compound in Maghanbougou.

2

Sanin and Kontron have no country (faso), only the bush, that is, wherever game animals live. They belong to no clan, to no race. Sanin, to whom no woman ever gave birth, to whom no man ever made love, nevertheless conceived and gave birth to Kontron, whom she initiated into

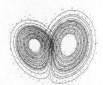

the secrets of things visible and invisible in the bush. To her Kontron as an adult returned with perfect devotion the affectionate care with which Sanin protected his youth. Archetype of the hunter, Kontron tracked down every type of game known and unknown to men. He even killed evil spirits. Nothing in the bush was strange to him; and from all beings and things he drew knowledge applicable in countless situations. Chaste Kontron remained, and pure as gold. Human beings who imitated him became his "children": all hunters are children of both Sanin and Kontron and brothers of each other. . . . It is sacrilege to assume that Sanin and Kontron were wife and husband, as do certain traditions from the region of Segou. Sanin is the mother and Kontron the son, affirm the Malinké hunters.

> —Youssouf Cissé, as published in "Notes sur les sociétés de chasseurs malinké," *Journal de la Société des Africanistes* 34, no. 2 (1964): 177–178.

3

Kontron always hunted with a bow. His arrows were made of bone—a secret he later revealed to initiated hunters. He only missed once. The tree that received his arrow, the balimbo tree, always has a dry part. When a pact is made with a spirit of the bush, a bronze ring is demanded by the spirit, who then shows the man how to look through it and see game. The ring is a token of their fidelity. Sanene was also a hunter. Though Kontron died before guns were invented, Sanene used them. It is their daughter, Komifolo, who initiated men into the art of hunting. She is the little bird who began things.

> —The Ancient of Bandougou, July 18, 1980, Bougouni

4

Now for the story of Sanené-Kontron. A father, Mari, had five sons. The youngest, Sané, was very ugly. "Kontron" is what his brothers, who were farmers, called him. *Kontron* means the spur of an animal's hoof. "You are useless as a Kontron," they used to taunt him. His father's name in full—Mari Fa, contracted to Marfa—means "powder gun." Kontron began to go to the bush. He was gone from three in the morning until eleven at night. He took the daughter of his aunt to wife. Her name was Deniblé, meaning "Red Woman." Each night Kontron brought back game to his wife, who never saw him by daylight. He always placed the meat in *n'tiankara* leaves; but one day, sensing it was to be his last, he wrapped the meat in *néré* leaves instead. The next day he arrived at the crossroads. There was his wife! She saw him! "You ugly

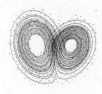

thing," she cried, "how could I ever have lived with you?" Whereupon he transformed himself into a termite mound—the kind with a hat (a sort of mushroom-shaped umbrella) that you find toward the south where farmed land has reverted to bush. Kontron always has a hat of straw.[55] Deniblé in turn transformed herself into a tontegi tree, which always grows beside termite mounds. Kontron's nephew, Nema ("Ease") called on Kontron there is his termite mound to help him with the hunt. It was Nema who established the first hunters' altar.

—Sekou Traoré, October 3, 1976. Bamako

To insist on a canonical version, as does Youssouf Cissé, is in effect to canonize one's own vision of the inviolate mother. Dreams are as a rule more complex, less sentimental, rougher. Though version 4 seems to be straying far from the paradigm, it has interesting things to tell us about feelings of inadequacy and rejection, which are the shadow side of the hunter's bravura. In this story, the Oedipal idyll of version 2 has been transformed into a cross-cousin marriage in the maternal line. A nephew, first initiated hunter, preserves the prototype of childlessness. Note that Deniblé is a desirable "red woman" like Buffalo-woman in the Yoruba story. The leaves in which Kontron wrapped the meat are used in the dyeing of mud cloth worn by women at times of life crisis and transition. N'tiankara leaves produce an ocher shade. Néré leaves, appropriate on the day of Kontron's discovery and demise, are used to produce a deep, wounded red. No motivation is given for Deniblé's fatal venturing into the bush. Did her sisters (as in the Eros and Psyche story) egg her on? Kontron is her demon-lover in "unreal" nocturnal time, but there is no place for separation and psychological transformation in this story. Both immediately are metamorphized into natural phenomena.

The termite mounds with umbrella hats crop up on well-watered land that farmers consider temporarily "sterile." At the crossroads the tree-wife shades and further shelters the little mound from rainfall. This is not the type of anthill formation used to "support" Sanene in Bouraba, southern Mali. In Bouraba the altar built upon the crossroads leading out of the village is an ample, reddish mound crowned with antelope horns—unmistakably a feminine image. The small one's hat looks like a prepuce.[56]

This fourth version, curiously, omits the name Sanene. One assumes that when she became a tree, Deniblé became known as Sanene. This transformation into a protective tree reveals her secret identity as "the mother who cannot be touched." Sekou Traoré's version has bent around to connect up with Youssouf Cissé's, but it works through a tough terrain of significant detail in order to get there.

To conclude with the crossroads, Sanene-Kontron's irreducible expression:

> The sacrifice occurs at the point of union. Where the roads *cross* and enter into each other, thereby symbolizing the union of opposites, there is the "mother," the object and epitome of all union. Where the roads *divide,* where there is parting, separation, splitting, there we find the "division," the cleft—the symbol of the mother and at the same time the essence of what the mother means for us, namely cleavage and farewell. Accordingly, the meaning of a sacrifice on this spot would be: propitiation of the mother in both senses.[57]

How, then, as a woman is it possible not to become deeply involved in rites of the hunters?

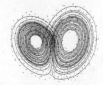

Buffalo Is Being Seated

To go back to the fall of 1976, the day following the hunters' get-together in Maghanbougou, when Sedou Camara played the praising harp and it rained on the corrugated tin roof, Baru took me to visit Sekou Traoré, a retired army officer and hunter. After telling two hunting myths—his version of Sanene-Kontron and a summary account of the Buffalo of Do, which his own ancestors had "vanquished" (see below)—Traoré hospitably led the way into his trophy room, where he invited me to select a gift. Impossible. Seeing that room in my mind's eye, I realize that of course all those animals had been killed gradually, one by one, over the years, but at the time what appeared was the residue of a single slaughterer gone berserk, as if one had opened Bluebeard's closet door. All those horns, heads, skins, tails, claws: an appalling sight. Misinterpreting my stunned reluctance as shyness, Traoré made the choice for me. And what did he pick but a massive buffalo head, whose crinkly, smelly condition suggested a rather *ad hoc* job of taxidermy.

Heinz Macher, in whose home I was boarding, threw up his hands in mock horror. "You and your hunters," he said; "this time you have gone too far. Buffalo are protected in Mali. Were I still in office, I would shoot you on sight. Should the police get wind of this, which [puckering up his nose] they soon will, jail is your destination. A Malian jail. Have you any idea what that's like? You think of traveling," he went on. "Forget it. With that thing stowed away in the Rover, you'll never get through customs. You won't cross any border."

"All right, Heinz, I hear you; but still, this thing is very precious to me. Have you got a saw?" From somewhere in the clutter of the back loggia he produced one, and never mentioned the topic again.

Covering both buffalo head and saw with the contents of my laundry bag, I drove off down the Sotuba road in search of a fairly secluded place wherein to accomplish the deed. Pretending, whenever anyone passed by, to be doing my washing, I gradually succeeded in sawing off the horns. (A really sharp hunting knife would have been the better tool.) Then, flushed and palpitating like a criminal, with mental apologies to Traoré and Buffalo-woman, I threw the gruesome head into the Niger, thrust everything else into the laundry bag, and regained the familiar safety of the old Rover. The flattish horns, fitted with heavy socks at the bottom of my suitcase, survived many a customs search at many a frontier, eventually to take their rightful place on Oya's altar. Thus did Do Kamissa, Buffalo-woman of Mali, link herself up with the Buffalo goddess of the Yoruba. And from a pair of contraband, crescent-shaped horns took shape this chapter.

The story of Do Kamissa and her "double,"[58] Sogolon, mother of the great hero Sunjata, is readily available to everyone interested in West African oral traditions.[59] Traoré's short-short version in no essential way differed from Niane's classical account, except for the names he gave to the Traoré brother-huntsmen, whom he said were Oúelé ("to call") and Toro ("to accomplish," i.e., "to answer"), which well suit their respective roles in the legend and beyond that a pan-African definition of sorcery! Recently, Youssouf Cissé answered my call by sending a far more detailed, leisurely account telling of the interaction between these hunters and the Buffalo-woman, which he obtained from the late Wâ Kamissoko, bard of the village of Krina. What is reported here is a composite: the standard story with interpolations from Wâ Kamissoko, as transcribed and translated into French by Cissé.[60]

Because a certain heir to the kingdom of Do refused to share his inheritance with (or acknowledge the seniority of) his elder sister, she exercised her sorcerous power to devastate the region and its people. No one could guess the identity of the ferocious buffalo within whose range no hunter could come without losing his life. The king of Do

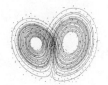

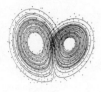

offered half his kingdom to whomever the beast would fall to. Hearing of all this, the Traoré brothers decided to take up the challenge.

[Wâ spells out the following intermediate steps:] In accordance with custom and good sense, the Traoré brothers informed their chief of hunters, Fara Koro Makan Kènyi (otherwise known in the literature as Naré Makan or Maghan Kon Fatta), and asked for counsel. Makan, a hunter-king ruling over loosely organized lands lying between the Niger and its Sankarani affluent, led the young men to a diviner even more foresighted than himself. The old diviner foresaw the way the young hunters could successfully overcome the Buffalo of Do, and he also predicted the birth of a great hero as a result. To realize this prediction, the diviner told the Traoré brothers they must accept as prize for their deed a woman rather than half a kingdom—a woman with seven deformities (blemished skin, hunched back, asymmetrical features, etc.). As pious hunters present prize game to a chief, the brothers must in the end present this woman to Fara Koro Makan Kènyi. For it was he, of the Keita clan, who was destined to sire the future founder of the empire of Mali. Fame alone would have to satisfy the Traoré.

Sacrificial ingredients were prepared. The diviner did a "work" for the young men, which consisted in specially preparing a grilled lamb's liver and some hallucinogenic tobacco. With these ingredients in a bag and with instructions to exercise unfailing deference (beyond common courtesy) to a grouchy old woman they would meet, Woulani and Woulamba set off for Do country.

On the outskirts of the settlement there was a small hut where Do Kamissa lived. (The reason for lodging her thus is that an elder sister, should she grow old without any children of her own, is problematic. It is the senior brother to whom falls the responsibility of providing for her. Yet if she lives in the thick of his compound, she will try to run things too much.) The Traoré brothers spied the old woman breaking up termite hills to use as chicken food. They helped her. She responded sullenly. They continued to help her. They offered her some grilled bits of lamb's liver (a great treat for old ladies), which she ate with pleasure, but without thanking them. They continued to do chores—fetching water and so on. "Whether you do, whether you don't, makes no difference to me," she said; but they persevered in their kindness. Every day they made themselves useful. Every day they offered her a tasty treat. Finally, sensing she was softening, they filled their pipe with fragrant *dyanaba*, blew smoke in her direction, and were not surprised when she asked for a puff or two. Hmmmmm, now she was mellow. She began to talk to them. They told her of their mission. "Know that I am the Buffalo of Do whom you seek," said the old woman. "Know also that I may be killed by no ordinary means."

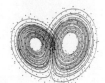

The old woman said she would permit the brothers to take her with an arrow fashioned of a distaff, weighted by a spindle, and shot from a bow bent from the sort of wooden spatula one uses to beat cotton into a fibrous mass. She gave them these things and also magical means of taking flight from the buffalo's charge. She gave them sticks that, when thrown, would turn into a dense forest. She gave them a stone's throw of potential mountains. She gave them an egg whose shell, albumen, and yoke thrown down could create a triple river—black, white, and red. (It is the triple river that flows between life and death.)[61] And finally she gave them three pieces of charcoal with which to produce a great obscurity. (It is from this magic that hunters like Ouana Togolo create the dark-thread-wound *dibi koro*.) "When you sight me on the banks of the pond at Dyi-N'Tan-Kongo (Place-of-the-ten-waters) our gazes will intersect (as at a crossroads). You will know me by my horns—one silver, one gold," she said.

Here accounts differ. Some say it was at the pond (the great pond where Sanene swore to be true to Kontron in version 1) that the younger, "accomplishing" brother took aim and sped the distaff-arrow toward the flank of the buffalo. Some say Woulamba grabbed it from Woulani. Some say the elder brother ceded the weapon. According to hunters' protocol, the one who sights is of equal importance to the one who kills, and sometimes in marvelous tales there's a third "brother" who runs into the bush, dangerously following in the tracks of the wounded animal until it falls.[62] Others say the brothers allowed for play between the great buffalo and themselves, equipped with the magical distancing and flight procedures she herself, in her old woman's form, had given them, to take her finally as they stood in sorcerous obscurity at the base of the giant tree.

In any event, Woulamba cut off the gleaming horns and tail as trophies, while Woulani, "the caller," praised his younger brother with such eloquence that he became ancestor of all hunter-bards, whose singing not only generates reputation as again and again felled game is brought before the mind's eye, but also helps restore the hunter's soul-force (*nyama*), which becomes depleted in the process of killing even a "consenting" animal.[63] The brothers now presented themselves before the king of Do to claim their reward. Instead of half the kingdom, the king of Do agreed that they could have the pick of all the unmarried women. According to Wâ Kamissoko, the brothers were accompanied by a little hunting dog called No-matter-how-distant-the-day-(it-will-eventually-be-now) to help them flair out the young woman inhabited by the soul-double of the now-defunct Buffalo of Do. (In another version, Fa-Digi Sisòkò's, they are accompanied by a cat.) All the lovely unmarried women were led out. No response.

"There must be some missing."

"Well, come to think of it, there is one," admitted the wily king of Do, "but you wouldn't want her—Sogolon, 'the warty one.' "

"Well, let's have a look at her anyhow."

So slowly Sogolon was led out in front of the crowd. She kept her eyes downcast. Not only was she disfigured by warts, but her eyes were set slightly askew in her face, one leg was a bit longer than another, one buttock was higher than the other, and her back was hunched. "This is the one for us!" cried the brothers.

So they led her, veiled, according to some reports, back to the territory of Manding along the banks of the Sankarani affluent, into the compound of Naré Makan, hunter-king of the Keita clan. After the wedding was when Makan's troubles began.

"She will be an extraordinary woman if you manage to possess her," had been the Buffalo of Do's advice to the young hunters. Some versions (finessing the diviner's orders) have the brothers try unsuccessfully to pin her down and enter her. Fed up, they decide to give her to their chief (surrogate father). In either case, again we have that paradox of wife as "dead flesh" or as "maybe mother" with whom legendary hunters, ever since Pishiboro's younger brother, have been assigned to grapple.

Each time Makan attempted to draw close to her, Sogolon's body began to bristle with buffalo hairs. All night and the following day the bride and groom remained closeted while crowds of busybodies hovered outside awaiting the announcement of consummation (the telltale spot of blood on white cotton bedcover). Finally, in desperation the groom took down his hunting bag, spread forth sand upon the floor (for Naré Makan was also a brilliant diviner), and began to trace signs. This piqued the woman's curiosity. Reading them, pondering, all of a sudden he jumped up, seized his sword from the wall, and threatened to take her life. Why? "It is the mantic earth's counsel," he replied. "A virgin of the Konatè clan from the kingdom of Do must be sacrificed here for the future of Mali! Prepare to die!" Terrified, Sogolon fainted, causing the Buffalo-woman's wraith to congeal in her body without being able to change it. Thus the hunter-king took her as an inert human woman.

When Sogolon came to, she had already conceived Sunjata, greater-bodied than a horse (so) and stronger than a lion (diara)—whose names combined yield his own. All praise to the hero of many names, Simbon ("hunter's whistle," the ultimate homage paid to a hunter and Sunjata's favorite appellation), Konatè-Keita, Lion. . . .

The natural enemy of the buffalo is the lion, totemic animal of the Keita. Within the intricate texture of this epic version of what surely was once a simpler "animal bride" tale told by hunters' bards, further aspects

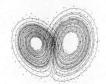

of the mediating role of hunters are discernible. First, on the level of political organization, out of the interaction between hunters and animal, a new type of man is born: a statesman capable of uniting the diverse tribes into one Mali. The events are plotted on an imaginary horizontal leading from Makan's position between the Niger and the Sankarani eastward to Do and back again as the hunters return with their booty—a modified Buffalo-woman just over the border of feasibility in marriage. The king of Do has transgressed against the feminine by denying his elder sister her rights, a denial duplicated by his sequestering of Sogolon, whose blemished skin and disproportionate anatomy reflect his disfiguring perception of women. In bringing Sogolon out into the light, a sequel to their successful wooing of Do Kamissa, the Traoré brothers bring anger and vitality into the compound of a rather quiescent Makan. (In Niane's version he's resting on a mat; in Wâ's version he's immature, unsure of his divinatory talents.) Before a hero of Mali can arise to unify the various clans, the collective soul, represented by Makan, the modest hunter-diviner-king, must incorporate the strength of "wild" women. Buffalo and Lion, antagonists, must coalesce.

Do Kamissa's persona is that of Mousso Koroni, "The little old woman with white hair," which is how the Bambara imagine the "dominant" feminine principle in her crone phase—the only aspect of her permitted to cross the threshold of consciousness. To this day, here and there in Mali groups of elder women with special sorcerous powers get together in her name. Their associations are protected by the hunters, who learn how to "do things," in Moussa Traoré's words, from them.

To the power of transformation into an animal, shared by gifted women and extraordinary hunters, two other modes of shape-shifting and altered consciousness have been joined in the Malian epic tale of Do Kamissa a.k.a. Sogolon, progenetrix of Keita kings. These are "doubling" (or "wraithing") and spirit possession. In other words, the magical aspects of the tale would seem to be woven of strands appertaining both to a very old traditional belief system (still in practice in the bush) and to a vernacular Islam that acknowledges hosts of spiritual agencies—some personal, some clannish, others wildly at large in the world and apt to intervene in order to right an imbalance by instigating animal attacks, epidemic, and elemental disasters.[64]

Although in principle both men and women have countersexual spiritual doubles, and although mediums of both sexes may be possessed by exotic spirits, in practice it is almost always women who prove susceptible to the activities of unseen beings and who work with them to achieve status and to make a cultural contribution otherwise denied them.

A double or spiritual-companion will resist sexual relations with a real partner (relations that aren't pleasurable if one has an excised clitoris and are extremely painful to someone routinely submitted, as a child, to so-called "pharaonic" infibulation—to have one's vagina partially sewn together). A woman possessed by a Buffalo wraith (or djinn in Islamic parlance) will put up a real battle on her wedding night, as Sogolon did. (The man will experience, even hallucinate, her as hidebound, horned, and hoofed.) Yet an animal nature coming to the fore in bed is apparently held to be an exciting inducement. Such a beauty as the Queen of Sheba is said to have had hair on her ankles—circumstantial evidence of her belonging to a sorcerous world of shape-shifting and psychic power that Solomon coveted.[65] A tough hide and hairy legs is also a sign of the resistant woman's power to survive parturition and delivery of a strong male heir.

Makan had recourse to sword-threat, followed by occult readings of cowries guaranteed to intrigue Sogolon; but there are less violent and less mind-boggling ways of calming the resident wildness in a woman. Possessing spirits and wraiths in the regions we are talking about are particularly susceptible to scents—fine aromas borne like the spirits themselves on the wind. Though on the human level the pipeful of *dyanaba* is calculated to soothe Do Kamissa's anger and render her amenable, and though from a more esoteric point of view the hunters are initiatorily including her in a common reverie blurring distinctions between self and other, they are also routinely using perfumed smoke to placate a powerful wind-borne djinn who appears on the plains as a buffalo.

Not only is shape-shifting sorcery originally the province of women in Bambara culture; so is wisdom. The distaff-spindle combination that Buffalo-woman gives the hunters as the only possible means of her destruction is an icon of the feminine state of being receptively wise. The spindle winds up threads of discursive cotton until the spindle looks pregnant. Conversely, the more we talk, the more we rationalize experience, the further we get from unmitigated vision. In augmenting the world, we conceal its mystery. So we have to unwind again. From distaff to spindle the thread goes, thence onto a bobbin for weaving, a man's job in Mali. Women spin again and again. From the distaff flows the thread around the

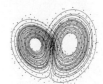

bulky little spindle. "Such is life; one thing ends; another begins."[66] This is why Do Kamissa chooses the weapons she does as she willingly gives herself up to a new dispensation. A few good turns, as we say, from the courteous hunters turned her on to her own fated spindle. What will be woven, by men, is the social fabric and its accompanying illusion of permanence.

If woman's wisdom accedes in the replacement of one form by another, then how does Buffalo-woman (surely only superficially duped by the crunchy lamb's liver, the sacred hemp smoke, and the young men's overdeferential behavior) know when her time is up? When does the augmentation of any particular whorl complete it? The Bambara, like the Dogon, gauge accomplished epochs according to the revolutions of an all-but-invisible star, the relatively minuscule companion of brilliant Sirius.[67] The word for "buffalo" in Bambara is *sigi*. Sirius is called "Buffalo-star," but it is the cycle of its dark companion that is called *sigi*. This cycle takes sixty years to complete. (The fifty-year cycle of Sirius is not considered metaphysically important.) It is as if the time-span of the visible star or of the visible person were regulated by, indeed, identical to, that of the invisible companion, or "spiritual double."

Sigi also means "being seated." When a Bambara man reaches the age of sixty, tradition permits him to celebrate by being ceremonially enthroned. He is given a cap whose flaps stick straight out on a line with the crown of his head like buffalo's horns. There he sits, a personification of elder Buffalo-woman, leader of the herd. Thus *sigi*, associating the plenitude of the human being with the astral cycle of sixty, is "the résumé," in Youssouf Cissé's words, "of all mythology."[68] Among the Dogon, the *sigi* is a collective ritual during the course of which all men are seated on special stools to hear a recitation of the creation of the world, thus every sixty years magically to renew it. So seated, the Dogon are costumed not as buffalo but as embryonic water spirits, androgynous replicas of their god of equilibrium and reflection.

Such cyclical thinking, whether the model is a bright star and its dark companion or distaff and spindle, implies that on the way to completion things turn into their opposites in order to bring less toward more. At the final phase of initiation into the mystical life, according to the teachings of the Bambara Koré society, consciousness is so transformed that the predatory king of the beasts is perceived as the embodiment of calm deliberation. Relinquishing their solar heat, lion-and-lioness, beyond

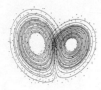

gender now, become infused with the virtues of elemental water, which holds the ethereal sky in contemplative suspension. "Lioness," sing the adepts of the Koré society, "enlighten us on the vastness of clarity." Man's feminine soul-double, *dya*, homophonically present in the name of "lion" (*dyara*), having been separated (by the circumcisor's knife), now rejoins its partner on a mystical level. Thus the renewed self opens itself to penetration by the otherness of god.[69]

If the Lioness accompanies the adepts on their journey to a higher consciousness, what possible transformation awaits Buffalo-woman, in whose guise the social personality of Bambara men becomes sexagesimally seated? Useless to search for her along esoteric corridors of the Koré society. One meets many animal guides in the course of reading Dominique Zahan's careful study of the Bambara initiatory process, but no buffalo. Why? one initially wonders. It would seem there's no refining her, this buffalo goddess. She needs hide. She needs horns. She remains fleshy. She has to be presentational, be an event. If, in Mali, she followed Oya's logic, she would wind up the sorcerous animal phase of her existence and go on to become a mask. It's true, she does. But I was unable to anticipate the reality of this idea. Then, there it was.

In late May 1980, I was fortunate enough to be able to see the animal masquerades of the Bambara Sogow society arrive by canoe at the town of Jokoro, just upstream from Markala on the main branch of the Niger. The sun sets suddenly in those latitudes. The twilight is very short. And it was precisely then, during the interval between fading light and darkness, that the bulky forms chose to appear silhouetted against a wash of hazy orange along the low horizon. Already the eastern sky, behind the village, was dark. To the sound of distant drums accompanying them, the masquerades—a black jumble of tall necks and broad backs—glided along in black slivers of canoes, as though dreamily crossing the threshold of memory, as though the stuffed animals of childhood, lined up along the shelf dimly lit by the orange nightlight, were reappearing in another realm of the imagination.

At their landing, part of the waiting population praised them, dancing into the nearby performance area. From the opposite direction (inland) came lengths of straw matting unrolling to enclose them, these gigantic animal structures, their angular frames stuffed with straw and covered with bright cloths, so that each pranced and bucked in its own space like the captive unicorns of medieval tapestry. The enclosing yellow

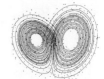

straw mats were from waist- to shoulder-high, on the human scale. A circle of men supported them, moving all the while. And so the profane were kept from crowding in too close upon these rampaging factitious beasts. Thus were hidden the ankles and feet of those who carried the weight and manipulated the marionetted aspects of the complex illusions—unless the watcher happened to be perched on a flat rooftop looking down on the scene. The heads of the masquerades were carved and brightly painted. Some of these moved on their necks. And upon some of the animals, animated statuettes were perched like cattle-birds.

The buffalo was hugest. Her wooden head carried carved human twin figurines between the horns. Upon her massive back, covered with indigo batik, floated a little Bozo fishing canoe whose oars worked by wires controlled from inside. Majestically she rolled and strolled on four human feet within the ample confines of her straw enclosure. The idea conveyed to the viewer was that of a vast animal and flowing river in combination: a single generative force.

Although the masquerades all arrived together, they performed serially, retiring between times behind the Sogow cult house, where a woman of a "certain age" could visit them. After a while upon such occasions a certain giddy weariness sets in, especially if one is a stranger with no particular place of refuge. Impressions get blurred; the dance goes on and on. About 2:00 A.M. people began to seat themselves along the principal path leading out of the public square and into the heart of the village. (Crowds of others remained seated about the square itself.) I remember slumping

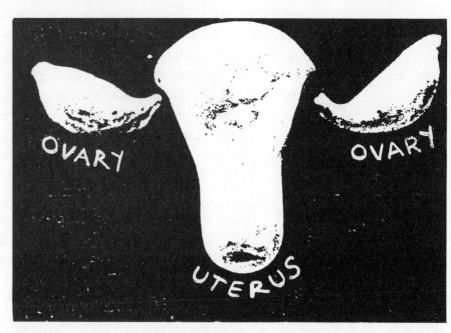

Human uterus and ovaries. Source: *Birth Atlas* (New York: Maternity Center Association, 1968).

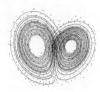

sleepily against a reassuring wall. Along the path runners appeared carrying torches. After them, inching and heaving itself along the sand, followed a great snake: yards of gunny sacking sewn together and stuffed with straw and men. How were they able to breathe through the burlap, the straw, and the dust they raised up? Somehow they did, and here it was, the great Python of Bida undulating along the path into the open. Illuminated sporadically by torches, the snake took a few dramatic turns about the space, during the course of which both front and back ends, undifferentiated like those of an earthworm, rose up two meters and sank down to squirm again with the rest of it. What is theater not capable of? From the moment of arrival by canoe to the finale of the great snake propelling itself along the spinal column of the village to the enlarged base of its brain, our interior world all the way back to its origins took shape.

Another mask the Buffalo permanently wears inside all of us blessed with woman's bodies is that depicted in the drawing. So when those sixty-year-old Bambara men sit down and put on their flaring caps, they have indeed come full cycle—their heads to espouse that from which they were born.[70]

This constellation of Bambara buffalo meanings is reinforced by data from the powerful initiation societies of the neighboring Senufo, which the anthropologist Anita Glaze has collected and interpreted. Not only is the buffalo an important visual motif in Senufo sacred art, but its name (*noo* in Senufo) is consistently used to designate key ritual events and objects. For example, there is a Poro drum called *noo* that graduating initiates ceremonially pass on to the succeeding group of novices, thereafter described as being "seated upon the *noo*."

> Thus it may be said that among the blacksmith and Kufolo Poro groups a primary meaning of the buffalo motif is the celebration of advancement and regeneration in the Poro cycle, the path to adulthood and fulfillment. All Poro initiates are considered "children" of the deity "Ancient Mother," and Poro instruction unfolds in the sacred grove, her domain. Only a tonal change distinguishes the words for "buffalo" and "mother."[71]

There is a time in woman's life span when, her productivity no longer magically threatened by blood sacrifices necessary to empower rituals, she is retroactively given full membership in men's secret societies and invited to accompany them into the sacred forest, graceful access to which all along had been her animal counterpart's special competence. Her proven capacity to bear and nourish children is of crucial importance in a male-dominated endeavor to achieve spiritual parturition of an entire age group: the birth of men from an enclosure of boys. Wise woman of the human herd, it is she who leads the way back through the thicket. Indeed, if the truth be known, in traditional African societies generally, as Glaze points out for the Senufo, the closer that spiritual leaders of both sexes move to critical situations vis-à-vis the unseen world, the "more secretive objects and events become, and the greater the role of women (real or mythological)."[72]

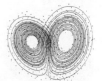

is a "feminine" animal. At the beginnings of the art of analogous thinking, then, hunters' shed blood is equivalent to women's.

Five or six million years ago the various species of buffalo as we know them began to diverge from their parent bison stock, carrying with them the connotative complex of "wounded wholeness" originally associated with the largest of "feminine" animals. Occasionally, as on the painted wall at Aouanrhet in the Sahara, a goddess appears horned. Gradually, on the African continent a distinction came to be made between a younger goddess antelope and an elder buffalo, and the disk that imaginations saw glowing between those curved horns was variously solar and lunar. Having reached the completion of her cycle, the Buffalo of Do showed one horn of silver, the other of gold. But in the beginning, as in the theriomorphology of Oya, the wholeness envisaged by the horns belongs to the moon and is a passing phase only. It is a moment

"The woman with the horn," from Laussel. Lalanne Collection, Musée d'Aquitaine, Bordeaux, France. For a while, she was visiting the American Museum of Natural History, New York. Limestone engraving, 42 cm. high, 30,000–22,000 B.C. Reproduced with the kind permission of the Musée d'Aquitaine.

of completion grown toward, ecstatically acknowledged, only to be gnawed away by darkness.

The right hand of the limestone "Venus" of Laussel holds a temporally notched (or "time-factored")[74] segment of the nocturnal cycle of wounded wholeness. "Call me," says this single horn from the caves of the Dordogne. "Call Oya, and I will answer because I, like you, am always torn between two surfaces. Where outer (which repels impurities) and inner (which nourishes) placenta join, there you will find me dancing up a storm. Between the woman alone with her loss and the animal wounded in the forest, I am ambassador. When you reach sixty, you can sit down and be feasted and drummed for. Woman of Laussel, you with your sagging breasts and worn face, see, within my horn a disk appears in low relief."

She began with the moon, for how else could the woman have seen the bond between visible part and invisible cycle of the whole? So in the guise of a bison Oya approached this ancient grandmother. To hand came crescent's avatar. Was not this horn the original "symbol"?[75] Thus to wind up our meditations upon Buffalo-woman and her Hunters.

Notes

1. In reflecting upon my own very modest experiences of diurnal and nocturnal hunting in Mali in the company of hunters to whom the world is magically alive, I have been buoyed and inspired by Merleau-Ponty's work on bodily perception of the world's "body": *The Primacy of Perception*, ed. James M. Edie (Evanston. IL: Northwestern Univ. Press, 1964), and *The Visible and Invisible*, ed. Claude Le-fort (Evanston, IL: Northwestern Univ. Press, 1968). I also have been aided and supported in my thinking by Paul Shepard's *The Tender Carnivore and the Sacred Game* (New York: Scribner's, 1973); José Ortega y Gasset, *Meditations on Hunting* (New York: Scribner's, 1972); James Lovelock, *Gaia: A New Look at Life on Earth* (London: Oxford Univ. Press, 1982); "Goddess of the Earth," *Nova* #1302. WGBH

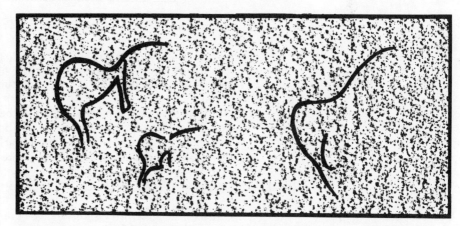

"Women-Bisons" from Pech Merl (Lot, France). After plates 76 and 77 in Lemozi, Amedée. *Pech Merl. Le Combel. Marcenac.* (Graz, Austria: Akademische Druck-und Verlag, 1969).

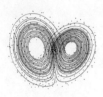

Educational Foundation, as broadcast on PBS January 28, 1986; and David Abram, "The Perceptual Implications of Gaia," *The Ecologist* 15, no. 3 (1985): 96–103.

2. Marcelle Thiébaux, *The Stag of Love: The Chase in Medieval Literature* (Ithaca, NY: Cornell Univ. Press, 1974), pp. 106–108. This is a superbly written book whose subject matter runs curiously parallel to African hunters' tales, as do the classical stories of pursuit and transformation from which the medieval stories derive.

3. The title of one of his essays, collected in LeRoi Jones, *Home* (New York: William Morrow, 1966).

4. In Judith Gleason, *Leaf and Bone: African Praise-Poems* (New York: Viking, 1980), p. 91.

5. Elizabeth Marshall Thomas, *The Harmless People* (New York: Vintage Books, 1958, 1959), pp. 52–53.

6. This "triangle," constructed on the model of Roman Jakobson's phonemic analysis of speech-learning, pervades Lévi-Strauss's studies of Amerindian myth. In brief, all human societies process raw food by cooking—an elaboration by cultural means. Moreover, there are various categories of cooking: roasting, boiling, smoking. When we eat, we intake "nature" according to cultural specifications and social conventions. Therefore we find throughout the world, food and its processes used as classificatory tools of social differentiation, inter- and intragroup organization, and resulting behavioral prescription. Certain people eat certain foods cooked certain ways on specified occasions. This is a way of telling them apart. Analogously, there are certain "roastable" women. See Edmund Leach's discussion in his *Lévi-Strauss* (London: Fontana Books, 1970), pp. 21–35.

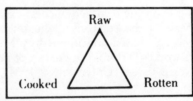

7. Barbara G. Walker, *The Crone* (San Francisco: Harper & Row, 1985), p. 10.

8. Ortega y Gasset, *Meditations on Hunting*, p. 120.

9. Adolf Portmann, "Biology and the Phenomenon of the Spiritual," in *Spirit and Nature*, Bollingen Series XXX (Princeton: Princeton Univ. Press, 1954), pp. 342–70 *passim*.

10. See Robert Farris Thompson, "Icons of the Mind: Yoruba Herbalism Arts in Atlantic Perspective, *African Arts* 8, no. 3 (Spring 1975): 52–89.

11. Xenephon, *L'art de la chasse*, texte établi et traduit par Edouard Delebecque (Paris: Société d'Edition "Les Belles Lettres," 1970), p. 17.

12. Victor Turner, "Themes in the Symbolism of Ndembu Hunting Ritual," in *The Forest of Symbols* (Ithaca, NY: Cornell Univ. Press, 1967) pp. 280–98.

13. Artists associated with Oshossi include the consummate draughtsman Carybé—to whom all praises.

14. See "Bamana Hunters" in Gleason *Leaf and Bone*, p. 91. This is a recurrent theme of Sedou Camara. See *The Songs of Sedou Camara*, vol. 1, text

from Charles Bird with Mamadou Koita and Bourama Soumaouro (Bloomington: Indiana Univ. African Studies Center, 1974), e.g., lines 104, 105.

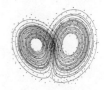

15. See Victor Turner, "Nkula" in *The Drums of Affliction* (Oxford: Clarendon Press and International African Institute, 1968), pp. 55–88.

16. See Shepard, *The Tender Carnivore and the Sacred Game*, p. 239.

17. Leo Frobenius, *Mythologie de l'Atlantide* (Paris: Payot, 1949), p. 180.

18. Wâ Kamissoko's narration of the genealogy and dynastic history of the Messalen, recorded, transcribed, and translated into French by Youssouf Tata Cissé. Unpublished manuscript, pp. 64, 70. My gratitude to Youssouf Cissé for allowing me to read and quote from the manuscript.

19. Youssouf Cissé, "Notes sur les sociétés des chasseurs malinké, *Journal de la Société des Africanistes* 34, no. 2 (1964): 175–226.

20. This unfortunate traditional practice is widespread throughout Africa. In their article "Female Circumcision: An Overview," Leonard J. Kouba and Judith Muasher present a table showing estimated percentages of women who have undergone this and even more damaging operations on their genitalia. Eighty percent of the women in Mali were estimated to have been thus mutilated. Attempts by international health and women's organizations to publicize the harmful effects of female circumcision have largely gone unheeded because excision and infibulation are not considered a mutilation by the groups who practice them. *African Studies Review* 28, no. 1 (March 1985). See also Fran P. Hosken, *The Hosken Report: Genital and Sexual Mutilation of Females* (Massachusetts: WIN News, 1982), and *Rites*, a video by Penny Dedman, 1991, distributed by Filmmakers Library, 124 E. 40th St., New York, NY 10016.

21. Pascal James Imperato and Marli Shamir, "Bokolanfini, Mud Cloth of the Bamana of Mali," *African Arts* 3, no. 4 (Summer 1970): 32–41. Sarah Brett-Smith, "Symbolic Blood, Cloths for Excised Women," unpublished manuscript, 1980.

22. Bruno Bettelheim, *Symbolic Wounds: Puberty Rites and the Envious Male* (New York: Collier Books, 1954, 1962).

23. Like the Yoruba kings' crowns discussed in the previous chapter. See also Robert Farris Thompson, "The Sign of the Divine King," *African Arts* 3, no. 3 (Spring 1970).

24. From the introduction to Gleason, *Leaf and Bone*, pp. xiv–xv.

25. See Dominique Zahan, *Antilopes du soleil* (Vienna: Edition A. Schendl, 1980). There is a lovely praise of the bounding kob on p. 118, line 4.

26. According to research by P. J. Munson, presented at the Conference on Manding Studies, S.O.A.S., London, 1972, discussed by Nehemia Levtzion in *Ancient Ghana and Mali* (London: Methuen, 1973), pp. 12–13.

27. Ortega y Gasset, *Meditations on Hunting*, pp. 49–50.

28. Thiemoko Diakité interpreted these words into French for me and also those of the Ancient of Bandougou. Mariko's character, as may be seen from the photograph, is of a profound beauty. He knows where he is. No sentimentality there!

29. Robert Duncan, "Passages 13" in *Bending the Bow* (New York: New Directions, 1968), p. 41.

30. Lorna Marshall, "The !Kung Bushmen of the Kalahari Desert," in *Peoples of Africa* (New York: Holt, Rinehart & Winston, 1965), p. 267.

31. S. A. Babalola, *The Content and Form of Yoruba Ijala* (Oxford: Clarendon Press, 1966), p. 20. An alternative myth, from the repertoire

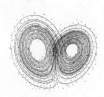

belonging to the "white gods" associated with the town of Ile Ife, speaks of a chicken as performing this office.

32. Praise of the duiker, recited by Odemiyi Apolebieji, collected and translated by S. A. Babalola, pp. 88–91. I have slightly modified the translation of these lines.

33. "Donson Makan," is the repertoire of Amari Jara of Nonko Kumo, collected, partially translated into French, and annotated by Dosseh Joseph Coulibali: "A propos de trois récits de chasse," *Études Maliennes*, no. 3 (Bamako, Mali, 1973): 47–53.

34. This story is summarized in Pierre Verger, "Notes sur le culte des oriṣa et vodun," *Mémoires de l'Institut Français d'Afrique Noire*, no. 51 (Dakar, 1957): 403.

35. R. G. Abraham, *Dictionary of Modern Yoruba* (London: Hodder & Stoughton, 1958), pp. 174–175, and Ulli Beier, *Yoruba Poetry* (Cambridge: Cambridge Univ. Press, 1970), p. 80.

36. Ortega y Gasset, *Meditations on Hunting*, p. 76.

37. Sedou Camara, *Songs*, line 11 and *passim*. This is one of Camara's favorite expressions. The form of these aphorisms—"If you're looking for an *X*, start with a *W*"—is how the bard brings hunters' tracking-sense into the world of everyday moral sense. It is the logic of appropriate cognitive beginnings.

38. *Syncerus caffer* (Cape buffalo). Smaller types are *Syncerus caffer nanus*. R. Malbrant. "Note au sujet de la classification des buffles africains," *Bulletin du Museum d'Histoire Naturelle* (2d series), vol. 7, no. 5 (Paris, 1935).

39. My principal sources on buffalo field-life are Anthony Dyer, *Classic African Animals* (Tulsa, OK: Winchester Press, 1973), and Emile Gromier, *La vie des animaux sauvages de l'Afrique* (Paris: Payot, 1963). The scene described in this is in effect a translation of Gromier's beautiful passage on p. 225 of his book.

40. G. J. Afolabi Ojo, *Yoruba Culture: A Geographical Analysis* (Univ. of Ife and Univ. of London Press, 1966), p. 38. Speaking of Oke-Igbo, a forested area in Ondo (east of Oyo state), within whose precincts can be found "The Forest of Spirits" immortalized by the Yoruba novelist D. O. Fagunwa, Ojo has an interesting note on the name of this hunting place. Originally thought of as a farthest outpost for farm plots and base for hunting expeditions, it was called *Oko Igbó* (distant virgin farmland). Later, when people were impressed by its hilly topography, the name was corrupted to *Òkè Igbó* (densely forested hilly area). Thus the character of a place can shift with its name, a name reflective of human perception. Oke-Igbo is a typically Oya place—a boundary, observable two ways.

41. An earlier version of this story was published in *A Recitation of Ifa* (New York: Grossman, 1973), pp. 305–12.

42. Pierre Fatumbi Verger, *Yoruba Medicinal Leaves*, pamphlet published by the University of Ife, Nigeria, n.d., pp. 12–13, 24–25, 38–39.

43. Babalola, *Yoruba Ijala*, p. 95, n. 1.

44. This discussion is in effect a dialectical "answer" to an essay by Karen Barber, "How Man Makes God in West Africa: Yoruba Attitudes Towards the Orisa," *Africa: Journal of the International African Institute* 51, no. 3 (1982): 724–745. It is a stimulating article from which I learned much. Of course the argument *au fond* goes back to the Greek Sophists.

45. Babalola, *Yoruba Ijala*, pp. 318–19.

46. Donald E. Kalshed, "The Limits of Desire and the Desire for Limits

in Psychoanalytic Theory and Practice," a paper delivered at the Fordham University conference "The Fires of Desire," April 6, 1991, pp. 18–27 *passim.*

47. Kalshed, "Limits of Desire," p. 20.

48. Germaine Dieterlen, "Mythe et rites des chasseurs Soninké," unpublished manuscript. I do not have a copy of this manuscript, only notes taken under pressure of time. For any inaccuracies, may I be forgiven.

49. Victor Turner, "Color Classification in Ndembu Ritual," in *The Forest of Symbols,* p. 66.

50. See Solange de Ganay and Dominique Zahan, "Un enseignement donné par le komo," in *Systèmes de signes* (Paris: Hermann, 1978), pp. 151–84.

51. George Santayana, "Love," cited by Joanna Field (Marion Milner), *On Not Being Able to Paint,* 2d ed. (Los Angeles, J. P. Tarcher, 1983), p. 29.

52. Ironically, as Lewis Hyde has shown, the pattern to which he was attracted (the legend of Wagadu) fit Pound, both person and poet, better than he knew. See Lewis Hyde, *The Gift* (New York: Vintage Books, 1983). chap. 10.

53. I owe this and other uses of "vernacular" in its cultural rather than strictly linguistic sense to Jean-Louis Bourgois, *Spectacular Vernacular: A New Appreciation of Traditional Desert Architecture* (Salt Lake City: Peregrine Smith Books, 1983).

54. Eviatar Zerubavel, *The Seven Day Circle: The History and Meaning of the Week* (New York: Free Press, 1985), *passim.*

55. As does Zaka, the Haitian *vodu.* See the discussion of the "palm fringe" syndrome in the chapter "Brother Palm-Fringe" in Part Two. Clearly this little termite icon is part of it.

56. Compare Ndembu termitary symbolism in circumcision and funerary and hunting ritual: Victor Turner, "Symbolism of Ndembu Hunting Ritual," pp. 294–295. The small, phallic-looking termite mounds can be used by the Ndembu as symbolic representations of the larger ones. "The symbolism of the termitary includes in its exegetical meaning references to burial practices peculiar to hunters, to the hunter's stealthy pursuit of game, to his vigilance, to his leonine traits . . . to the feeling that his proper 'home' is in the bush (represented by the termitary 'hut') rather than in the village. Besides these senses there are overtones of fertility and virility." (p. 95).

57. C. G. Jung, "The Dual Mother," *Symbols of Transformation, Collected Works* 5, par. 577, p. 371.

58. There are many ways of discussing this phenomenon, and some of the African ways of thinking of it will be discussed below. The Buffalo nature of Do Kamissa would be described by Jung as an "autonomous complex." "I have frequently observed that the typical traumatic affect is represented in dreams as a wild and dangerous animal—a striking illustration of its autonomous nature when split off from consciousness," says Jung ("The Therapeutic Value of Abreaction," *Collected Works* 16, par. 267, p. 132).

59. Available in English: Djibril Tamsir Niane, *Sundiata: An Epic of Old Mali,* trans. G. D. Pickett (London: Longman, 1965); Camara Laye, *The Guardian of the Word,* trans. James Kirkup (Glasgow: William Collins, 1980); John William Johnson, *The Epic of Son-Jara* (Bloomington: Indiana Univ. Press, 1986).

60. See above, note 18. Much of the text to follow is paraphrase rather than strict translation. Though they will never read it, I would like to dedicate this account to Nicoro Kamissoko, Fanta (Wâ's widow), and Lasana (his son). Nicoro, Wâ's mother, is in her mid-nineties.

61. The three rivers in African thought are interrelated processes.

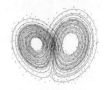

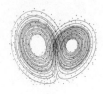

Perhaps purification, strengthening (vitalization), and disintegration-transformation best convey their tendencies. Turner (*The Forest of Symbols*, p. 57) aptly compares them to the Hindu "strands of life" (*guna*). Symbolically, before the hunters can kill the Buffalo, she will have had to pass through these three color-phases.

62. Compare the three brothers of Part Two in the chapter "Masquerade as Monkey Business": the first saw the corpse; the second covered it with a shroud; the third, instead of bringing it home, tried to sell it, then abandoned it in the bush. This three-stage process, as personified by three brothers, is a widespread African folktale format. Remembering that when the game is brought home it is transformed by cooking from decaying flesh to food, one can correlate these three with the white, red, and black rivers (see note 61). White is vision; red is killing; black is the flesh transformed.

63. In his "Notes sur les sociétés de chasseurs malinké," Youssouf Cissé devotes several pages to a most interesting discussion of *nyama*, this vital energy that a being (even a dead one, and possibly over several generations) can emit through space in a directed way. When a being has been wronged, wounded, or killed, its *nyama* pursues the perpetrator. In order not to be overwhelmed by *nyama*, the hunter fortifies himself with amulets, undergoes purificatory rituals, immediately cleanses the fallen animal with his whisk as he begs its pardon, and also relies upon praise-words to build up his own spiritual resistance. The "word" has enormous power. The utterance depletes the bard, who must be rewarded by the praisee in order to right the balance. I have discussed this verbal strengthening mechanism at some length in the introduction to *Leaf and Bone*.

64. A. J. N. Tremearne, *The Ban of the Bori* (London: Heath, Cranton & Ouseley, 1914), pp. 97–131.

65. Tremearne, *Ban of the Bori*, p. 407.

66. Dominique Zahan, *Sociétés d'initiation bambara* (Paris & The Hague: Mouton, 1960), p. 250.

67. See Robert K. G. Temple, *The Sirius Mystery* (New York: St. Martin's Press, 1976), pp. 35–51, which contains an essay by Marcel Griaule and Germaine Dieterlen on the Sudanese Sirius System.

68. Personal communication.

69. The so-called tirades of the Koré society express this mystical union. They appear on pp. 257–77 in Zahan's book, cited above. An English translation of part of them appears in *Leaf and Bone*, pp. 159–163.

70. The diagram is from Robert Dickinson and Aham Belskie, *Birth Atlas*, 6th ed. (New York: Maternity Center Association, 1968). Many thanks to Quassia Tukufu for pointing out this picture to me.

71. Anita J. Glaze, entry 19, *Face Mask*, Ivory Coast Senufo, catalogue of exhibit: *For Spirits and Kings: African Art from the Paul and Ruth Tishman Collection*, ed. Susan Vogel (New York: Metropolitan Museum of Art, 1981), pp. 41–42.

72. Anita J. Glaze, *Art and Death in a Senufo Village* (Bloomington: Indiana Univ. Press, 1981), p. 48.

73. André Leroi-Gourham, *Les religions de la préhistoire* (Paris: Presses Universitaires, 1964), pp. 104–105. What happened to the horse in Sudanese thought? It is not an indigenous animal but came across the desert with various invaders, beginning with the Romans, much later with the Moroccans. In the traditional rituals of the Bambara Koré society, the horse, retaining associations of high-spirited turbulence, erotic pull, noetic aspirations, and fatality that it is

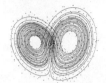

universally thought to embody, particularly symbolizes the pursuit of esoteric knowledge and eternal life. It is linked to the feminine principle of fire and wind known as Nyalé. See Zahan, pp. 162–71. Its obvious secular associations have to do with elite status and the waging of war.

74. This is Alexander Marshack's term. See Alexander Marshack, *The Roots of Civilization*, (New York: McGraw-Hill), 1972).

75. A symbol is literally a "throwing-together" of two parts. When joined, they match up. The word was originally used of a clay seal, which a man would give to a messenger along with his message. When the messenger returned, the seal in hand, he had been recognized in two places. We use the word to mean a throwing together of visible and invisible parts. There is no fixed meaning. Our minds have to match up that which we have, as it were, in hand and the other part, deeply implied. Psychologically, the symbolic process is a unifying one, consistent with its literal origin. Holding a horn and allowing the moon, a temporal process experienced in their own bodies, to fill itself out imaginatively must have been a wondrous putting of worlds together.

part four

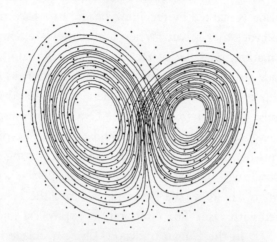

observing the passage

O that
Life might flow toward beauty
Day-long and through the night
    casting away all customs
    strayed beyond bounds of justice
Men, pure and reverent
Might respect the gods . . .
      —Euripides, *The Bacchae*

Surga una gratitud
¿En cuantas direcciones?
Se despliega la rosa de los vientos.
      —Guillén

All who worship Orisha wear beads. The first stage of affiliation with Orisha is marked by receiving beads. In Africa there is no big deal about the beads themselves. When and if they are appropriate, one simply goes to market, buys the correct beads, strings them, and puts them on. Oya's beads are thin, cylindrical, brownish-maroon in color with perhaps a few red ones added for emphasis. There are at least two Yoruba names for Oya's beads: *oyadokun* (*oya di okun:* "Oya becomes rope") and *oya romi* ("Oya pours into me").[1] The first would seem to be typical of the way she transforms herself into rather than merely affiliating herself with things. The second suggests that the beads and the person who will wear them are as part to whole: as she pours herself into the beads, so the wearer will be filled with Oya. The connotation is physical and intimate.

In the Cuban tradition, Oya's necklace is more elaborate: for example, nine brown beads, one red, followed by nine of her special brown beads striped vertically with two thin black lines outlined in white, followed by a red bead, and so on. For ritual purposes there is a heavy *collar de mazo*, so called because short strands of beads of the correct number are joined in bunches by a single large bead and these bunches form a continuous, lengthy cable, punctuated by beaded tassels. The *mazo*, worn diagonally across the chest like a bandoleer, is put on when the initiate appears before the community dressed as the Orisha-in-person on the second day of initiation and again when he or she is "presented to the drums." Indeed, not one but five *mazos* are put on criss-cross at this time and, as David Brown points out, it's a weighty burden, for each *mazo* can consist of as many as 12,000 beads and weigh over five pounds![2] Each *collar de mazo* spends most of its time draped upon the sacred covered tureen in which concentrated power of the Orisha resides. So it would seem that it's the Orisha who is appropriately wearing such a weighty ornament, not the person—except upon rare occasion (serious sickness, for example) when fullest possible protection of divinity is needed. Then, if a *mazo* belonging to Obatala is not available, the guardian Orisha's is put on.

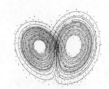

In the first chapter of this section, Oya's necklace will be taken as a symbol of commitment and service to the goddess. In Brazilian practice there is a special necklace of the bunched type, the *runjebe*, that belongs to Oya, which carries her weight of responsibility for the imprinting of correct ritual behavior and which also plays a striking role in mortuary ritual. This particular necklace bears much of the symbolic burden of the first chapter, which focuses on Oya's role and that of her mediums during the course of a funeral ceremony observed in Ile Ase Opo Aganju *terreiro* on the outskirts of Salvador, Bahia, in 1985. The reader is asked to imagine that despite interpolated explanations, stories, even reveries, all the while the funeral is going on from indicated start to finish.

The second chapter in this section, "Moving Oya," presents ongoing inquiry into modes of singing and dancing Oya in the Cuban Santería tradition. The intention here is to move the reader as close as possible (without benefit of audio- or videocassettes) to the expressive mode of participation and the receptive mode of listening to what certain gifted musicians and dancers have to say about what they are experiencing as they approach Oya musically.

In the final chapter, "Oya of the Nine Pieces," Oya is variously broken down into temperamental components and situational modalities. What, then, might a "unified field theory" of Oya look like? The reader is presented with a couple of diagrams, a conversation, a gesture, and a story.

Ora of the Necklace

January 30, 1984. On the way to an *axêxê* at Balbino's. About an hour out of the city the bus turns off the highway and slows to negotiate a narrow road. The road winds past the polo grounds, past country villas discreetly hedged by jacaranda and hibiscus, past rows of simpler houses frankly fronting intersections. At last the bus swerves around a corner recognizable as the place to get off: blunt edge of this quiet little town with the beautiful name Lauro de Freitas. An enormous ficus, several hundred years old, shades the crossroads. Apart from that tree, it is the sort of town that upon first arrival will always seem familiar: squat, stucco masonry shouldering the heat of anywhere—the Mojave desert, southern Algeria, the Yucatan, or northeastern Brazil, where in fact it happens to be. Useless to wonder which year this or that solid segment was first plastered over, whitewashed, or repainted for the first time in more subjective coloring. Some of these thick walls now sweat pale blue, others pink; and, shimmering in the heat, across the seaward side of the intersection dangle silver-tinseled holiday greetings: *Feliz Natal.*

The dirt road to Balbino's begins here, heading straight for the dunes, then at the last possible moment veering left along a sand track with an African name, Rua Sakété. The thick late-afternoon sun throws these white dunes into contoured relief against a vivid blue sky. Sweating under a backload of slant heat, one pushes on through soft drifts, bordered on one side by the tattered remains of laundry snagged along a barbed-wire fence and on the other by a homey series of front porches.

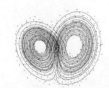

The purpose of an *axêxê* ceremony, held the eighth day after a cult member's death, is to send the disquiet soul of the deceased away to begin its process of transformation. The word (*àṣẹṣẹ́* in Yoruba) means a severing and neutralizing of "ashe"—an energy infusing and radiating from all things. Ashe may be increased or depleted. Not all things and beings have the same mode or strength of it, but there is an interchange of this energy between people and things. Human personalities are webbed to special aspects of the places they frequent and inanimate things they use; these local projections and absorptions of ashe are intermixed with those of the Orisha a human being carries and serves. From such an intensely inhabited world, leave-taking is difficult.

All African religions cope with this difficulty by shifting the soul's attachment from here to "the other side" of a symbolic river or beneath a reflecting surface of water. First of all, there's a dramatic severance from the commonplace. The breaking of household objects used in daily life by the now-dead person begins a process completed only after an aspect of the freed soul has been called back into a ritual container placed in a house-hold shrine so that its beneficent ashe may be periodically solicited. Close family members and members of the deceased's age group have their own special responsibilities in these rites of severance. Members of an occult society into which a person may have been initiated are responsible for cutting ties made fast through ritual participation; it is they rather than the biological family who will sponsor the complex funeral ceremonies. For the funeral is a means of validating the whole organism of which the individual, no matter how deeply ensconced, was but a transient part. It is upon such occasions that the values and symbols of the society are given their finest and most sonorous artistic expression. It is then the saints come marching in.

For example, hunters' funerals, performed by the brotherhood, take the occasion of necessary severance as an opportunity to celebrate the venatic art per se and for lively commemoration in song and story of great hunters long since dead. The Bambara *donsonton* (to which we were introduced in the previous section) perform danced pantomimes of the hunt before breaking the pots in which the dead hunter's magic had been stored. Yoruba hunter-bards (*oníjálá*) interweave praises of animals and lineage history of the deceased with item-by-item eulogies of his hunting equipment, including shirt, hat, and breeches. As each item is invoked, it is put into a large basket, which will eventually be carried into the bush.

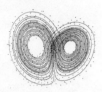

To leave such things around would be to risk the contamination of lay-persons.

Worshipers of Orisha store the ashe received at initiation in various ritual containers and iconic representations of the gods. Periodically the sacra within the containers are given herbal washings and strengthened with the blood of sacrificed animals. The situation at death, therefore, is rather complicated. Not everything can be destroyed or carried into the bush, but only those things from which the indwelling spirit of the Orisha has determined to flee. If a spirit wants to continue to reside in its consecrated vessel, its will has to be respected. I have known cases in Africa where the Orisha or other spirits tended by the deceased have simply flown into the head of a relative and possessed him. So he has to tend the shrine. Even a ceremonial petticoat worn in a state of trance may have a certain transpersonal static clinging to it, which means it cannot be summarily confiscated. A preliminary stage of the *axêxê* is therefore devoted to the questioning of all sacred paraphernalia of the deceased by means of the cowrie-shell oracle. If an Orisha's ashe resides in the thing, then it will have to be entrusted to the care of a cult colleague or blood relative identified by divination. This may seem strange to those accustomed to legacies in which the individual human intention prevails beyond its disappearance.

Axêxê. Something snapped. Break it again. This raw edge of loss is preeminently Oya's territory. No other Orisha wants to have anything to do with funerals. Orisha, as forces of life, they say, don't mix with death, no more than oil mixes with water. Oya, with a foot in both worlds, is a notable exception. But because substitutions are always permissible in Yoruba religion, should a carrier of Oya be unavailable, a medium of Ogun or of Babaluaiye may be assigned to do Oloya's work at an *axêxê*. (See the chapter "Brother Palm-Fringe" in Part Two.) But whereas these dark hunter-brothers of hers are competent in the arts of death-dealing and death-avoidance, they cannot preside over the subsequent phase of transformation into subtle existence as ancestor-spirit.

To witness Oya at work in this crucial context was reason enough for hastening along Rua Sakété to take part in the *axêxê* of a Brazilian priestess personally unknown to me. And furthermore, how better than at a funeral ceremony to celebrate the integrative affirmation of Candomblé—this African religion reconstituted on Brazilian soil with an elegance perpetuating the historical epoch of its cruel arrival? For naked

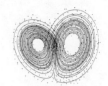

the Africans came out of the slave ships they called *tumbeiros* (moving tombs) to clothe themselves in visions of ball gowns worn to serve their sustaining gods. For me, there was yet another motive, tied to personal loss. Exactly one year previously a phone call had announced the death of my *madrina*. Though she had died in Puerto Rico, the first phase of the funeral rite, which in Santería is called *etutú* (atonement)[3], was necessarily held in her house in the Bronx. That event continued to haunt me. I had no idea, as I hurried there, how closely the preliminaries in Balbino's *terreiro* would parallel those undergone in the Bronx, but I had a vague sense that whatever was going to happen at the *axêxê* would complete a cycle of severance else left jagged.

The familiar bedroom in the Bronx had been crowded with as many of Sunta's "children" as could make it there on a wintry Sunday morning. Dressed in white, everyone perched on the pushed-back bed or craned to see from metal chairs rented for the event. All the marvelous clutter amid which Sunta operated had been stowed away in bureau drawers, closets, cartons. What was left? Her *soperas* (covered tureens) and a few pieces of sculpture—some from various *botánicas* around town, some from Africa itself. These things were neatly arranged along the sunny windowed wall.

Time to begin. One by one these things were taken up and placed before a Cuban diviner, who asked the shells whether this or that Orisha was there. In only three cases was the answer yes. These *soperas* were set aside. The rest, the empty ones, remained clustered on the floor. Without further ado this diviner, cock of the roost, took up a machete and began smashing them to bits—*whack, whack*—sending shivers along the base of the skull. The message was clear enough: death does violence.

But there was more to come. Suddenly it was the assignment of the four "oldest" women in the room to take up Sunta's *eleke* (sparkling ritual beads). One by one they were to be taken up and literally pulled apart. The necklaces, strung on cotton thread, are delicate. All that's required is a yank or two, and the tiny particles of color fall into a charcoal-smeared calabash, from which there can be no return. Circuits of vitality ripped to shreds. To break them was to "own" the violence of death in a painfully dramatic way. Neither Obatala's nor Oya's necklace was thus broken, for Sunta wore these two every day. (Obatala ruled her head, and Oya was her "mother.") Did they go into the ground with her unbroken?

The shards of pottery, the polyglot of beads in their dismal container, everything broken or smashed was quickly packed by white-suited, white-capped men into a cardboard box, rushed out of the house, thrown into the trunk of somebody's car, and driven off to be dumped, so they said, into Long Island Sound. So that was that.

At once the bitter rivalries riddling the house resurfaced. Certain backs turned. Exclusive clusters of mourners formed. Those women especially close to Sunta wept. Very few embraced. People were exchanging telephone numbers, promising to keep in touch. People were swearing *sotto voce* to have nothing in the future to do with X or Y or Z. Some people got rides. Others walked in heavy coats along icy sidewalks to the elevated train station. Thus, like the white beads of the missing Obatala necklace, all those whom Sunta's personality had more or less held together dispersed to the four quarters. A week later a mass was said for her Catholic soul in another part of the city in a church she did not frequent. There was to have been a feast of some sort back at the house. A few stalwarts took a long bus ride from Washington Heights across to the South Bronx. But you could have cut the mood over there with a knife. Whatever it was didn't come off.

As often happens when a strong leader dies, there is nobody capable of taking disinterested charge because the leadership has been exerted precisely in harmonizing the various dissident elements of the group, to which therefore a certain expressive license has been given. One isn't aware of this at the time. The real skill of the leader is hidden—the ability to be all things to all people, to be the resonating core. In any event, what I woefully realized was isolation—the failure to have formed any meaningful alliances within the group that whirled about Sunta. Our friendship had been personally rewarding, reciprocally, but extraneous to the whole, from which I could only remain aloof. That meant I had no way of truly (as opposed to chronologically) "coming of age" in Santería. Yet without community, religion cannot flower in a person. However, it would be a long time before essential compatibilities would spontaneously surface to form nuclei of communal commitment, affection, and grounding.

The neighborly front porches give way to a row of stubby fence posts: whitewashed tree branches stuck in the ground and wired casually together as one might improvise a corral for miniature horses. The gate is wide open, inviting one to enter the *terreiro* in the relaxed, though somewhat tentative manner of a welcomed, even expected person who doesn't know what to expect. From a distance it's a fact that nobody is sitting around the stone table under the tree in front of Shango's shrine house where Balbino and his cronies, sacrificers and drummers, like to clack away at domino games during off hours. The wide door to the *barracão* is ajar, but no sounds come forth, so it's probably better to continue crossing the open, sandy yard, past tree and table.

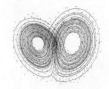

The north end of the enclosure is marked by a row of buildings running from Rua Sakété to the foot of the dunes. Dominating the north-western corner is Balbino's residence. No one to be seen along the L-shaped veranda. Beyond the main house is an outdoor cooking area, almost hidden by a miniature grove of dracae and euphorbia plants, which announce a series of sanctuaries housing ancient gods of earth, iron, and forest. Among these is wedged a freshly constructed bungalow belonging, as hand-lettered words on the stucco facade proudly announce, to EGBOMI SOFIA.

Sofia, a stout senior priestess from Balbino's parent cult house in the city, comes out here to assist him as *mãe pequeña*. When called to ceremonial occasion, Sofia may now spend the night here in relative comfort, together with whomever else Balbino invites to share it with her. This is a make-do arrangement that rather annoys Sofia. As soon as Balbino can afford to build his own guest house, the elderly woman's privacy will be better respected.

With certain misgivings, therefore, one slips inside to put a bag down beside the two others already there. Tin-roofed, rather than tiled or shingled like the others, Sofia's proud new home away from home is like an oven, urging one quickly into the quiet yard.

Out of sight of driveway and *barracão*, domesticity discreetly flourishes. Upon every bush that has managed to push its way up through the sand and endure to adulthood, crinoline skirts have been stretched to dry like gauzy mushrooms. It is a wondrous sight, stirring feelings of tenderness, amusement, aesthetic awe, together with premonitory sensations of the ghostly. As snails secrete translucent paths, so these crinolines might have been vaporously emanated by dancing goddesses, disappeared now over the dunes. Instead of evaporating under the sun, their pirouettes congealed.

Ah, here is Yvonne, stalwart arms filled with neatly folded laundry, coming into view along a path from the dunes. Before the sun goes down, what Yvonne is carrying back for her group, placed upon the crinolines collected from the bushes, will blossom into exquisite white petticoats, overskirts of batiste, dotted swiss, or voile, graced with blouses of hand-made lace and head-ties of fine handkerchief linen. For those who serve the African gods enter the *barracão* fresh and full-flounced as roses, camellias, dahlias. Yvonne, Iansã, sister, there you are! Here, let me help you . . .

It would be possible to expatiate for hours on those beautiful Candomblé costumes to which so much time and energy are devoted, as though the sisters were their own gardeners producing each year more radiant perennials. What one sees at the beginning of each ceremony are shimmering moments slipped on over the starched rhythms of devotion, images growing rounder with each swirling performance as years spiral outward from the core commitment. What one doesn't see at the moment of entrance into the *barracão* is the economics of the women's situation: the poverty, the self-reliant thrift. Nor does one see the strain, alleviated by humor.

Traditionally, those committed to serving the Orisha vend snacks of African origin, in particular spicy bean cakes fried in palm oil, which are called *akará*. Up and down the streets of Salvador, Bahia, and along the beaches one sees these dancers of the gods seated at low stalls shaded by umbrellas. Beturbaned, wearing many waist-length strands of bright beads over lace blouses, these picturesque Bahianas in their full white skirts do not solicit, rather they attract customers, as the marvelous food they cook, redolent of Africa, melts in the mouth. "The world is our market," sing the African Mothers, those gifted with powers placing them at the very center of things. Yes, the world *is* their market, but they also inhabit the crossroads, or certain trees in the bush, and when one wants to placate them in such places one leaves a portion of their favorite food, *akará*.

This is Oya's favorite "dry" offering as well. On her special day of the week one places on her shrine those very bean cakes the Bahianas sell to earn money with which to buy the cloth they wear to celebrate the entrance of gods and goddesses into their bodies. Thus, Oya may be said to patronize the self-sufficient economy of their worldly lives. Nor is this the end of her witchcraft with regard to bean cakes, which upon sacred occasion can be transformed into the cosmic essence whose homely vehicle they are. In the course of certain rituals, puffs of cotton drawn out into wicks soaked in palm oil and ignited are swallowed by priestesses of Yãsan-Oya to dramatize their mastery of fire. Thus is enacted the myth of Oya's quest for the power of lightning, a bit of which she carries under her tongue. The name of these little fireballs the priestesses of Oya swallow is also *akará*. In Cuban practice they may be fed an Oloya to validate her trance!

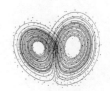

"Go on into the *barracão*," Yvonne says when we have put the laundry down on the bed in Cici's cottage, which she shares while on duty here in Lauro de Freitas. (Yvonne lives with her large family of children in the city of Salvador.) It turns out that the ritual potteries have already been broken inside the sanctuary and that now they are throwing the cowries for the dead sister's ritual costumes. "We'll talk later. Come back afterward and we'll make coffee." The *axêxê* drumming won't start until after dark. Meanwhile Yvonne and Cici have a lot of ironing to do. If any of the things being interrogated fall to their lot, Sofia will see they get them.

But who would have wanted them, these dingy workaday housecoats, these wrinkled sleeveless blouses? But because the woman had worn them here on sacred premises, they could be positively charged. At one point they held up a faded, once garishly flowered dirndl. This, worn over crinoline, must once have welcomed her Orisha into a shrine room where offerings were being made for him.

Had we not all been sitting, legs stretched straight out, on straw mats, one would have thought us to be at a rummage sale: bargain day along Second Avenue, the thrift shops teeming with those for whom free enterprise just won't work. Where are the beautiful lawns, the batistes, the voiles, the damasks that one had been observing for weeks taken down from clotheslines or carefully lifted out of hampers and trunks, or billowing from beneath food vendors' umbrellas, or swirled to the drums in ceremonies? Were they all but veils of illusion to be transformed at the wearer's death into ill-fitting rags crying for suds, for a long bleach in the sun, for gentle sprinkling followed by wedged pressings of an old-fashioned iron?

When Inanna, Sumerian goddess of morning and evening star, descended by choice into the underworld, she had to pass through a succession of gates, at each of which she was stripped of a beautiful garment or ornament until finally she was naked—nothing but a chunk of meat hung on a hook by order of her angry shadow-sister who rules the world below. The Hanged Man of Tarot is similarly emptied of superfluous knowledge. So one struggles to divest the person of its hampering precepts and withering excuses for not living up to them until we reach the innermost garment of the soul—despair. Off with it!

Those who carry Orisha are apt to forget that they do so through no merit of their own. Nor is the god responsible when things go badly. The same wind that swells the sail can turn and topple the mast. Sobering thoughts like these came to mind as night descended upon Balbino's *terreiro*. Never having known or even seen the woman thus stripped of her

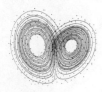

garments enabled one to view the process with the shadow-sister's cold eye, and with that detachment came a growing sense that something in her moral life had gone terribly wrong.

The clothes indicated that she had been a rather recent initiate whose ruling Orisha was Babaluaiye—or Omolu, as he is popularly known in Brazil. There under the heap of wash-dresses his authority had vacated were the raffia skirt and veil of his ritual costume. A person has to be very strong to carry Babaluaiye and survive. And apparently she wasn't up to it. In some way she had betrayed her god. Since Babaluaiye specializes in causing and curing nervous disorders affecting the skin, the nature of the god seemed to be actively participating in what was going on here: a skinning off, as it were, of bandages. Even more strangely, it was precisely the time of year when his festival is celebrated in Brazil.

The Catholic image borrowed by Afro-Brazilians—first to conceal, then to elaborate, the meaning of Babaluaiye—is Lazarus. In popular chromoliths distributed throughout the Western Hemisphere, we see the old man wearing a purple penitential cloak, leaning heavily on two canes, and attended by a faithful dog who licks a running sore on his right thigh and a second, grayish hound whose nose touches the knuckles of his left hand. Never officially canonized, this Lazarus of the Latin American world has nevertheless become a saint. Churches bear his name. At the very moment of working through that pile of clothes in Balbino's *terreiro*, there was a statue of Saint Lazarus being carried through the streets of the barrio called Federação where, on a promontory overlooking the sea, stands the church dedicated to his miraculous misery. Why during the solemn week of his festival should the old man have chosen to desert his wavering child? Perhaps because his power then was everywhere increased to the breaking point.

Balbino throws the cowries directly on the hard-packed sandy floor of the *barracão*. Here he has a natural advantage over the Cuban diviner, who had to sprinkle dust on the linoleum in order to perform his job properly. But the magic circle within which they are thrown is delineated in exactly the same way: two concentric circles, about eighteen inches in diameter, the inner drawn in charcoal dust, the outer in chalk.

Normally shell divination in Brazil takes place on a board covered with white cloth and encircled by necklaces comprising the spectrum of Orisha. Thus coiled and intertwined the bright necklaces represent the rainbow serpent, Oshumare, whose image in Africa is carved along the edge of the diviner's wooden board. To cast the shells within a space demarcated by carbonized and calcified materials is to take a look into the void.

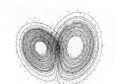

Back to Cici's place for that cup of strong, sweet coffee. It is pleasant in here with all these preparations going on. Cici's little girl, sucking her thumb, sits on my lap while her mother heats up her supper. Cici, daughter of Obatala, is about forty years old, short, thin, nervous, bespectacled, with a confidential manner of talking. Cici is extremely intelligent, with a sophisticated knowledge of the religion she serves with humility and practical devotion. Had circumstances permitted, she would have become a professional translator. She knows many languages, even some Russian, which is why she named the little girl she raises Tatiana. Now she is determined to learn and teach Tatiana Yoruba so that the meanings of the cult songs can be understood and passed on to the next generation. One worries about Tatiana, who seems to have some kind of developmental deficit or endemic emotional disturbance. Yet Cici's patience and forbearance are Obatala's own, and her character is capable of handling difficulties. One senses that they have surrounded her all her life.

Whenever there has been a chance to chat, Cici has generously volunteered information that she knows will be of interest. Now, in the midst of dressing for the funeral ceremony, as she takes it down from a nail on the wall in the partitioned-off bedroom of the one-room cottage, Cici begins to talk about *runjebe*, the special necklace consecrated to Oya.

Only senior priestesses holding the rank of *mãe de santo* may wear this necklace, only those who have performed their "seventh-year obligation," a ceremony during which a priestess receives the power to initiate others. It is a power symbolized by the *deka*, a basket containing the implements (scissors, razor for cutting and shaving the hair) and medicinal substances (including the sacred paints) used during initiation.

The *runjebe* is made up of forty-two large fastening beads, or *firmas*, between which are strung bunched strands of little ones. There are always nine beads to a strand of Oya's necklaces, but there may be either three or nine strands to a cluster. The small beads are maroon or brown, and thirty-nine of the *firmas* are bright red. The remaining three, at the knotted end of the necklace, are color-coded to signify the wearer's own major and minor Orisha and the major Orisha of the priest responsible for the wearer's initiation.

When a *mãe de santo* dies, she is buried with the *runjebe* necklace in her mouth.

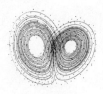

Runjebe. What is the meaning? The word is derived not from Yoruba but from the Fon language of the ancient kingdom of Dahomey. *Hun-je,* "spirit-beads." *Gbe* as a particle placed at the end of a word signifies intentionality—a keen focus derived from the art of hunting: *gbě.* An alternative form and meaning of the final syllable, *gbe* ("a bowing" as of the head—gesture of submission), would stress obedience to the spiritual world rather than refinement of concentration. Either is possible. Both meanings convey responsibility of vocation, the acceptance of constraint in a cyclical mode.[4]

Two weeks after Cici took the necklace down, pronounced its name, and described its function, I had the following dream. In reality it was the eve of my departure for Nigeria, but in the dream I was already there. I was setting out alone for Dugbe market (in Ibadan) in search of beads. That was all, and it was strange, for I usually go to Dugbe market with a friend to bargain for cloth. I take the dream to mean a search for beads with which to make my own equivalent of the *runjebe* and a shift of focus from cloth to beads as immemorial ornament of the goddess.[5] The "beads" in no literal sense I take to be elements of "practice."

Although the beads of the *runjebe* are not "told," their consecutive pattern may instructively be compared to that of the rosary with its fifteen "decades" of small prayer beads punctuated by larger ones. The ten Hail Marys of each unit are preceded by a Paternoster and followed by a Gloria, both represented by the same large bead: in the end is the beginning. The rosary is also an emblem of the great Hindu goddess of many names. Perhaps it is derived from articulated vertebrae of the Great Snake coiled head to tail: the "great round" continuously spoken in segments, praise-bones strung on a sounding thread. As all things are held together in a moving circle, so holding a rosary one cannot lose the thread of meditation formed into a circlet of "well-formed" mantras.[6] The language of the Hail Marys reinforces the tactile image of the spherical beads: "Hail Mary, full of grace, blessed be the fruit of thy womb, Jesus." Hail Vac, Vedic goddess of speech linking heaven to earth and thoughts to the vibrating forms of all things. Hail Oya of the fiery tongue whose roots plunge to the origins of ritual.[7]

The *runjebe,* then, shares some of the meanings of all rosaries: a procession of miniature nows, representing rounded "hours" in their original sense, units of time not divided mathematically into sixty minutes but rather stretching to encompass the task at hand. The rosary speaks of completion of the lived day between sunrise and sunset. It speaks of the lunar cycle, of seasonal shifts of consciousness. Each bead is lustrous, consistent. But being an African necklace, the *runjebe* with its bunched strands joining at each prominent bead and dispersing again, also speaks about people in groups. The *firmas*, the large beads, are like leaders. The proliferation of strings suggest lineage lines passing through ancestral nexus.

Since chiefly necklaces of this multistranded structure are common in West Africa, it would seen that its authoritative design derives from these. But how did the *runjebe* as a "rosary" of entitlement to service of the spirits find its way from the ancient kingdom of Dahomey to Salvador, Bahia? I have a theory that it was brought to Brazil—the idea, the pattern of it—by a woman of rank, a queen, whose preoccupation with ancestral continuities matched Oya's own.[8]

Yvonne (Oloya) preparing for the *axêxê*—February 1983.

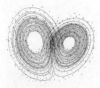

It is a tale whose truth is encoded in the strands of the *runjebe*, telling of continuities halted but unbroken, of responsibilities gathered into a single hand and relinquished so that another hand could take them up, of paths whose destination—so far as the human eye can see—is always a returning. When the mouth can no longer speak or sing, Vac, the Vedic Oya, fills it with an unbroken string of beads: the ultimate compliance.

Time pulls such moments away from us. Twenty-four months, ninety months have gone by since, crowded into Cici's cottage, three women, laughing like schoolgirls, put on layer after layer of white petticoats by kerosene lantern light. From inside the *barracão* just a few yards away, unseen drums urge the latecomers on. And the one who is only a visitor steps back to take a picture of Yvonne.

The placid, broad forehead and wide cheekbones tilt downward in concentration. Slightly below the looped fall of her copper-colored Oya beads, with elegant fingers that belie the stalwart contours of face, shoulders, harvester's arms, Yvonne is disentangling two braided raffia cords, each about a meter long, preparatory to winding them about her forearms. These cords, called *contragun* ("against Egungun"), are worn as protection against those very spirits of the dead whom it will be Oya's task tonight to confront. The moment in retrospect is appropriate. A few seconds earlier and Yvonne would have been slipping on the raffia *moka*, worn as token of initiation, whose pom-pom now floats across the cascade of glass beads. A few seconds later she will look up, turn away, and reach for her lace-edged head-tie. You can see a corner of it hanging from a clothesline beyond the compass of the photograph. And when she ties the scarf about her reluctantly combed, chignoned dark hair, almost all of the back-country wildness coursing through Yvonne will have been effectively concealed.

Now for the shawls with which we are supposed to cover our beads. They, scintillating with the colors of life, are not permitted to "see death." The visitor is unprepared. But Cici is right on top of this minor emergency. She pushes up the lid of her trunk, gets out a sheet, bites the edge, rips it in half—all a single phrase of acted thought. Over the shoulders goes the white cloth, loops across the chest to dangle its free end over the right shoulder. "Come on, everybody, Balbino will be furious," says a neighbor (from another cottage back by the dunes) who joined us five minutes ago. We shove open the wooden door and step out into the perilous darkness.

Oddly, there are no spectators to speak of—only the family of the deceased sitting along a bench on the north side of the *barracão*. Opposite them, along the eastern wall, stands the row of high-backed chairs reserved for cult dignitaries or for the ancestors, should they choose to appear. These chairs are like the thrones in the palace at Abomey—not in design but in meaning. Like everything else in Balbino's *terreiro*, the chairs are painted white. Normally the chairs would be amply filled by *mães de santo* from affiliated Candomblé houses in the city and by secular patrons of the cult. But tonight only Balbino and two assistants are seated there, and the image of absence is very strong.

To the south are placed the white-painted drums. Across from them, on an ordinary occasion of this sort, Candomblé dancers in skirts of all colors would be standing ready to go on; but tonight, because it's an *axêxê*, straw mats have been set out, and upon them some twenty-five or thirty white-clad members of Balbino's house are kneeling in an attitude of prostration. The latecomers take their places.

Foreheads against fists clenched to the earthen floor, we assume the position all will maintain, even while singing, during the first half of the *axêxê*. It is an attitude assumed by Hecuba and the chorus as they pound the earth at the conclusion of *The Trojan Women*. It is a posture resumed after each round of the "dance of life" game in which this first movement of the ceremony culminates. So *that* was the reason for all the small change!

"Small change." An explanation has to be inserted here. On the way out of Cici's cottage, Cici, Yvonne, and the neighbor grabbed waiting cupfuls of coins, hastily knotted into handkerchiefs. To put into a collection plate, the visitor supposed, confidently patting the little change purse pinned to the waistband of her underskirt. But that couldn't have been full enough for what was required; so when we had found our places on the mats, the always resourceful Cici reached out a bulky loan of antiquated *centavos*.

After the *padê* had been performed in the center of the hall, Balbino—young, slim, in white clothes cut African-style—got up to dance before his congregation. Son of Shango, he dances with great elegance. Just as he was hitting his stride, everyone rose from their mats and rushed forth with handfuls of coins. Sofia, the visiting *mãe pequeña*, stoutly arose to dance in his place. And so it went. One by one all the members of the house came forward in order of their years of initiation. And as each dancer pushed the provided rhythm into the subtler contours of personal

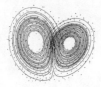

style, the rest of the group rushed to fill her outstretched hands with the small change of acclamation. Then, like a foamy wave, the well-wishers would retreat, leaving the soloist alone for a few seconds more as another readied to take her place on the "strand of life."

"You're mortgaged to Death, but we'll buy you back!" As upon a common surge of gratitude for a particular person's way of being, that sea of white-skirted humanity rewards the vulnerable one with the clinking of riches. And the dancer facing the menace of darkness all by herself as the waves retreat does so with excess of vitality. She begins by saluting all four points of the compass and then, sustained by the distant drums, executes her solo rapidly, for there isn't much time. Her body outdoes her. She goes for broke. And the energy comes back to her in coin. As the dance of life progresses, four women are replaced by Oya.

The dancers taken by Oya do not return to their mats, but rather stride here and there through the vast space of the *barracão* and out through the barnlike door into the night. It is a night taboo to everyone else. No one is even allowed to pee except under Oya's escort. Hands on hips, with that restless stride of hers, Oya in four different guises takes turns patrolling up and down in front of the door. If it is her whim to return to dance amid the throng of small-change-bestowers, she does. Or she might suddenly be moved to rush out into the darkness, howling like an animal.

After the dance of life there is a break. It is possible to go and stand by the door. Transfixed by the sound of her deep, guttural howling, as though protecting her young from unimaginable horrors only she can keep at bay, one imagines such a howling heard by neolithic dwellers on the Palatine Hill before ever Rome was built by descendants of those twins fostered by an ancient wolf-woman returning now to howl across the dunes of Lauro de Freitas.

The sound Oya makes when she howls is conventionally called *Heyi!* (Yoruba) or *Hei!* (Brazilian). It is a sound welling up from inside a person in trance at the moment when the possession stabilizes itself and becomes recognizable. Other divinities announce themselves vocally in other ways. Oya's visceral signature is *Heyi!*—a cry repeated in a stylized (nonguttural) way by acclaiming worshipers. One greets Oya with the phrase *Éépàà Heyi. Éépàà* is a salutation heard in other contexts—the Oro cult and Egungun, for example—where an otherworldly apparition inspires awe and dread, but at the same time pleasure in its manifestation. Recognizing the power with respect, it verbally constrains it. The *Heyi* part of the expression belongs to Oya alone. It is an echo, as we have said, of her own primary utterance. What does it mean?

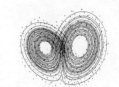

The phenomenon is accounted for by the Ifa oracle as part of a complex of meanings falling under the sign Ìrẹtẹ̀ Ògúndá, most of which caution the client to revive neglected ties to the Ancestor. For example, the following lines depict a condition resulting from such neglect:

> Rain never falls again
> Penis has withered into whips all over town
> Vaginas have dried up like leather bags
> All the little rivers are dying of thirst
> And all the streamlets have put on garments of dried leaves.[9]

It is a condition easily magnified to global scale so that we may better see what Ifa is driving at. Whether by stockpiling nuclear armaments and irresponsibly failing to deal with the radioactive waste, or by industrial ravaging of the environment, the present generation in power ignores the probable plight of future inhabitants of the planet. And Robert Jay Lifton's therapy for such a fearsome prospect is remarkably Ifa-like in its urging us to mend "the broken connection" between ourselves and those who have gone before.[10]

The oracle's etiology of Oya's gutteral cry presents us with a glimpse of the rampaging ancestral goddess threatening, because of neglect, not to dry up the world but to destroy it.

the origin of heyi!

shooting-arrows-puts-Hunter-in-doubt
Torrential-rain-disperses-the-King-of-Ife's-market
[Are proverbial names of priests who]
Consulted Ifa for Olúgbìjì, the good person
When he found himself in the midst of rebellion.

There is an Orisha, the diviners said, In your family—
Orisha Owner-of-fire.
O, said Olúgbìjì, This is Oya. She has been
In the family a long, long time.

Then you should offer her, the diviners said,
Two-hundred portions of pounded yam, a lot of gbẹgiri soup,
A white goat, six cocks and twenty-one stones.

Oya took these things. She got herself ready.
People pleaded with her: Oya dakun! ("Oya, we beg you!")
But Oya didn't listen, because she was determined

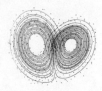

To destroy all Olúgbìjì's enemies, completely.
Saying Oya dakun! did not good. No stopping her.

If you keep this up, people said, You'll destroy the whole world.
You'll simply have to learn to accept pleading.
Go buy a slave, Oya, they advised her. He'll know how to respect you.
He'll know all your prohibitions [and let people know when they risk
Offending you]. Besides, he'll make your name even more popular.

The slave's name was Ehin (Tooth).
That's an awful name! said Oya. It ought to be Heyi
[Close enough to the original].

After that, whenever Oya got furious, people would call Heyi,
Which is what a person possessed by Oya calls, Heyi!
But the possessed person doesn't call, doesn't know;
It is Oya herself who does the calling.[11]

As is often the case in Ifa texts, the fanciful diviners' names are in effect diagnostical. What's the matter here? Abreactive arrows shooting automatically off in all directions and flooding of ego's transactional "world" (market) with affect. The client's presenting symptom is loss of control over his situation: rebellion inner and outer. The literal meaning of his name, Olúgbìjì, is "The-one-who-carries-the-tornado." Because he cannot recognize what aspect of the Oya-complex he's caught up in, the diviners refer to another facet, the fiery, in order to spark his soggy confidence, hoping thereby to get him to acknowledge neglected obligations to his inherited Orisha. This he does. Now the diviners go on to prescribe an offering that will animate Oya's warrior side, including ammunition "borrowed" from Shango. Once ritually served, Oya's visceral loyalty knows no bounds. She lashes out, prepared beyond all exigencies of the situation to destroy everything that is *not* Olúbgìjì with her pelting stones.[12]

Olúbgìjì as a conscious personality has vanished from the story. It is Oya who stands furiously before us now, refusing supplication. This turbulence at the bottom of everything, like the world's psychotic core, unconscious cause of what's been going on in Olúbgìjì's compound, in the hunter's forest, in the king's market, now grandiosely prepares to make the world her playground. Acting-out is the only language available to this force. But the human community will provide it with a stimulus barrier or "voice" of its own choosing. Because the only mode of relationship acceptable to this tyrannical element is being-in-charge, the differentiated intermediary will have to be a nominal "slave." But subtly the slave can, and always does, assume a modicum of control.

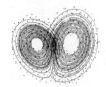

In this case, by insisting that the goddess be well treated in accordance with her own dietary laws and behavioral prescriptions, Oya's advocate in effect will be holding *her* to an unstated bargain. Pampering a specified number of vagaries will create corresponding channels of responsibility. (Thus it is possible to come to terms with one's own or another person's madness by honoring its presence in a limited number of non-life-threatening instances.) As a sort of public relations person, the slave will keep Oya's grandiose designs symbolically satisfied so she won't have to demonstrate what she can do by wreaking social havoc. And the community, which stands to benefit from Oya's incredible energy in its midst, will join in the chorus of acclamation, praising the Owner-of-fire to the skies.

The slave's name is "Tooth." Why? To be bitten by the animal within is to be transfixed in a mutual act of identification.[13] What the animal within wants in so biting through is recognition of its own thwarted needs—"Tooth" being the agency of this notice-giving. As Oya's intermediary at the jagged frontier of consciousness, "Tooth" transfixes us, passion's prey, as the hook transfixed Inanna, reduced to mere meat in the underworld, as the talons of Venus transfix Phèdre in Racine's drama. Now comes an interesting shift in the direction of censorship. We think of the unconscious contents of our minds as displacing their messages into tolerable format. The Yoruba story imagines that the autonomous complex herself rejects the naked notion. It is she who renames it, keeping the phonemes intact but rearranging them in order to conceal her own remorse. Thus *Ehin* becomes a toothless ejaculation of animal pain: *Heyi!*

Once uttered, the cry belongs to the community that tunes ears to hear it. *Heyi!* isn't the cry actually heard, but what the Yoruba language-culture makes of such an inchoate howl. And the responsive community elaborates this shaped sound (howled by Oya's holy victim-carrier-slave) into acclamation of that suffering's numinous source: *Ẽeyi! Ẽépàà Heyi!* Thus, unknown otherness at the core of Being is recognized and sustained within the limits of ritual. Analytical psychology can respect the tooth, the howl of pain, and theomorphize the source, but it cannot provide a listening community within which to placate and praise. And the God of Western religion died, as Pan before him, of a severed connection with the animal.

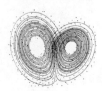

I want to know you, Unknown One,
You who are reaching deep into my soul
And ravaging my life, a savage gale,
You Inconceivable, yet related to me!
I want to know you, moreover to serve.[14]

To Nietzsche's tortured plea there was no responsive *Heyi! Ēépàà Heyi!*

Now to attempt to splice broken threads of discourse. As we already know from a previous chapter, Oya is the only Orisha to arise out of the animal. And only she is willing to assume a mediating position between the living and the dead at funerals, because her animal nature protects her. Of the contamination of dread, the animal is "forever healed"[15] because Death stands somewhere behind it, or inside it, not out there in a projected future. And furthermore, it is the species that survives the individual animal. In the goddess Oya, animal wisdom and ancestral representation coalesce.

Indeed, her most intimate habitat is the ancient part of the human brain that programs the following types of learning: establishing territory, seeking shelter, homing; mating, breeding, imprinting survival techniques on offspring; forming social hierarchies, selecting leaders, establishing interspecies communication systems over considerable distances.[16] To dismiss such patterns of instinctive living as stereotyped behavior seems perilously arrogant. If we experience her turbulence these days along the seam between the potentially sterile though infinitely clever front part of the brain and that ancient part where fundamental patterns of survival and enculturation originated, it is because her capacity for guidance is socially neglected and ideologically factored out of mainstream cognizance. But Yoruba oral traditions recall that when you're "going to the forest to bring home leadership," you rub buffalo horns with camwood (red dye) and present them to Oya.[17]

Heyi! encodes an intimate story of the relation between the goddess and the one into whom she pours herself. It tells us how that "slave," her paradigmatic initiate, in turn gets a grip on Oya and maintains her within psychologically tenable and socially useful parameters. But *Heyi!* as part of the bunch of stories belonging to Irete Ogunda has a broader message. To avoid the horror of guns everywhere going off by themselves, we need to recenter ourselves where ancestral messages are telling us the simplest things, like homing for the homeless and selection of competent leaders. Let the old bulls retire to the mud wallows! Let seasoned buffalo-women find the path to regeneration.

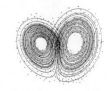

So once upon a time that night in Lauro de Freitas, Oya in quadruplicate patrolled the dangerous out-of-doors and kept us all within. For a long time. The break stretched on and on. The next part of the *axêxê* couldn't happen until something or other got settled. What was it? Rumors floated about the hall. There had been some difficulty with the family of the deceased, who had surreptitiously kept back certain things that should have reverted to Balbino, as *pãe de santo*, for him to distribute by means of divination. Because of this violation, the Egungun cult representatives present had informed Balbino that the ancestor who was to materialize for the occasion (indeed, had been hired by the family to do so) refused to have anything to do with the funeral. But this would ruin things for everyone. The ancestor would have to be pleaded with. Therefore, chaperoned by Oya, the entire congregation filed out and around to the backyard of the *terreiro*.

> The sacred Egungun precinct (*igbale*) is a white-painted shed about the size of an outhouse. The moonlight shines white upon the dunes behind the shadowy shed. In the stillness you can hear the gruff, guttural voice of Baba (Father) Egungun haranguing the company, particularly the dead woman's relatives. Between the Igbale and the rest of the group—white-clad, white-shawled, huddled together about ten meters' safe distance from the shed—stand four Oyas in a well-spaced line. Truce-bearers of our capitulation to ancestral demand, these Oyas hold their ground. Hands behind their backs, restlessly rocking back and forth on their heels, they answer Baba's hoarse tirades with an occasional howl: *Heyi! Heyiiiiii!*
>
> White dunes in the white moonlight. All colors have been drained from the world. The whiteness of the costumes stands out in relief against the shadow cast by the dunes. Behind, the invisible sea, whose moon-tides formed this gleaming barrier. The damp air diffuses this white light, in which attentiveness is so thickly suspended.
>
> Eventually an interpreter for the ancestor emerges from the Igbale. It is Yo-yo of Engenho Velho quarter in the city. Flanked by Yvonne's and Regina's Oya, Balbino (who as a Shango priest is ritually terrified of Egungun) approaches Yo-yo to negotiate. More growlings from the outhouse Igbale. Finally an agreement is reached. Baba will appear at the *axêxê* if the family returns the stolen paraphernalia immediately.

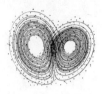

They leave—a pitiful, shadowy group, escorted by a stark-white Oya. We stand there huddling closer against the chill in the air until we hear a car go off down Rua Sakété. Then, shepherded by our wolf-mother, we turn back to the *barracão*.

The *axêxê* is under way again. Four *oje* (Egungun initiates) in crisp white shirts, pants, and caps enter to perform their sacrifice to the ancestor exactly where we had performed our dance of life. The pottery jug gradually filling with coins is replaced by a box wrapped in white and set upon an improvised stretcher. It is a miniature coffin containing the broken potteries from the inner shrine together with all those dingy things the cowries earlier had consigned to oblivion. To these eventually will be added the contaminated items kept back by the unscrupulous family.

When the rites despatching these things have been completed, Yvonne's and Regina's Oyas act as pallbearers. Out the door and into the bush goes the white-covered box, and with it, in memory, all Sunta's things as well, the homey *soperas* so brutally smashed, the necklaces so easily broken.

Now we remove the shawls from our shoulders and wrap them over our skirts, African style, in order to dance the rhythms of all the Orisha—except for Obatala. The dancing continues. Steps, gestures, demand of the visitor entire concentration. After the Orisha cycle is complete, we dance and sing the ancestors. When Baba Egungun finally arrives in his silken pink and blue panels of swirling cloth, the effect after these hours of whiteness is startling: Day-Glo of the afterlife. Everyone in ritual fright disperses to the edge of the hall, leaving Baba to rush about and cavort all by himself. The community salutes and praises while he, as is his wont, warns and chastises in that gruff voice of his. To these admonishments we respond with the sort of tolerant fondness shown irascible old human codgers—great-uncles and grandfathers. This affection for the ancestor, mixed with awe and forbearance of the old guy's eccentricity, brings him around at last to bestow his blessings. These are scooped up in a physical sense. One laves one's face with them, coats one's arms.

Now Baba asks Oya to dance with him. All four rise to the occasion, but Yvonne is strongest. She is a magnificent dancer. In terror, a pallid Shango, Balbino, hides behind Yvonne's skirts. What's going on now is a play, and it's very funny—Baba dashing around playing hide-and-seek with Balbino.

Having performed with incredible vitality, covering the entire space, for an hour or more, Old Square Head, with his flapping pink and blue panels, emblazoned with little mirrors, retreats to the Igbale for refreshment. *Cachaça*, lots of it. Throwing our shawls about our heads, we form a circle to dance, stooped with empathetic old age, for Obatala. In the end is a new beginning.

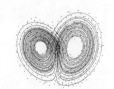

Obatala, or Oxala as he is known in Brazil, is the creator god. God of the white cloth, all the Orisha are reflected in him. He formed our bodies, so the myth goes, out of clay. Some he formed while drunk on palm wine, which accounts for various misshapings of body. His worshipers are the ones who lay out the body at the end of life. It is they who wash it and put on the white cloth of burial. Cici, who carries Obatala, had said this as we were dressing for the *axêxê*:

"Whenever there are heavy tasks, having to do with witchcraft, ghosts, confrontations with powerful forces in the bush, it is up to a daughter of Oya to perform them. What I have to do is very sad. It is a task few would want. But then, one has no choice in such matters, does one?"

Candomblé ceremonies always begin with a *pade* for Elegba and end with a cycle of songs for Obatala. Yet, visually, Obatala had been celebrated throughout. Why not then end the evening quietly with a shared cup of malt beer in the cottage of Obatala's daughter? Because Yvonne won't let things trail off that way. Coming out of her Oya trance, far from stupefied as one might imagine, she's hyping us up for a bawdy song:

> *A fu lele a de-o, a fu lele*
> *A fu lele a de-o, a fu lele*
> *Oya cara bel oko, a fu lele*
> *Oya bamba la yi le, a fu lele!*

> Storm wind is arriving, strong wind
> Storm wind is arriving, strong wind
> Oya likes a good hard lover, strong wind
> Oya dances a wicked bamba, strong wind!

Moving Oya

The material in this chapter represents work in progress on Oya's songs and dances in the Cuban tradition of Santería. Included here are, first of all, a series of conversations with people variously involved on a high level of competence in the performance of this music in religious and/or folkloric settings as well as in the teaching and/or documentation of drumming, singing, and choreography for the Orisha, Santería style. These conversations are followed by the presentation of a series of song texts honoring Oya in the Lucumi language, which is a condensed and elided form of "old" Yoruba, altered over the years by continued exposure to local Spanish pronunciation and idioms. The third and fourth parts of this chapter are musical transcriptions contributed by Esther Gleason and charcoal drawings of Xiomara Rodrigues dancing Oya by Susan DiMirjian. And finally, we have the first draft of "Oya's Songs: An English Version."

Because the field research represented by the conversations and song texts is taking place right here in my hometown, many people, including friends and family members, have been knowingly and unknowingly involved on various levels. Besides the interviewees and other formally acknowledged contributors, I would like to express gratitude to my dancing chums and teachers at Lezly's and at Boys Harbor. Without community, the practice of any religion, certainly an African-derived religion, is impossible. A core group of those who take, give, and drum for classes at the above-mentioned and equivalent sites form in effect such a community—perhaps the only sort of congregation that I'll ever be able without reserve to be a part of.

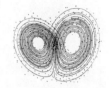

Because the vocabulary with which practitioners talk about their music in its ritual context will be unfamiliar to most readers, it seems appropriate at this taking-off point to give a brief description of some of the elements of that music and that context while making free use of their relevant terms of art (with definitions).

The musical offering to Orisha begins in the *igbodu*. This word, which means "sacred wood" in Yoruba, in our corner of the New World has come to mean "inner sanctum"—practically speaking, the small room in a Santera's home set aside for Orisha paraphernalia and activity. If there isn't such a room available all the time, then one is periodically cleared out to serve as *igbodu*. The service in this inner room consists of preliminary drum salutations to each of the divinities. The double-headed sacred *batá* drums, or *fundamentos*, are three: *iya* (the mother), *itotele*, and *okonkolo*. (An alternative and musically simpler orchestration for ceremonies may be provided by *güiros*, a group of percussive netted and beaded gourds, called *agbe*. The *güiro* band includes a conga drum and an iron bell-gong.) During this first part of the ceremony, popularly known as the *oro seco*, the drummers station themselves before a tiered altar and lavish display of food, flower, and candle offerings prepared for the Orisha being celebrated. If it's an initiation that is being played for, the musicians will face the "throne" within which the new initiate (*iyawo*) has been seated, costumed to represent the Orisha he or she will now be serving. Although the salutations are brief, these concise musical expressions are thought, by drummers especially, to be the sacred core of the ceremony, perhaps acoustical embodiments of the divinities themselves.[18]

When the salutations are complete, the musicians move outside into a public space (practically speaking, living room or carport; ideally, a patio) for the *oro cantado*, during the course of which voice now joins drum in the salutation of a prescribed order of Orisha, two or three songs each. Here one must hasten to say that the first Orisha to be saluted, no matter what the occasion, must always be Elegba: intermediary between everyday and spiritual worlds, the one who opens the way, but who without proper recognition may block it and cause all manner of confusion. The singing format is call-and-response throughout, the *akpón* (soloist) being needfully answered and sustained by the educated, communal voice of his *coro*. As the rhythms are played and the songs sung, initiates in attendance are expected to come forward and dance for their own Orisha.

After the *oro cantado* has been completed, seamlessly begins the ceremony's third and relatively open-ended phase, whose purpose is to bring down the Orisha, primarily that Orisha being celebrated upon this particular occasion. As the various sequences of songs for a plurality of Orisha unfold, the gathered community begins to dance. If a dancer shows preliminary signs of possession, the *akpón* will close in with a strategical series of chants that, as we shall see, are designed both to beguile and to provoke the hovering Orisha to manifest itself in that dancer's body.

conversations

I

PROTAGONIST: Oya has two sacred salute rhythms: the one whose name I don't know and *Oya bi ku,* which occurs in the context of salutations for Egungun. The second part of the first rhythm is almost identical to the second part of Agayu's salute rhythm. The conversation between Iya and Itotele is the same. Only Okonkolo is saying something different, and that's a very minor difference.

INTERVIEWER: I wonder what this hidden, yet explicit musical connection means, John? Maybe it has something to do with the river. Oya, they say over there, controls the Niger. Religiously, it's the river of death. In the chromoliths we see Agayu as Saint Christopher carrying the Christ Child across the river. He's the ferryman.

P: Chris (Oliana) used to say that Agayu was pushing a heavy, heavy burden. Like Sisyphus's rock.

I: Funny, that's what Xiomara says about the part of Oya's dance when she's cleansing: throwing her hands, her arms down, up and down again. It's a tremendous effort. Her face becomes so pained. She says *all* the dead have to be cleansed and that there are so many of them . . .

P: The rhythms can be taken in more than one way. They can be understood as "language," which could mean that none of the rhythms is anything more than a set of praises for the Orisha; therefore, a praise can be almost the same for different Orisha.

I: Like "Oya, you're a *heavy* lady!" "Agayu, you're a *heavy* guy!"

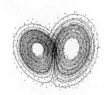

P: But the rhythms are also meant to convey an actual feeling or impression of what the Orisha's essence is. What I get for both Agayu and Oya is a very controlled, almost meticulous type of feeling. It doesn't, particularly in the opening sections, sound in the least uninhibited. Both of them (in the rhythms) sound controlled to the point of calibration. Everything is in precise place. It's like clockwork—no exuberant spirit—steady and even. In none of the salute rhythms for Oya is there really anything that conveys the essence of wind.

I: And oddly, perhaps that's why Xiomara says she loves to dance Oya. This of all the Orisha dances is her favorite, she says, because its movements are so precise, its gestures so definite. This sense of order is what, I imagine, frees her to be so stupendously dramatic when she takes on Oya's character . . .

P: In the *salutes*, it would seem, the graveyard aspect is paramount. *Oya bi ku.* ("Oya gave birth to death")

I: I wonder why that is? What are the rhythms that can be played for her songs?

P: First, the one whose name we aren't sure of. Then there's *yongo* and *chacha lekpa fun*, and *yesa*, listed in order of speed. Songs build up in intensity. They get shorter. The rhythms become more intense. The four I've specified aren't the only ones. This isn't an exclusive list. There are other possibilities.

I: Like that curious case you mentioned in which one of Oya's songs goes to the third part of the Osain salute. I don't see how you guys do it—the memory it takes, the instant responsiveness. As soon as the singer opens his mouth you have to be there—slap—with the correct entry for the correct pattern. I can't even recognize what it is I'm hearing. Can't you give me a simpleton's way of distinguishing between her alleged *Ewi pa mi* (which I think was what Puntilla called it; I should have asked him to spell it) and her *Oya bi ku*? And which is the one that sounds like rain dripping off the roof into a bucket?

P: Sure. Ka king king BA. That's *Oya bi ku*. King kon ki ki. That's the one I don't know the name of. I think it's *Oya bi ku* that you hear ping-pinging into a bucket.

PROTAGONIST: *E wimi loro* (2*). That's a *rezo* (prayer). *Ayiloda yo oku o* (3); that's a *canto*. People sing it every day. Its meaning is an offering—to let the Orisha know they are going to start a feast. It goes in the *oro*. It's expressing admiration, this *o-ku-o*. It isn't so much about death as it is respect for the powerful Orisha.

As the words of the songs in question are mentioned, he sings them a couple of times in an incredibly sweet voice, as though to enter their world for a bit before politely responding to what would appear to be extraneous questions about literal meanings. At one point during the course of the conversation, a car with a huge noisy radio pulls up in front of the building. We are on the fourth floor. We don't see anything. He raises his hand as though to silence the awful racket, which stops accordingly. Joan, the friend who has come with me, quickly glances over, and we both smile. But Puntilla makes nothing of this "magic," simply goes on softly singing and talking. Somewhere in the back of the apartment a parrot whistles shrilly but not too loudly in its own limited vocal world.

P: *O mesa loro* (4). Yes, yes, I know the Yoruba numbers, but what that really means is an agreement: "I eat with you; you eat with me." *O lele* (6). It's something she eats. It's made with cornmeal. You use a *garbillo*.

I think that's what he said. I don't recognize the word. Tamara, his wife, can't think of an English equivalent. He jumps up and runs to the kitchen, which must be just around the corner of the parlor, for in a couple of seconds he's back, triumphantly, with a sifter.

P: So you sift it, parboil, then you wrap it in the skin of a plantain and cook it that way. *Kala kala* (6). That's also something she eats. Oya has a lot of foods. Everything she eats you can also put in the hole (for Egungun).

I attempt to explore the "Agayu connection," which John had pointed out in the salute rhythm. And to begin, for the second time I ask him the name of that pattern. I think he says *ewi pa mi*. There's a rhythm for Shango that sounds very like it: *ebi kpa mi* ("Hunger is killing me.") But he starts to sing, so I forget to pursue my confusion.

---

*The numbers in parentheses refer to those used in song texts.

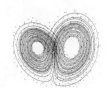

P: *Shola kini ba . . . Oya Oya o Takua* (19) [he sings]. That's a song for Agayu with a *complemento* for Oya at the end. No, it isn't a *tratão* [treaty] between them. With Shango there are many *tratãos*. For example, *Oya Ga Ga Ga* (28). *Ga Ga Ga*, that's *pecho*. Shango looks at her, laughs, and says, "Look you, woman, with those pants you are wearing. Look at your chest!" [Sings it again several times with all of us laughing and joining in the chorus.] Here, the *tratão* is also a *puya*. He is taunting her. This is *fundamento*.

I love this idea of "treaties" like cross-riffs between certain Orisha who are placed close to each other along an invisible spectrum. A mythological way of expressing such a relationship is marriage. But why couldn't that rhythmic overlap between Agayu and Oya also be considered an "alliance" of some sort? Tamara, who serves Agayu, acknowledges, "Yes, they both have the same number." And yes, yes, says Puntilla, they both have a lot of colors. In fact, it turns out that the satin overskirt, with its panels of nine colors, that Xiomara wore when she danced Oya as part of Puntilla's folkloric group had been given to her by Tamara. It was part of the Agayu costume Tamara had worn seated on the throne as a new initiate. And one never wears those costumes in life again.

P: There are other *puyas* we sing for Oya, for example, *Iba loya peregun*. You've made saint, haven't you? Well then you know that *peregun* is the last plant to go into the *osain*. So this song is telling Oya she had better hurry, she's the last one to come down.

I: It's like the famous *ewe ikoko* (15). You sing that to force her down. You call that *malanga* leaf ("arum") in Spanish. Well in Yoruba it's the leaf of cocoyam, also broad and flat, which answers to the name *ewe koko*. This Yoruba guy from Nigeria [Jacob Olupona], a professor, well he was at that ceremony you played last Sunday in Brooklyn. You told me to go to it, and I'd learn something. Well, I did. *Ewe ikoko* was the one song he recognized—words, melody, everything. In Yoruba that song goes, "*Ojo pa ewe ikoko*," which means "(Let) the rain drench the cocoyam leaf!" And here's the interesting part. He says they sing it on all sorts of musical occasions, when a sort of peak of excitement has been reached, a saturation point. Even a pop group could sing it. "Let the rain come down!"

P: Over there they've lost a lot of traditions. They can't understand our songs because they have forgotten them. Our ancestors came to Cuba with traditions that we have preserved, just as they were then. *Ewe ikoko* is saying to Oya [i.e., to the person the singer feels is resisting possession],

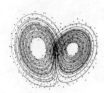

"Hey woman, what is the matter with you? You didn't really get initiated properly on the head?!" You know, you remember where they put that *ewe ikoko*? I can't say more direct because she [indicating Joan] hasn't made saint—yet.

I: Yea. It's got money wrapped in it. ["That's *right!*" says Tamara, laughing.]

P: *Omi o baba agba akara jeun* (29). This is another kind of provocation, one might call it a test. It tells Oya, "Now that you're down here (if you are really down here) go eat those fiery cotton wads over there!" And these people in New York they don't know what you're singing, even if they really are possessed and could eat fire.

I: But you'd think that if Oya indeed were down, despite the ignorance of the horse, *she'd* know what to do. ["Maybe," says Tamara, equivocally, "maybe."]

III

INTERVIEWER: Emilio, I wanted to speak to you because you seem to have a special gift. At that bembé in Brooklyn, it was very clear: the need for Yemaya to be there for her feast, and nothing was happening, so Puntilla put you in, like a pinch hitter. And your voice was so insistent, your manner so directly engaged, as though you could actually see the Orisha before she came, and you were harassing her and at the same time seductively reeling her in. For me, the scene could have been taking place in Niger, Africa, and you a guy they call the *sorko* over there. As I said on the phone, I would like to ask you about some of the Oya songs and what they mean to you. But I think it's fairer to let you have your say first on your own terms. I mean, suppose you were to start off from scratch to tell people who have no idea what this bembé business is all about what your role is, and anything else you want to put into the book.

PROTAGONIST: A singer is hired to work a *tambor* [bembé, ceremony]. The mode or motive of a tambor is to do *ebo* [perform an obligation, make an offering to the Orisha]. Sometimes the tambor works itself, and it is the job of a singer to direct it accordingly. What the singer wants to do is to invoke possession. He has to work the people and the Orisha. When you are going to work the Orisha, you are in effect working the person who is going to dance the tambor. If you know who is dancing, and you know what ticks that person off, it's easy, but you don't always have that luxury. A good singer will always utilize those songs that are slower in nature and that are considered the *fundamentos* of that Orisha. There are beautiful songs that would never be utilized in a *tambor de*

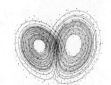

fundamento. The core songs are called *tratados.* These themes can take you in many different directions. If you know the person dancing the Orisha, you will work the theme that you know will accomplish the task. If you don't, you will use a *tratado* [sequence of songs] that you particularly like, because then the chances are that you will work it very well, and the Orisha will pick that up.

For I'm sending it out to the Orisha. I don't do that consciously, it just happens. If you don't begin to see the manifestation of the Orisha, then you try another *tratado.* You don't begin with an insistent song, of course, you work slowly in the beginning. Sometimes an Orisha can give you a very hard time. You can use beautiful songs, but after a while all that sweet stuff doesn't work. That's where the *puyas* come in. You don't use them lightly. They are like your ace in the hole. The veteran singers know how to pace themselves. But it could happen that you're caught off your guard. Once the Orisha is almost there, that's when you begin to pray. You want the actual possession to happen while you're praying. It makes it much more religious—not just one, two, three, and the Orisha's down.

The quality of voice helps, people enjoy the singing more, but it isn't essential. What really gets you through is how knowledgeable you are. The singer has to be a musician. He has to know when he's on *clave* and what to do if he gets off.[19] The worst mistake of a singer is to be tentative. After you do your research, you determine how you want to sing the song. Forget how the other guy sings it. Once you have established the chorus, you can alter the words; but you can't lose the chorus. If you embellish, you have to know the meaning of the words you're using. Embellish and then return. A good singer can turn the song around 360 degrees and then come back to it, all the while keeping in *clave.* That's what differentiates the men from the boys.

Oya has her *tratados* [sequences of songs]. You can begin a variety of ways. *Yakota,* for example, is a slow-paced rhythm. It goes with *Yansan wa me o* (21) and *Oloya de* (7). *Ayiloda* (3) can be played with *tui tui* (a rhythm Oya shares with Shango), or it can be played with the prayer-flavor, laid-back [to the nameless salute rhythm]. As for the words, the same word can mean different things in different contexts, depending upon which Orisha you're singing for. I wish I could have gotten into the semantics of the thing, but that would have been a whole different career. If I knew the meaning of every word I sang that would make me a richer person. But even if I lack that knowledge, I feel all the joy of the experience.

Oya? I see a beautiful woman who is dark skinned with long black hair and with many faces. *Ekwele ule o . . . ekwe ule.* That song is for Olokun, but I think of Oya that way.

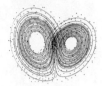

IV

Several conversations are going on here simultaneously. Xiomara is at the moving edge rather than the still center of this storm as she stomps and whirls about the room in dialogue both with the music resounding through the speakers and with the character of Oya she's easily—though with great physical and emotional effort—portraying. Darting in and out of her path, clutching the minuscule Sony tape recorder, Brunie is attempting to elicit verbal comments from Xiomara as she moves her extended arms to form various minisecond poses (crossed high above her head and slightly forward from her face, for example) and to execute various sweeping motions accompanied by down-flicking or by rotational gestures of the hands. And all the while those tremulous, solid, flowing shoulders are speaking continuously like the ostenato of the smallest batá drum, while her robust torso, like the prow of a ship in choppy water, releases emphatically to the crest of the wave, retreats to the hollow, releases emphatically again its own syncopated time. Over in the corner, where sufficient light is coming in from the air shaft, Susan is conversing with charcoal pencil on drawing paper, for surely only this medium can arrest what's going on while at the same time conveying a sense of its dynamic. Though the amount of light in the room isn't sufficient for the speed one would need for a good series of "stills," nonetheless my eye is riveted to the viewer of the faithful old Nikkon. Whatever comes out, no matter how dim, blurred, grainy, will ultimately be of use to Susan in her work. Xiomara's costume is incredible. Over a tight-fitting burgundy satin bodice and matching circular skirt there's an overskirt consisting of various solid-color panels that fly out when she spins. On her head is a gold satin turban, and in her hand she holds, variously, black flywhisk or wooden machete. (We tried the little copper sword from Brazil, but it proved too delicate for the task of fighting off all those negative energies in defense of her living children.) Toward all four directions she briefly positions herself, cleansing the dead with her "broom" on their way across the great river or, reaching high instead of sweeping diagonally down, summoning all the four winds to whip up a storm. She succeeds. The music stops, and breathing heavily for a few seconds, Xiomara stands immobile in the center of the room, wipes her face with her handkerchief.

PROTAGONIST: Because she is affiliated with death, Oya must always be consulted at that time. It is a terrible responsibility. She is breath: the first to go in, the last to go out. I am sweating, but it isn't hard, not really. It hurts me if I don't do it.

INTERVIEWER: You say the movements are traditional, that as a trained professional you learned from those who had mastered them. You say the songs tell your upper body what it should be doing. You respond to the rhythms, the tempo automatically. What is it, then, that you personally add to make Oya come alive on the stage through you?

PROTAGONIST: *Mi sentimiento, mi corazón.*

V

INTERVIEWER: Richard, you teach us a beautiful dance for Oya, which for me has a special message about maintaining balance in the midst of turbulence.

PROTAGONIST: The movement is representing Oya traveling through the wind mounted on a horse. In one hand she's holding a peace flag in the other the reins of a horse. Or, with that upraised hand she's feeling the wind.

It's in 6/8. You transfer weight on 1, the downbeat. For 2, 3, you shift, pull in, and fall to the left on 4. The weight-transfers sway the body from right to left. I am reacting to the rhythm of the wind blowing. The body comes close to falling and then lifts, twists. Yes, you release down, then pull up. In the center there is a contraction. The movement ripples upward, causing the head to vibrate. The energy in the center makes the body tremble. What I'm showing here [as he releases to the side] is what we call *puyando*—the mimicking of the Orisha.

Oya is a very intense Orisha. There's a strength, a maturity, a peaceful, vibrant kind of energy. My experience with Oya goes back to 1972. My mother was very ill. Caridad Torres, my *padrino*, took me to a bembé for Oya. An old priestess with twenty-three years in Oya got possessed. She saw me, stopped and said to my padrino that she was sad because a daughter of Oshun (that was my mother) was going to leave this world and go into the world of truth. She said she would let me know when the time came. Two weeks later my mother was in the hospital. We, the family, were taking turns sleeping in the room and watching over her. In the middle of the night I was suddenly overcome by a wind of cold. I got up and checked the windows, the thermostat. Everything was all right. My mother felt warm to the touch. Then I realized that what I had felt was Oya's warning me, as she had promised. In less than nine hours my mother was dead.

VI

PROTAGONIST: One comes down, that sets them off. People get excited. They all want to come at once. They don't have control. There is confusion. They don't understand *fundamento* tambor. People here are crazy. But I try to keep to the tradition.[20]

INTERVIEWER: *Fundamento*. What exactly does that word mean?

P: Aña is an Orisha who lives inside the drum. Aña is *fundamento*. A drum that isn't *fundamento* is *abericolá*. This means uninitiated. It can also mean someone who doesn't really belong. When you see batá drums played in a folkloric situation, they've got to be *abericolá*. The *fundamentos*, you take them out only when you are going to feed them in preparation for playing a tambor [religious ceremony]. And you can only play up to 9:00 P.M. When you are finished, you put it back in there [pointing to the closet to the left of the front door where the sacred drum is stored]. *Fundamento* lives in twilight, in the semidarkness. It hates the sun. It can't take rain.

If a person is going to play *fundamento*, you have to ask Aña if it is all right for him to do it. But just because he plays, like Pepe, it doesn't mean he has the secret. Few people know what *fundamento* is. You have to follow many rules. No drugs, no drinking or sleeping around. And the night before a tambor you can't have sex with your own woman. Very few in New York have *fundamento*, are able to, though there are quite a few who go around saying they do. Ask a so-called *fundamento* where he was born. He will mumble something. He won't be able to tell you. I have all the paperwork. You have to know who made the drum, who backed it up. They know from Cuba who gave birth to me. I am lined up with the drum. When they want something serious done, they call on me. It's true, Aña, the drum, is a religion inside a religion.

Puya? When you pinch somebody it's a *puya*. It is used to provoke— teasing hard. [Like goading a horse] They get upset, and they come down.

Puntilla gets up to go answer the phone. While he is out of the room, my colleague Pacho tells me that in Spain flamenco dancers are famous for singing all sorts of insults to the Virgin Mary—so she'll come down, we suppose.

P: If you don't have the Orisha dancing on your head, and you are having an *ebo* [in this case, "musical offering"] for your Orisha, you have to provide a dancer who can become possessed. That's what the person who calls me has to provide. I bring the drummers and the singers . . . The music is always going out toward the person. The person is going through a certain state. The Orisha is beginning to manifest in a certain way. The singer responds by positioning himself, and the drum also positions itself accordingly.

VII

PROTAGONIST: My work has been with Felipe Alfonso, retired [and recently deceased] *akpon* of Conjunto Folklórico Nacional de Cuba. . . . Though some of the other top akpons may interpret them differently, and therefore break the written words in different places, I have written the songs down word for word as Felipe sings them. We hope that this adds to your work.

INTERVIEWER: Dear Jerry, I certainly appreciate your help in correcting my transcriptions. Using, for the most part, your word divisions and spellings brings this effort more or less in line with your tremendous work. However, though I accept the idea of paradigms, I resist the practice of standardization in oral traditions. For example, I wouldn't dream of cutting out Lazaro Ros's rezo introduction on account of its deviation from Alfonso's version. Ros's is very beautiful, as I'm sure Alfonso's is. Had I been familiar with both, maybe I would have had to ask Oya which moved her most! Please here take credit where credit is due; and where there are differences or mistakes in orthography, realize that you aren't in the least responsible.

Protagonists of the Conversations

I. John Amira.
II. Orlando "Puntilla" Rios
III. Emilio Barreto
IV. Xiomara Rodriguez
V. Richard Gonzales
VI. Puntilla [encore]
VII. Jerry Shilgi.

OYA

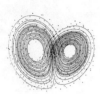

A note on sources and sequences: Some years ago, when we were working together in a context familiarly known as "The Play Course," I asked John Amira where I could get hold of some good Santería music. Kindly, he prepared two tapes, medleys including songs of all the Orisha. Only two selections for Oya were included, one of which especially moved me. Not knowing anything about *tratados/tratãos,* or *sequencias,* as John prefers to call them (reserving the former for "treaties" between Orisha), I called this offering by Lazaro Ros "Long Song for Oya," and from time to time would work on transcribing the lyrics phonetically. Now I know that "Long Song" consists of two *rezos* (prayers), followed by two *cantos* appropriate to the *oru cantado* situation. I have left Ros's performance intact as a series (1–6).

Next (7–12) is a recorded performance by Lazaro Galarraga with (to my ear, anyhow) superb tonality and flow. Following is a short(ened) sequence (13–16) sung by Julito Collazo on one of the tapes John gave me. Number 17 usually occurs along the same song-road as 16, so I have placed the *Eru Ana* version of it in this position.

In the fall of 1990, in preparation for a modest musical offering by the Oya *egbe,* José Manuel Guinart recalled some songs onto my tape-recorder. Jerry Shilgi and Felipe Alfonso edited José Manuel's contribution into more standard form, appearing here as 18–25. (Songs 21–24 are usually performed in this order as a complete *tratão.* Number 25 has not undergone surveillance by Shilgi because it only recently resurfaced on a separate homemade tape.) Numbers 26–31 were contributed by Puntilla during the course of his first interview. I heard 32–34 sung by Louis Bauzo during an Orisha dance class he organized. I later noted them down phonetically, and months later Louis was kind enough to clarify muddles. Louis also helped reconstruct 35 from a remembered performance by Puntilla. I can't recall when I first heard the little phrase-song listed as 36, but number 37 is a refrain sung by Jose Manuel at the conclusion of his own enthusiastic rendition of 13. Far from exhaustive, this collection is only a beginning.

As what Puntilla would call a *complemento* to these songs in the Cuban tradition, I've attached a coda of three from Brazil. The first (39) is a beautiful nonliturgical song for Oya from the film *Tenda dos milagres.* Elisa Mereghetti brought the recording (Dudu Moraes sings it) back from

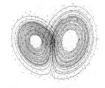

Brazil and Lisa Lipkin arranged a simplified version for us all to sing in "The Play Course." Numbers 40 and 41 are traditional *candomblé* songs that Jose Manuel and I reconstructed from old recordings.

In sum, the order in which the texts appear on these pages is the result of personal encounters with the songs, most of which were heard (or, more precisely, listened to) for the first time not separately but in longer or shorter sequences, one naturally calling up another. What is this "naturally?" It would seem that certain songs are linked in sequences by sound and individual word association, others by rhythm or intuited meaning, and the larger groups by precedent, which in turn conditions the feeling that a singer will lend them. Conversation III gives us a sense of how an effective singer in a ritual setting responds to the medium's mood and gauges her process; or is it the Orisha's vagaries upon this or that particular occasion that he's responding to? Thus the song-roads reaching toward and bringing the Orisha home become engraved upon communal consciousness. Fortunately, these various metonymical attempts to define and locate Oya and her compatriots haven't yet hardened into the canonical, which is the danger looming whenever an oral tradition begins getting written down. An acknowledged "standard" stands midway along the frontier between flexible and rigid; and no one, involved in this "reduction to writing" can ignore its existence. For example, Jerry Shilgi/ Felipe Alfonso took the songs to follow and divided them into the following groups: (A) The *rezos* in reverse order, first 2, with its chorus, Ee Oya wimi loro, then 1, with the refrain, Ayaba te mire o. (B) *Oro cantado* as placed here, (3) Ayiloda, then (4), Oya de. (C) Jose Manuel's sequence, (21) Yansan wa mi o, (22) Bobo wa ñale, (23) Bobo brakata, (24) Akara sa ba ori. (D) A *sequencia* consisting of (7) Oloya de, followed by (8) Oya de o, (19) Oya oye o, and (5) Ere mi ocha, and concluding with (18) Mawo ya ro. (E) Another road, including (16) Eeee a, (6) Kala kala wo, (17) Oya wima wima, (14) Oya Oya ile o, (9) Oya eri wo ya, and (10) Oya eri wo mariwo ya. (F) A final group in the following sequence: (15) Ocha ewe ikoko (a famous *puya*), (20) Shola kiniba (complimenting Agayu), (12) Adie kwele (another *puya*), (13) Oya mi loya, and (11) Oya oya.

A second example, this time of spontaneous patterning of songs in a secular situation, may be provided by Puntilla, who at the conclusion of an *ad hoc* picnic supper in my apartment, led his band and their followers in a generous burst of eighteen songs for Oya, nonstop, with improvised percussion (including a kitchen pot hit by a spoon as clave): (7) Oloya de, (8) Oya de o, (10) Oya eri wo mariwo ya, (28) Oyaga ga ga, (16) Eee eeee a, (6) Kala kala wo, (17) Oya wima wima, Bembe Oya and Oya o (uncollected), (35) Oya 'n sama tere rema, (32) Lamba o, Omo l'Oya (uncollected), (19) Oye oye o, (12) Adie kwele, Awa to (uncollected), (13) Oya mi loya, (37) Longoro ya, and a repeat of (35). The message here is that there are always more songs than one knows, and playful streams of consciousness preside over their occasional arrangement.

Superscripts in the texts refer to notes at the end of Part Four. For comments on number 26, which can be sung for other Orisha, though for some reason Oya seems to "own" it, and on many other songs as well (*puyas* and *comidas,* mainly) see Conversation II. Lucumi words in transcription normally appear unaccented, which makes it difficult in the process of translation to refer them back to their Yoruba roots; but this won't affect the casual reader. In general, vowels should be given a latinate value; but where Spanish orthography has dominated standard Yoruba pronunciation, I have usually anglicized it: "Shango" rather than "Chango" and "ewe" (leaf) rather than "egue." All phrases not attributed to the *coro* (chorus) belong to the *akpón* (lead singer).

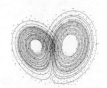

(1) Oya, Oya mbero
Oya mo rere
Akamala oye
Oye weko nunko nunso
Woye woye obinisa
Oya mi lode o
Osi kreta kun foya la meta
O duro ba lo ye o
Ara 'ya wo ee

coro Ayaba te mire o
Ayaba te mire o
Obini a ima
Ayaba te mire o ee

(2) Ayaba ayaba u lose wele oke
Dibi kua diña le
Loje loje loje loje
Lo baya mala wola wona
Iya kekesele
'Ya kekesele su adoso yoso yano
Igwa kekeke ee
Ee, Oya wimi loro e
Ee, Oya wimi loro e
Oya kara owi sa leyo
Eki ma yoro
Eke ola

coro Ee, Oya wimi loro e
Ee, Oya wimi loro e
Oya kara owi sa leyo
Eki ma yoro
Eke ola

(3) Ayiloda ya oku o
Towo mode ke eyo ayaba[21]
Ekifala oye o
Towo mode ke eye ayaba

coro Ayiloda ya oku o
Towo mode ke eyo ayaba

(4) Oya de (m)ariwo
O mesa loro yoko ro

coro [repeats the stanza]

(5) Ere mi ocha
Oya lokwa (a)kara ko loro

coro [repeats the stanza]

Ere mi ocha o loya lo
Kwa kara ka loro

coro [repeats the first stanza]

(6) Kala kala wo
Oni o kala lawo olele

coro Oya(n) kala
Oni kala lawo olele

Oni kala lawo

coro   olele
Owimi owimi

coro   olele
Oya mesa meji

coro   olele
Oya mesa menon

coro   olele
Kala kala wo
Oni kala lawo olele

coro Oya kala, oni kala lawo olele

(7) Oloya de
Iwa ri wa shekeshe[22]
Oloya de
Iwa ri wa shekeshe
Ago ima ago lona
Oba osire, Oloya de

coro [repeats the stanza]

(8) akpón and coro
Oya de o, a-ina

Oya mada she ku bere

coro Oya de o, a-ina Oya de

(9) Oya eri wo e
Oya eri wo Oya osi

coro [repeats the stanza]

(10) Oya eri wo mariwo ya
Oya eri wo mariwo ya

coro [repeats the stanza]

(11) Oya oya, Oya oya
Oya yewe ayiloda

coro Aye be ogun
Ayiloda

(12) Adie kwele umbo mo le ya

coro   ko ko ko

(13) Oya mi loya[23]

coro Oyo mi loya

[entire unit repeated 3 times]

Oya mi loya uga bembe

coro Oya mi loya uga bembe

[entire unit repeated 3 times]

(14) Oya Oya ile o
Oya mo ba loro ke

coro [repeats the stanza]

(15) Ocha ewe ikoko

coro   Oya Oya[24]

(16) Eeee eee a
Eeee eee a
Oya kala ayiloda ma rere o[25]

coro [repeats the stanza]

Ayiloda

coro   ma rere o

Ayiloda

coro   ma rere o

(17) Oya wima wima[26]
Yansan wima wima
Shokoto pengpwe ala we ri Oya

coro [repeats the stanza]

(18) Mawo ya ro, mawo ya ro[27]

coro Teyeye mawo ya ro
Mawo yao Oya teyeye

(19) Oya oye o
Iba ko ke iña le takua

coro [repeats the stanza]

(20) Shola kini'ba[28]
She 'ru baba mi

coro Oya Oya o Tapa

(21) Yansan wa mi o

coro Ayiloda
Obini sa ba eri[29]

(22) Bobo wa ñale

coro Oya ma oloya

(23) Bobo brakata

coro Ma foya de
Obini sa ba ori

(24) Akara sa ba ori[30]
Akara sa ba ori

coro [repeats the stanza]

(25) Koro unle o kara kara

coro [repeats the line]

(26) Awa ra ni koko
Awa ra loyu re
Awa ra loyu re
Mole ya Oya, Mole ya Oya
Ocha wewe ikoko

coro   Mole ya Oya
Ocha wewe ikoko

coro   Mole ya Oya

(27) Iya loya ee adie adie Oya[31]
Iya loya ee adie adie Oya

(28) Oya ga ga ga
Shango kwe lu laiye[32]

coro Oya ga ga ga

[entire unit repeated]

Okodo lo mi shokoto
Baba sise awa o

coro Oya ga ga Shango kwe lu laiye

(29) Oya bi ku oni lewa wo
Oya bi ku oni lewa wo
Omi o baba agba akara jeun

(30) Iba loya peregun
Iba loya ko wa ile

(31) Alafi Oyo e
Shango alafi Oyo e
Bamba okete ile Shango
Bamba okete ile Shango
Iba loya ima loya e
Iba loya ima loya e

(32) Lamba o
Lamba o sile

coro Oya de we lamba o

(33) Farara kun fa
Farara kun fa
O tutu mama iso loya

Omo loya

coro Farara kun fa

(34) Oya uye o
Bati ba o ma se masho
Oya le we

coro Se masho
Oya bi ku

coro Se masho

(35) Oya'n sama tere rema[33]

coro [repeats the line]

(36) Oya de i-ye

coro [repeats the line]
Oya de mariwo ya

coro [repeats the line]

(37) Longoro ya, longoro ya
Longoro i tomi loya

coro [repeats the stanza]

(38) Bariba ogwe dema

coro Mole Yansan a moleya[34]

Songs from Brazil

(39) E l'Oya
Oba shiré oba sharé loja
E loya e loya
Oba shiré oba sharé loja
E loya oooo
Eee eee [repeat 4 times]

(40) Oba tile o, oba tile
Tani loya e?

coro   *Oya e, Oya e*
Tani loya e?

coro   *Oya e, Oya e*

(41) O tani to
Mi Oya o
O tani to mi Oya

coro A eeee o tani to, mi Oya

Musical Transcriptions

Note: In transcribing these songs, small concessions had to be made for the sake of clarity and for maintaining the basic song structure. Songs 7 and 13–14 had different ornamentation in the repetitions, quite complicated "taking off" from what I conceived as the basic thematic material, and I chose not to include this improvisation in the transcription. Similarly, in song 39 I was concerned to present the paradigmatic melody beneath and continual variations of the soloist. I notated the melodic prayer sequence in song 1 as faithfully as possible, without feeling the need for metered measures because of its chantlike nature. An *x* appears in place of a note when the vocalist's tonal quality is guttural, making precise identification difficult.

I was interested to learn while doing this project that the real difficulties lay in the complexity of the songs, not in any "irregularities" rhythmic, melodic, or tonal that would make conversion to Western notation next to impossible. The manuscript was notated in its final draft and designed to the scale of the book's pages by Timothy McKeown. John Amira's comments on the rhythmic configurations underlying the songs were most helpful as I moved from first to second draft of the manuscript. The reader may find it difficult to sense where the verbal emphasis lies, but this is a problem built into the construction of music in relation to words in these songs, and it is hoped practice and intuition will overcome it.

—Esther Gleason

Xiomara dancing Oya. Charcoal drawing by Susan DeMirjian.

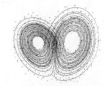

(1) "LONG SONG FOR OYA"

OYA

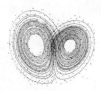

(page two)

O-ya kara owisa le-o   E-ki ma yo-ro   E-ke o-la   Ee O-

ya wimi lo-ro e-e   Oya kara owi sa le-yo   E-ki ma yoro E-ke O-

la   A-yi-lo-da ya o-ku-o   To-wo mo-de ke e-yo a-ya-ba

CORO

A-yi-lo-da ya o-ku-o   To-wo mo-de ke e- yo a-ya-ba

SOLO

Ye-ki- fa-la O-ya o   To-wo mode ke   yo a-ya-ba

CORO

A- yi-lo da ya o ku—o   To-wo mo de ke   yo a-ya-ba

SOLO

O-ya de—e   ma-ri-wo   O me-sa lo— ro   yo-ko ro

CORO

O-ya de—e   ma-ri-wo   O me-sa lo— ro   yo-ko ro

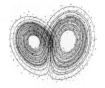

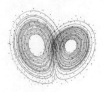

(13) "OYA MI LOYA" (page four)

SOLO CORO 3x

O- ya-a mi lo-ya o-ya-a mi lo-ya

SOLO CORO (14) SOLO

O-ya mi loya u-ga bembe O-ya-a mi loya o-ya o-ya ile o

CORO

oya mo pa loro ke O-ya oya ile o oya mo pa loro ke

(7) "OLOYA DE"

SOLO

O lo-ya de i wa ri wa sheke she O loya de iwa ri wa she

ke she Ago ima go lona oba o shire o o-ya de-

CORO

e o lo-ya de i wa ri wa sheke she ago

im-a go lo-na oba shire-e o o-ya de

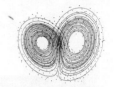

A note on the English version of the songs: The translations are equivalents only—within the precincts of vocabulary appropriate to the praising of Oya, whether in the solemn *rezo* mode or in the teasing vein of the *puya* or midway between. The Lucumi originals carry a double semantic load: (1) that of the "old" Yoruba praise-poetry and abbreviated chants from which they were derived and creatively reconstituted under stress in oppressive social and political circumstances, and (2) that of certain segments of a continuing Afro-Cuban experience which the religious notion of "Oya" could naturally be coopted to express and symbolize. Which is to say that mysterious Oya (like other Orisha) had to be reimagined within an interactive complex of spiritual forces that don't correspond point by point with her limited affiliations in Africa. Already implicit in Ifa as a regulative agency, borrowed and adapted to Afro-Cuban purposes from the Catholic canon of saints and their folkloric "portfolios," the Lucumi "pantheon" housed in *casas de ocha* represents a complicated and geographically diffused Yoruba

Xiomara dancing Oya. Charcoal drawing by Susan DeMirjian.

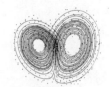

belief-system in microcosm. In like manner song repetoires for the various Orisha are constrained for the most part to short verses of highly condensed material which cannot be entirely resolved into Yoruba equivalents.

Yoruba "reversionists" think differently, I realize. But to me the Lucumi liturgy as sung today is a beautiful cultural expression in its own right; and although in these free translations I have allowed, to the best of my knowledge, detectable Yoruba words to surface and illuminate, I have been at equal pains to transmit an emic (or here-and-now consensual) sense of their texture, dynamic, and various rhetorical strategies.

The risks I have taken have been in the service of what I have sensed to be the tone of the song in question. Although aware of the *clave* swing between polarities trochaic and iambic, I have in no way literalized this notion, but I got so I could hear the Lucumi syllables swinging, and certainly the reader will notice how the upside and downside of Oya's personality are often paired in the same lyric, even within the same line.

Extending this notion, one can see how beyond the confines of formally constructed *rezos*, short *cantos* containing solemn encomia (like 19 and 32) and wistful pleading (in numbers 14, 33, 34, etc.) balance and thus implicitly give permission for license taken in gratuitous *puyas* (like 17 and 28), which seem less calculated to cajole Oya and her medium into the same cage than playfully, with the gods as vehicles, to air stereotypical tensions and attractions between men and women, thus intensifying the erotic atmosphere. Of course it can be argued that so to increase the libidinal temperature within sacred precincts, where the only possible way to go is into possession rather than into bed, is entirely consistent with bembé intentionality: to bring down Orisha. As Emilio eloquently conveys it, "working" Oya (or any other Orisha) is tantamount to vocal seduction. (Thus Don Giovanni, spelled by Leporello, plays *akpón* to initially reluctant Elvira and Zerlina, and the list of ecstatic missions accomplished gets longer and longer.)

To return to Oya's *sequencias*. Here within a collaged composition limited to about 200 lines (including choral responses) the tension between the major facets of her personality—feisty thief of fire/compassionate goddess of death—is dramatized to the point of incongruity. The former in Brazilian Candomblé is nicknamed "Oya of the mat," whose breaking-the-plates-with-her-buttocks dance provides heated commentary on her cool-eyed disinitiation of the deceased medium during *etutu* ritual. The ribald subtext of song-segments 22–25 was beyond the translator's

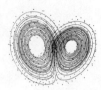

power of compression; but it's there on the back burner cooking up a storm. Reversing the direction of implication toward the spiritual world, with a food recipe as vehicle and reincarnation as tenor, we have the incomparably witty and beautiful *canto* 6. Again, mama's cooking, but in a different place; and we understand that warmth in the kitchen like desire's fire mystically retains its heat in the alembic of transformation from one state of being to another.

Food for thought and leaves for remembrance. Conversing with Puntilla as he lingered with relish over various recipes, I began to realize that an ancillary purpose of the songs is the encoding of correct ritual procedure. So although they seem quippy, the reader will be ill-advised to write off verses having to do with Afro-Cuban tamales (corn meal, especially guinea corn wine, is a sacred commemorative food in the old country), or *akara* (bean cakes are made with black-eyed peas in the Lucumi tradition) or malanga and peregun leaves as picturesque details of a folkloric religion. Where and in what order certain leaves with specific medicinal as well as symbolic properties are placed or processed in the course of initiation is information crucial to the finding of one's position in the vaster universe of all beings.

And finally, readers should be aware that the short-short songs are repeated until the chorus really gets going, at which time the *akpón* goes on to the next. Sounds and symbolic actions link them in *sequencias*. Taken as a whole fabric, the songs are remarkable for their range within such limited compass and for the ingenuity expended in expressing traditional themes in a few syllables with great zest, all the while ringing changes on the syllables in order to shift meaning and provide inuendo. The songs here translated are a verbal patchwork Oya, gradually constructed by a loving and witty community to fit a vigorous and occasionally plaintive music. Few who sing them now would be able to explain more than the gist of their meaning, but these lyrics continue to carry an intense emotional charge. May they be enjoyed even in this provisory English format.

Oya's Songs, an English Version

Long Song for Oya

(1) Oya Oya I pray, Oya
     For your blessings
     Illuminate me with intelligence

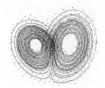

Lead me, so I won't get lost in the world
Carefully carefully, strenuous woman.
Oya, my fresh air
Let no ill winds blow in our direction
Stand steadily by your people
O secret of our survival.

coro Queen of the wind, behold me bending before you
Queen of the wind, behold me as reeds, grasses
Wife of fire
Queen of the wind, behold me bending before you.

(2) Beloved queen, tremble of leaves upon the mountain
Definitely you gave birth to death
Gently gently gently gently
Careening along the path of honor
Mother of sudden gusts
Mother of sudden whirrings
In an earthenware jar.
Ee Oya, speak to me plainly that I may know
Ee Oya, speak to me plainly that I may understand
Oya, strength to the elder, welcome!
Take our words now, but not our voices
Until tomorrow.

coro Ee Oya, speak to me plainly that I may know
Ee Oya, speak to me plainly that I may understand
Oya, strength to the elder, welcome!
Take our words now, but not our voices
Until tomorrow.

(3) Arise that I may fall before you
Great Queen, fondling your children one by one.

coro [repeats the stanza]

Arrive changes, turning up to down
Great Queen, fondling your children one by one.

coro [repeats the stanza]

(4) Oya stay, hidden one
Wild nine sit down calmly.

coro [repeats the stanza]

(5) Ground beans, my Orisha
Oya, come enjoy your favorite food.

coro [repeats the stanza]

Ground beans, my Orisha

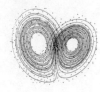

Oya, come enjoy your *akara*.

coro [repeats the first stanza]

(6) May we live to see our dreams unfold
Cornmeal wrapped, cornmeal boiled in plantain leaves.

coro [repeats the stanza]

Oya, owner of dreams
Cornmeal wrapped and boiled in plantain leaves.
Secretly shrouded cornmeal

coro plantain leaves
O speak to me rustling

coro plantain leaves
Oya nine-fold, nine-fold

coro plantain leaves

(7) Oya stayed
Trembling with little bells she came to her
Oya stayed
Trembling with little bells she came to her.
Clear the road, make way for fire! Queen
Of our festivity, O Oya stayed.

coro [repeats the above stanza]

(8) [*akpon* and *coro* together]
Oya came O, blazing with fire, Oya came
Oya will strike, flaming the grasses.

coro Oya came O, blazing with fire, Oya came.

(9) Oya, spare our heads
Oya, take care of our heads, O please!

coro [repeats the stanza]

(10) Oya, shred the fronds, save our heads
Oya, shred the fronds, save our heads.

coro [repeats the stanza]

(11) Oya Oya; Oya Oya
Lively leaves falling before you.

coro World pleads for your medicine, Oya
Please rise to the occasion!

(12) Chicken hesitates on the way to market.

coro cluck-cluck, no-no

(13) Oya my Oya

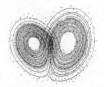

coro Oya my Oya [3 times]

  Oya my Oya can't sit out a bembe

coro Oya my Oya can't sit out a bembe.   [3 times]

(14) Oya, Oya's other country

  Oya, protect me when I meet you there.

coro [repeats the stanza]

(15) Malanga leaf, last to go under the throne.

coro Oya, Oya

(16) Eee eee a

  Eee eee a

  Tall Oya bestowing good fortune.

coro [repeats the stanza]

  Arise, Oya

coro windfall to follow

  Arise, Oya

coro windfall to follow.

(17) Oya talk talk, talking

  Yansan talk talk, talking

  Must be those short pants under your flounces.

coro [repeats stanza]

(18) Be careful, ferocious woman.

coro Calm down, take it easy, ferocious woman

  Take it easy, Oya, calm down.

(19) Oya we're honoring you

  Thief of fire from Takua

coro [repeats stanza]

(20) Emergence of honor—that's what enslaves me, Father.

coro Oya Oya O Tapa.

(21) Yansan, I'm on my way

coro Uplifting you

  Strong woman, save our heads.

(22) Come dance, everyone![35]

coro Oya, over the edge.

(23) Everyone's letting go.

coro Oya's coming down

  Strong woman, save our heads.

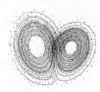

(24) Hot *akara*, save our heads. [twice]

coro [repeats the line twice]

(25) Stiff resists, lively comes on strong.

coro [repeats the line]
Decisive woman, round the corner faster now

coro Grinding those beancakes all the way home, catering woman.

(26) We bought you with malanga leaf
Face to face we made an honorable agreement
Eye to eye, face to face an honorable agreement
Binding sky to earth, earth to sky, Oya
Malanga leaf goes under the throne

coro Binding sky to earth, Oya
Malanga leaf goes under the throne

coro Binding sky to earth, Oya.

(27) Mama Loya eee, chicken on the way to market   [2 times]

(28) Oya, plump plump plump
Shango's playing your boobs in the world.

coro Oya, plump plump plump

"How about those bulges beneath *your* clothes?"
Asks Oya. He says "Papa's heating up."

coro Oya plump plump plump
Shango playing his favorite drums.

(29) Oya gave birth to death—owner of the beautiful secret
Oya gave birth to death—owner of the beautiful secret
Water seeps through the earth, come eat *akara,* ancestor.

(30) Peregun plant enters last of all
The house is waiting for you, Oya.

(31) King of Oyo ee
Shango is king of Oyo.
Bush rats grow fat in Shango's country
Bush rats grow fat in Shango's country
By your leave, Oya, we invoke lightning
By your leave, Oya, we invoke lightning.

(32) Honor is on its way
Honor is entering the house

coro Oya arrives, covered with honor.

(33) Dragging along in sorrow[36]
Painfully struggling

Come freshen our spirits, Oya.
Oya's children, we are

coro dragging along in sorrow.

(34) Oya, food-o
Newcomers can't cook, can't go
Oya, stir for us

coro Neither cook, nor go
Oya gave birth to death's kingdom

coro Neither cook, nor go.

(35) Oya—airfall—smashing, flattening.

coro [repeats the line]

(36) Oya descends, answering.

coro [repeats the line]
Oya remains behind the veil.

coro [repeats the line]

(37) Tearing everything up, tearing everything up
We'll have to start over, Oya.

coro [repeats the stanza]

(38) Searing medicine is on the way

coro Touch ground, Oya, in the market.
Spreading, this "medicine" is contagious

coro Touch ground, Oya, in the market.

Songs from Brazil

(39) E l'Oya
Plays to win, plays to lose in the market[37]
[repeat both lines]
E l'Oya oooo
E-eeee   [4 times]

(40) The queen has come to the house
Who is being proclaimed?

coro Oya-e Oya-e
Who is being proclaimed?

coro Oya-e Oya-e

(41) Rapid motion, my Oya-o
Is sufficient motive.

coro A eeee, o sufficiently rapid, Oya.

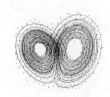

Oya of the Nine Pieces

Is there such a thing as an "Oya type" of person in everyday life? Some years ago a drummer who used to perform at ceremonies for the Orisha in New York thought about this question for a while, then confessed he could see no pattern. To begin with, there is a scarcity of evidence. Everyone knows countless Oshuns, a substantial number of Yemayas, but very few Oyas. The drummer could think of only four—three women and one man. To begin with the latter: "He was a quiet person, laid-back, kind, helpful." Of the three women, one was "energetic, a go-getter, a dynamic sort of personality." Another presented herself publicly as a quiet, well-behaved "little girl" type. But hers was a temper quick to flare up, dangerously. At home she was apt to draw a knife. Her husband, an Ogun, was always checking the kitchen drawers and under pillows for knives. They got into terrible battles, said the drummer, which this Ogun-husband often got the worst of. Finally, he had the good sense to get out of the house altogether. The third woman, married to an Elegba, was a nag, the drummer said, very uptight, always mothering her husband instead of relating to him as an equal. "Oya is unpredictable," commented the drummer's wife laconically.

Predictable, however, as questions and answers in the advice columns of tabloids are the patterns of maladjustment culturally open to women: the go-getter, the little girl who hides her violence in kitchen drawers or under the pillow, the nagging mother. Oya's convective currents have seized upon such women and wrung them dry. How, without

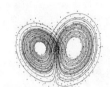

physical removal from the social conditions that reinforce them, could these women have been educated away from such patterns and toward the containment of Oya?

As the drummer was speaking of the quiet, laid-back man devoted to Oya, I thought of a Nigerian counterpart. Unusually retiring where expressive personalities are the rule, this Nigerian son of Oya spent most of his time alone or with his twelve-year-old son out on the farms an hour's walk from town. It was 1970. His was the first Oya shrine I had ever visited. The quiet priest was helpful. He and his son danced Oya to the batá drums for us in a secluded place. A big man, over six feet tall and solidly built, he danced with ineffable, placid grace. Oya's turbulence had found a nourishing home in his soul, her jagged bolts well grounded. The Oya priest had a wind cylinder (ancestor of the *palo de lluvia* used in Latin percussion) upon his altar in town. He played it so that I could hear Oya speaking (as I now interpret it) in a contained way. It was an intimate sound heard as he rotated the cylinder like an hourglass. It was like the rustling of leaves signaling the distant beginnings of a storm. He must have heard her speak to him like that out on the farms.

The drummer's response raises difficult questions having to do with performative aspects of the self in cultural context. Psyche is feminine. For a woman, ensoulment is an arduous, asymmetrical process, which does not necessarily involve finding a countersexual principle. It may mean discovering a definition of the feminine outside the culturally defined range of female roles in which the soul-seeking woman finds herself. Cross-culturally, women devotees of the spirits animating possession cults overwhelmingly outnumber men (and often the few men involved are ambivalent about their own gendered roles). Such cults from the Dionysian era to our own have been avenues of women's liberation, creative contribution to culture, and spiritual development outside the hegemonic confines of "organized" religion and ideology. This does not mean that the *thiasos* (sacred community) is disorganized, but it does suggest that, following Turner, its status is liminal.

What is at issue here is the extent to which the worshiper of an Orisha has been able to integrate the archetypal force into her total personality structure. When one is not aware of the presence of the Orisha in everyday life, then chances are the split in the inner world has not been healed. The Orisha possessing the person remains autonomous. Its appearance in ritual context enriches the community of participants for whom an

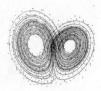

archetypal configuration is thus made visible; but despite the reassuring prestige attached to being the carrier of such power, the person herself remains undeveloped. Wounded, prone to inflation, to projecting unacknowledged psychic contents upon what are experienced as hostile, conniving others, the Orisha-carrier can remain childish, unreliable, even marginal so far as worldly matters are concerned. How does the desired integration take place, and what thwarts it?

The Orisha mirrors the hidden self. In the European process of psychoanalysis it is up to the client to find words to tell who she really is. Dreams, imaginings, drawings may hint at or provide forms for this gradual self-disclosure within the facilitating space provided by the analyst. In the Jungian mode, various configurations of the unconscious become identified and "owned" so that in becoming a centered whole, the analysand humbly finds herself to be a system of energies over which the willful ego's control is illusory. It is a transpersonal Self that binds the whole, and it is to this Self that the ruling Orisha corresponds.

Curious to see how the Orisha were functioning as quotients of deeper identity in the personalities of three highly trained academic women friends kind enough to cooperate in the experiment, I playfully administered the Myers-Briggs Type Indicator test to each of us (so we were four) twice. The first set of answers was on behalf of the head-ruling Orisha in question. The second set were "I"/ego responses. In all cases the Orisha appeared to be drawing the person out from profound introversion and helping her balance a constitutional way of relating to the world (through feeling, thinking, intuition, or perceiving sensuously) with a complementary approach.[38]

In the African system of therapy it is the oracle with the diviner as intermediary who tells the person who she really is; although it is up to the individual to fulfill a prenatally chosen destiny. The well-being of the group to which the person belongs is also a strong consideration in treatment.

In the relatively contained Candomblé communities, where initiation is understood to be continuous until the completion of the "seventh-year obligation," adepts undergo a process of Orisha-role exploration. Gradually the initiate assimilates an image of her own head-ruling Orisha, theatrically represented in trance without her conscious knowledge, but projected back upon her in daily life by others who, partly in fun, expect prototypical behavior from her. At the same time the adept is gradually

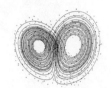

internalizing collective representations of the Orisha in various media: altar installations, drum rhythms, dance gestures, myths, folktales, ritual costume, and so on. She also gets to know others who carry the same Orisha she does, and so has living role models. Each divine personality has a range of expressions, or "roads"; within the particular variation alloted her by the oracle, the initiate is encouraged to develop her own style, and the Orisha itself is believed to control this evolutionary process by continual reinforcement of the initiate's vital potential.[39]

Like actors, Orisha-carriers are licensed to be a bit temperamental in their daily lives. An easy access to the unconscious, there from the start, has been cultivated in cult context, and it is not so easy to keep it from spilling over into nonritual situations. One may see such vagaries of behavior as informal rehearsals for prototypical roles that initiates ceremonially play in inspired trance states and also as adjustments of the true self to the world—to the world of the cult community first, then to the world outside. In time, an Orisha-based personality replaces the old depressed or hyperactive or hypochondriacal social mask that used to face the light of day with apprehension.

Because the integration of Orisha into the total personality occurs in a group context, the strength, cohesiveness, and collective wisdom of the religious community are of crucial importance. And the community requires space. A retreat is necessary. Affluent Buddhists and Sufis in the United States can afford sequestered terrain and extended vacations. Santeros have trouble making ends meet. Throughout the Caribbean, other versions of this core West African religion remain stable and supportive of evolution of character because of grounding upon the soil and in family tradition. A second diaspora to the continental United States has rendered the Orisha somewhat skittish. As these gods attempt to take root beneath the linoleum floors of cramped apartments and in the unsettled psyches of individuals attracted into their orbits, a certain turbulence shakes the flimsy walls. Self-knowledge tends to go by the boards, and acting out gets confused with archetypal enactment. Obatala eats too much; Shango chases after women; and Oya hides knives in her bureau drawers. Consonant with the materialistic society into which these African gods have latterly fallen, much of the energy expended in their worship gets literalized. Compulsive instructions are loftily given out on correct ingredients and procedures. A new fundamentalism incarnates itself in the display windows of proliferating *botánicas*. The Oya women

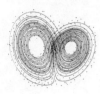

observed by the drummer may have set up their altars according to pre-scription, but they have not been able to center themselves in the eye of her tornado.

Within the range of characteristic Orisha-behaviors specified by tradition, divination provides the initiate with certain guidelines. There is also, as suggested above, and interplay between collective representations handed down by oral traditions and the Orisha-fulfilled lives of real people whose virtuoso embodiments of the type have enlarged it, lent it a mem-orable style; great stage actors leave their mark upon dramatic characters. There are many ways of playing Hamlet, and it would be difficult to rehearse the part without initial reference to one of the legendary inter-pretations. Although the aggregate of ways of being a certain Orisha co-incides with the number sacred to the divinity—twelve for Shango, eight for Obatala, nine for Oya—in practice the possibilities polarize about ex-tremes of age or temperament: either the sensuous, dandified Shango or the tyrannical thunderer; either the young Obatala or the ancient. Oya's nine ways are bifurcated into vitalistic or mediumistic directions.

In Nigeria these two aspects of the goddess are mutually exclusive. Shrines and activities associated with Egungun-Oya, Mother-of-the-dead who sees beyond life, are ritually avoided by cult members devoted to Oya-Ajere, Carrier-of-the-container-of-fire. In Brazil the Oya affiliated with Egungun is called Oya-Bale, whose name derives from *igbale*,[40] the sacred precinct where the dead in masquerade form materialize before go-ing out to perform in public. In Brazil the vital Oya, who carries her fire in a more explicitly sexual way than her Nigerian counterpart, has, as suggested above in the notes on Oya's songs, a popular Portuguese name, *Oya de esteira*, meaning "Oya of the mat," which she is imagined provoc-atively to carry about ready to unroll and spread down for any chance lover she fancies. It is this hetaeristic aspect of Oya that performs the "plate-breaking" dance: hands on hips, buttocks prominently extended in saucy rotation. However, as we have seen, plate-breaking, or crockery-smashing, also has its funereal reference. It is as though the sexy dance of *Oya de esteira* were compensatory for the shattering activity of Oya-Bale.

Another way of looking at these two aspects of Oya is in terms of her consorts. With Shango is associated her fiery, outspoken side, and with Ogun her inward-turning. In the words of the Brazilian social psy-chologist Claude Lepine, "When Ogun took the power of dominance away from women, Yansan (Oya) disappeared from this world, to inhabit the

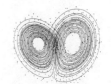

next."[41] This mediumistic other world of Oya's has a double locus. It is the forest to which the wounded human animal reverts: nature as a healing retreat from social trauma. It is also the mystical realm whose cyclical continuities similarly balance the stress of present existence. Between these interpenetrating vistas Oya-Bale vacillates like the wind. This is the invisible Oya who refuses definition. With patriarchal denial of her pre-eminence is matched her skittish (and "schizy") refusal to be anywhere.

Lepine has established a flexible typology or expressive profile of each of the Orisha. In theory she plays no favorites. Yet, obviously, there is personal involvement. Often, the more projective, the more insightful will be one's remarks on any topic. Lepine writes with illuminating eloquence of Oya. The kaleidoscopic goddess takes shape in her words as for the first time in a European language. Ten pages are devoted to Oya's modality. I doubt there are that many scattered throughout the various books and essays on Yoruba religion by the international community of scholars.

Although the grid upon which Lepine's analysis of Orisha characteristics is based devolves from the behavioral sciences, her language of description is popular. A distillation of what Candomblé worshipers have had to say about their gods, the impressionistic prose telling her readers who they are confidently echoes that of centuries of prognosticators informing us of the characterological significance of sun signs and planetary aspects. The hidden (and probably inadvertent) literary model of such seductive typological discourse is, of course, that of the astrology manual, cross-fertilized by contact with the symbolic biology of humors—hot, moist, cold, and dry. (Even Jung's psychological types are presented in this tone of voice). Lepine presents Oya as though in the grip of her own ruling planet: a compelling force in her own imaginative life.

She is connected to water as tempest and rain. She is connected to air as air-in-motion, which tears roofs off houses and fells trees; but her essence is fire, fire-in-motion, lightning. This relation to movement and fire make her divinity of women who lead intense erotic lives.

Associated with silence, Oya "speaks" fire. Or, having come from a distant place, she doesn't know the language of where she is. As divinity of forest and hunters, she is connected to animals and spirits of wilderness. She can transform herself into an animal evoking the idea of mortal peril for the hunter. She is linked to the first ancestor, semi-animal, of humanity. She is responsible for abundant game.

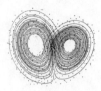

As queen of the dead, which she controls, she is responsible for the ritual "seating" of the male ancestors in the trunk of the Akoko tree. As dynamic principle of movement, in this context she represents the link between generations past and future.

Yansan represents a type of woman that is turbulent, nervous, full of initiative. She can be, at times, combative, authoritarian, impetuous, jealous, temperamental. She is independent, provocative, disobedient, but a dedicated wife. She represents a type of active, audacious woman who cannot find herself in domestic work, nor—like certain Yemanjas—in professional life. She has a penchant for the theater, for dramatic arts.

Oya-Bale wears eccentric clothes, vibrant colors, lots of jewelry.

Oya-Esteira is an adventuress. A fertile woman, mother of many children, she loves children; but being unsuited to domestic chores, she is not always a patient baby-tender.

Linked as she is to winds and leaves, the God of Medicine is her lover.

As Ogun's wife, she is a warrior-woman.

As wife of Oshossi, the hunter, she is part animal, part woman.

As wife of Shango, she is possessive and dedicated. She is the fire which empowers him.

Beautiful, even vain, exciting the jealousy of other women, she nonetheless prefers to live isolated in the country. There, silent and secretive, she observes and perceives everything.

As a river Oya is sensual and passionate.[42]

Thus, much abridged, but I hope doing no violence to her style, is Claude Lepine's vision of Oya. Could this be the same goddess who crowds the pages of this book? To read it by the light of a feeble bulb set high out of reach in the ceiling of a room in a Bahian boarding house was to experience a curious reversal of roles. She was saying things about Oya that pulled me to her as though for the first time. She became a romantic figure—a goddess of possibilities rather than of tormenting distractions. No matter that her various roads had already been marked in more corrosive ink. A sister's apprehension of them drew us into common orbit. It was like reading an advertisement for Oya and being tempted to answer it, or reading a novel and identifying wholeheartedly with the heroine.

Yes, it is reassuring to find the place where you live described by a foreigner as a tourist attraction. The hard pavement becomes for a while more springy under foot. Then comes the double-take. Can this neighborhood of intersecting streets really be what the guidebook is talking about? What seems in Claude Lepine's description an effortless play of

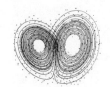

options can in reality be an exhausting struggle with priorities. This moving picture of the goddess flowing gracefully from sequestered forestlands to public masquerade ceremonies, from gypsy colors and gypsy necklaces to animal hide, from fire to air to water (without ground) catches the gleaming edges of Oya's personality but perforce ignores the wear and tear and the necessity for grounding. Does Claude Lepine know this now that she too, as I suspect, has come more nearly to inhabit Oya's kaleidoscopic environment?

To return to the notion of there being a certain number of "roads" for each Orisha, in theory nine for Oya (although this "nine" shouldn't be taken literally), on the personal level, how any individual who carries Oya will groove and into which road(s) depends upon the destiny of that individual, which awaits discovery within the guidelines specified by Ifa (if such a ritual consultation be made) and by "readings" performed with shells at the time of initiation. What concerns us here is metapsychological. Given Oya's unpredictability, her sudden shifts in direction and velocity, how can she be mapped as a coherent unity? The moral urgency of such a question for an "Oya person" is obvious. As an anthropologist friend is fond of saying, citing a Haitian proverb, "You have to learn to ride the horse in the direction it's going." But how to chart that maze of hoofprints yesterday and tomorrow? In an earlier chapter we discussed how, originally a ritual cleansing performance, Oya always resists anthropomorphism. Her "many faces" make her difficult not only to visualize but to conceptualize. (Note that Emilio, the singer, slid into a song for Olokun, the protean sea, in order to convey his feelings about her.) I have a problem with the usual notion of archetype, which seems so abstract and static because it does not allow for the fresh event that Oya always seemingly is.

To the rescue came the Lorenz attractor, tutelary spirit of contemporary chaos theory. Edward Lorenz, an experimental meteorologist and natural mathematician, thirty years ago grappled with the weather's unpredictability by building a model of a simple fluid system (composed of water rather than air) subjected to heating/cooling. Simulating the turbulence of his model on a digital computer, he accounted for its seemingly chaotic reversals of spin, and other matters, by a simple theory of exponential amplification: microstimulus generates sudden macrochanges. He

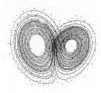

then went on to represent in the geometrical form of an attractor what the behavior of his convective currents was being pulled toward.[43]

The Lorenz attractor shows threads running parallel for a short time only to diverge radically, loop around opposite invisible foci, then pass the imaginary bisecting line again, looping in reverse direction. The lines of the diagram represent a tight sequence of moving points in a "state space," which as the points move and the situation changes, will be folded over and over again (as one folds dough to make croissants). Quickly the 10,000 points we see so close together that they seem a thread will form a peppery cloud of points. A single point on the surface represents any state of the (in this case, convective) system at any frozen point in time. But which is it? The point of putative prediction could be anywhere in the nebulous formation of dots, but the underlying butterfly pattern will remain, will keep on exerting its attraction no matter what in apparent randomness is happening.

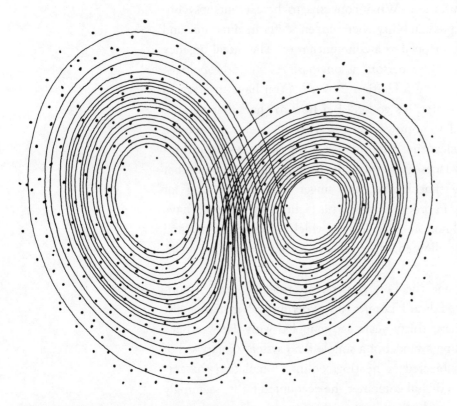

By analogy, here are Oya's fire-death polarities. And here also the positive-negative halves of *clave*, toward which all articulated sounds of the musical system perforce gravitate.

Another way of tracking Oya would be to look at the places she shows up along the continuum of the Ifa oracle, whose 256 combinations have been compared to a series of windows through which the various forces in the world speak to us situationally. However, the Ifa

Polarities of Oya (and *clave*) as suggested by the Lorenz Attractor. After drawings in *Scientific American*, December 1986.

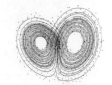

system, being an oral tradition, isn't standardized. Nor are the Orisha, for that matter. In one Nigerian town certain Orisha have great currency; in another they are peripheral, or known by different names. Diviners travel about learning stories, chants, and accompanying herbal remedies from colleagues, however, so consistency of associations clustering around each of the 256 *odu* is pulled forward. Avoiding the issue of cowrie shell divination and how it does or does not correlate with Ifa, focusing solely on Ifa stories about Oya collected in Africa, all but two of which can be found textually explored in this book, we can compose the following chart. I have inserted the combinations Obara Osa and Osa Meji in proper order but haven't put the relevant stories in because Oya is not mentioned by name, even though clearly the protagonist is suffering her effects and/or acting as she does. All the stories were collected from the Oyo state region.

Oyeku Owonrin—Here Oya is playing the bellows for Egungun to dance.

Odi Obara—Oya, working the bellows in Ogun's foundry, up and runs off with Shango, a handsome customer. At the end of the story Oya fights Ogun.

Irosun Osa—We see Oya with a red cloth over her head. Her children take the hint and establish Egungun masquerading and worship.

Obara Osa

Osa Ogunda—Oya, Buffalo-woman, assumes human form and is persuaded to marry Hunter (Ogun). Disaster results. But she gives her children buffalo horn with which to call her.

Osa Meji

Otura Ogbe—Because Shango didn't make the proper sacrifice in order to marry Oya, they fight. Oya also fights her co-wife Oshun. Both become rivers.

Irete Ogunda—Oya, on a destructive course, is persuaded to acquire a slave, Enin-Heyi, to act as impulse barrier and intercessor between herself and the community.

Ofun Osa—Oya, a tornado, is pacified with snails. A young diviner take her in, and she vomits up riches upon his floor.

Waiting for Emilio to appear for his interview, I sat talking to a Cuban *babalawo* (diviner-priest of Ifa) on the back patio of his house in the Bronx, where a *tambor* for Obatala was eventually to take place. Preoccupied with this question of mapping Oya, in her Ifa appearances as well as in her song-sequences, I asked him how he personally reconciled all her different guises as they show up in various *odu*. Marcos Vargas is not only an Ifa priest, but a priest of Orisha Agayu as well, and it's true that for the moment we were sharing a rhythm of thinking, orderly and clear. "Look at it this way," he said. "When you were sixteen you were a different person than you are today, you went running around, carefree. And when you were raising your kids, you were different again. You didn't get out much. Now you're working on a book, and that means you're not the same as you were different times in your life. It's that way with all those aspects of Oya—the animals and so on." (According to one of his *odu* she became a deer—but then, there weren't any African buffalo in Cuba.) "When I make an Oya I pull them together, summing up the ways she is and the [Ifa] places she speaks as if it were a whole life. Taking all these I make them one and set them upon the head of the *iyawo*" (person being initiated). As he was speaking, his hands were reaching out, pulling in various ingredients, and kneading them into a highly compressed biscuit.

Now to reverse direction from compression towards dispersal with a story collected by a very old friend, who is also a *babalawo*. Though he doesn't practice much, Ifa is always on his mind, he knows an immense amount. He heard this story in the same Nigerian town where twenty years ago the quiet Oya priest from the farms was playing the *palo de lluvia*, through which she speaks so softly.

The story begins with Ogun:

how ogun broke into seven pieces, oya into nine

The madman with steely bones
The terrible god who bites himself mercilessly
The terrible god who eats worms without vomiting!

It was Ogun who married Oya for the first time. Like a patient animal she used to carry his tools on her head when they went to the forge. On top of the tools rode a calabash containing food for their midday meal. While Ogun forged the tools, Oya worked the bellows for him, *whoosh, whoosh*. The sound of Ogun's hammer on the anvil—*king, king, ki-king, king, king, ki,* and all over again—worked in well with Oya's

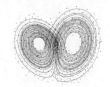

heavy breathing. But beneath this music was a hidden pulse beat, portending trouble, that both chose to ignore.

One day Ogun fashioned two very special rods for their mutual protection in this dangerous world we live in. "Here, you take this one, Oya," he said. "If ever you find yourself in great danger, strike with it! If it be a man who is threatening you, he will break into seven pieces. If it be a woman, she will break into nine." Ogun gave one of these magic rods to Oya and kept the other for himself.

Time passed. Then one day a very special customer called at the forge. It was

A man by the name of Shango
Who liked so much to be elegant
That he used to plait his hair like a woman
And he made holes in his ears
In which there were earrings, every time.
He would wear beaded necklaces
He would wear silver bracelets
He had too much elegance!

This gentleman was so charming that Oya, *whoosh, whoosh,* couldn't resist turning her head to look at him now and again. Nor could Shango resist Oya, for the Creator had given her a very powerful charm. Which is why she is known as *Oya-e-rií rií:* "Oya (so charming that) you can't take your eyes off her."

Ogun, bent over the forge and completely absorbed in his ironmaking, hadn't the slightest idea that anything like a flirtation was going on—until it was too late. First the bellows weren't working too well. There were breathless pauses. Then they stopped for good. Oya and Shango had eloped!

Where was Oya? The smith summoned everyone in the neighborhood with his gong, *king, king, ki-king, king, king, ki*—and asked them to help him track down the runaway. Everyone tried. They went off in all directions. Finally they came back to Ogun and reported, singing:

We went to the Egba of dogs in search of Oya
    But we didn't find Oya
We went to the Esa of hens in search of Oya
    But we didn't find Oya
We searched for her at the kola-nut depot
    Where she used to throw little pieces into her mouth
    But we didn't find Oya
We searched for her at the batá drum compound
    Where she used to dance the Elekete rhythm
    But we didn't find Oya

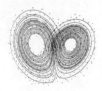

We searched for Oya where the coconut leaves never stand still
We searched and searched, but could no more find Oya.

So Ogun went off on his own. Finally his keen hunter's eye spotted the culprits. Amulets swinging upon his rough shirt, Ogun started off in swift pursuit.

Far off in the bush, Shango saw trees quivering. Birds were flying away, startled from their roosts. "What will I do? Ogun is my senior brother. In running off with his wife I have done a terrible thing. He is furious."

Oya said, "Don't worry, Shango. You just stay quietly over there and keep out of sight. Leave it to me. I can handle this one."

And so they advance, closer and closer, Ogun and Oya. Everything in the forest backs out of the way. Squirrels scramble up the trees the birds have vacated. The trees themselves hop close to the stream and bend down, covering their ears with their branches. Closer and closer they come. Now they're face to face. They raise their magic rods. *Pa! Pa!*

Each struck at exactly the same time. And as predicted, Ogun broke into seven pieces, Oya into nine. Which is why you find them scattered all over the world in our time.[44]

Suppose you find a fragment of one of these gods in your heart. Well, that's your business, not mine. A story might come of it. And when the story is told, like a wild bird you release it, this way, *Hepa! Heyi! Hepa!*

Notes

1. William Bascom, unpublished field notes, March 22, 1938, p. 3, and November 4, 1950, p. 4. My thanks to John Turpin for making these pages available to me.

2. David Hilary Brown, *Garden in the Machine: Afro-Cuban Sacred Art and Performance in Urban New Jersey and New York*, dissertation presented to the Faculty of the Graduate School of Yale University, 1988, vol. II, p. 401. This dissertation is a mine of information and should be consulted by anyone seriously interested in Santería.

3. Yrmino Valdés Garriz, *Ceremonias Funebres de la Santería Afrocubana* (San Juan: Sociedad de Autores Libres, 1991), uses the alternative Lucumi (Cuban Yoruba) pronunciation and spelling: *ituto*, and on page 66 defines the rite as one of dis-initiation. (I have here used the Lucumi spelling of the Yoruba word, *étútú*.) *Ceremonias* gives a meticulous description of mortuary ritual for Santería initiates and includes texts of songs and chants. Valdes plans to include a recording with his next edition. Retrospectively, after reading Valdés's account, I realize that I had missed certain details of the process in the Bronx, and that others had been omitted. The book may be ordered from the Sociedad, Apartado 4525, Antiguo San Juan, Puerto Rico 00902 for $12 plus mailing charges.

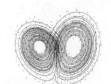

4. My source for the etymology of *runjebe* is R. P. B. Segurola, *Dictionnaire Fon-Français*, vol. 1 (Cotonou, 1963), pp. 87, 203, 234–35, 260. In her *Dicionario de cultos afro-brasileiros* (Rio de Janeiro: Forense Universitaria, 1977), p. 222, Olga Gudolle Cacciatore confounds (in my opinion) two types of necklace, *runjebe* and *runjefe,* and confuses the Fon meanings. The meaning of the latter would be "dark blue (or black) spirit beads."

5. In the course of doing research on Paleolithic goddesses, Seonaid M. Robertson wondered why, wearing nothing else, the goddess should wear a necklace. She finds this a widespread attribute of goddesses everywhere and comments that "this question has remained strangely unexplored by anthropologists" (*Rosegarden and Labyrinth* [Dallas: Spring Publications, 1982], p. 117 original ed. 1963). In the meditations to follow on the rosary, perhaps there is an implicit theoretical beginning to such research.

6. The thread that wove the Hindu fire sacrifice together was sound, uttered as "well-formed" speech. The Sanskrit language is etymologically "well formed." Thomas J. Hopkins, *The Hindu Religious Tradition* (North Scituate, MA: Duxbury Press, 1971), p. 20.

7. *Rita* means "the course of things" and by extension "the proper course of things" Hopkins, *Hindu Religious Tradition,* p. 12. The Beatles have fun with this idea by making Rita into a "lovely meter-maid" presiding over the meter of their song.

8. See Judith Gleason, *Agotime, Her Legend* (New York: Viking Compass, 1970).

9. My gratitude to Pierre Verger for sharing two rows of Ìrètè Ogúndá, which here appear published for the first time in an abbreviated English version for whose wording and the ensuing interpretation neither he nor the diviners from whom he collected it are responsible. Quotation is from P. Verger, unpublished manuscript, 1977, p. xxi b.

10. Robert Jay Lifton, *The Broken Connection: On Death and the Continuity of Life* (New York: Simon & Schuster, 1977).

11. Verger, ms. p. xxi a.

12. Here Oya is adopting the "Jakuta" aspect of Shango, which, like lightning, is associated with the kingdom of Bariba, located to the north of the present Republic of Benin. The stones, Neolithic celts, are believed to descend from the sky during thunderstorms.

13. C. G. Jung, *Psychology and Alchemy, Collected Works* 12, par. 186, p. 145.

14. In Walter A. Kaufmann, *Nietzsche: Philosopher, Psychologist, Antichrist* (Princeton: Princeton University Press, 1950), p. 371. Nietzsche wrote these lines in 1864.

15. The phrase is from Rainer Maria Rilke, "Eighth Elegy," *Duino Elegies: "Und wo wir Zukunft sehn, dort sieht es Alles / und sich in Allem und geheilt für immer."* This "animal's elegy" has been of tremendous importance in my own understanding of the connection between Oya-the-animal and Egungun-Oya.

16. Paul D. MacLean, "The Triune Brain, Emotion, and Scientific Bias," in *The Neurosciences,* ed. Francis O. Schmitt (New York: Rockefeller Univ. Press, 1970), p. 339. Again, MacLean's work has been invaluable in the thinking out of this *Heyi!* section.

17. From *Osa,* William Bascom, *Sixteen Cowries: Yoruba Divination from Africa to the New World* (Bloomington: Indiana Univ. Press, 1980), p. 249.

18. John Amira and Steven Cornelius, *The Music of Santeria: Traditional*

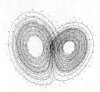

Rhythms of the Batá Drums (Crown Point, IN: White Cliffs Publishing, 1992), pp. 21–22. For a detailed description of sacred and festive architecture and decoration in Santeria, see David H. Brown, 1989, Vol II.

19. *Clave,* whether played with resonant wooden cylinders (*claves*) or with an externally struck metal bell or the flat blade of a hoe, is the rhythmical pattern that, superimposed upon the regular pulse (6/8 or 3/4) holds every articulated aspect of this music together.

The 6/8 clave sounds like this (all-caps represent hits of the clave):

ONE two THREE four FIVE SIX one TWO three FOUR five SIX (ONE, etc.)

Thus the pattern is completed in the course of two measures, rhythmically divided in such a way that the second measure is opposite in dynamic to the first. Amira and Cornelius brilliantly describe the phenomenon as a positive-negative reciprocity of polarities, one half balancing the other. "As the pattern is repeated, an alternation from one polarity to the other takes place, creating pulse and rhythmic drive" (*Traditional Rhythms,* p. 23).

So what Emilio means by "staying on *clave*" is that a solo-singer must maintain fidelity to these alternating dynamics across two measures. He can't sing a "yang" articulation of his variation in a "yin" place, but must keep these two energies ("plus" and "minus") in proper balance.

To use a metrical example from the world of poetic composition: The first part of *clave* is trochaic (− u) in feel and the second part is iambic (u −). The last two counts of the first part of the clave in poetic meter would be a spondee, which is a way of bringing troches to emphasized fruition or syncopated halt.

20. As David Brown points out, 1980–1982 "marked the beginning of a new era in the practice of Lucumí religion [popularly called Santería] in the United States." In 1980 Juan Raymat ("El Negro") and Orlando "Puntilla" Rios arrived via the Mariel boat-lift. Both had been "sworn in Aña" (see below) in Cuba. In 1982 Louis Bauzo was designated *olúbatá* or "owner" of the first set of sacred drums to have been "made from scratch" in this country. At the end of the decade there were at least five sets of sacred Bata drums, or *batá fundamento,* in this country and a sizable corps of "sworn-in" drummers equipped to play them. *op. cit. The Garden in the Machine,* vol I, pp. 137–41 *passim.*

21. Often *akpón* and *coro* sing the first two phrases of this song in unison before A. goes on to "*ekifala . . . ,*" which is a variation.

22. Alternative: *Ibariba* for *Iwariwa.*

23. We have transcribed the Collazo rendition. Shilgi reports that the more "standard" Cuban version begins with the *akpón* singing,

> *Oya mi loya*
> *Oya mi loya*
> *Oya oya (a)uga bembe*

and *coro* coming in with *Oya mi Oya.*

24. This is a shortened version. For the complete expression, including an elaborate solo introduction, see song 26. The meaning is discussed in the course of conversation II. After singing this song, Collazo returns to 14, then sings 7 and goes on to 16.

25. In some other renditions *kara* is used for *kala.*

26. On the *Erú Añá* tape I listened to, this song is third in a sequence

beginning with 7, going on to 16, and concluding with the present song. *Penpwe* is the way the Yoruba word *penpe* is pronounced. Shilgi hispanicizes the word *gue(n)gue.* In any event, it's *shokoto penpe* that Oya is famous for wearing. The words in combination mean "short (calf-length) pants" of the sort that Shango wears.

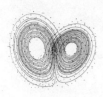

represents an introverted rational function. "She opens you up and gets you to making cognitive maps," as one of my co-subjects put it.

39. Gisèle Binon Cossard, "Contribution à l'étude des candomblés au Brésil: Le candomblé Angola," doctoral thesis, Faculté des Lettres et Sciences Humaines, Paris, 1970, p. 212.

40. A distinction should be made between *igbódù*, which refers to the sacred grove of Ifa (divination) and which became the "inner sanctum" of Santería practice and *ìgbàlè*, sacred grove of Egungun.

41. Claude Lepine, *Contribuicão au estudo do sistema de classificação dos tipos psicologicos no candomblé ketu de Salvador*, 2 vols., presented to the Department of Social Sciences, Faculty of Philosophy, Letters and Human Sciences, University of São Paulo, Brazil, 1978. Roneo.

42. Lepine, *Contribuicão*, vol. 1, pp. 222–32, *passim*.

43. "Chaos," by James P. Crutchfield, J. Doyne Farmer, Norman H. Packard, and Robert S. Shaw, *Scientific American* 255, no. 6 (December 1986); James Gleick, *Chaos: Making a New Science* (New York: Viking Penguin, 1987).

44. Pierre Verger (Odi Obara), unpublished manuscript, 1977, p. ix a. *Kabiesi!*

Glossary

NOTE: The terms of art relevant to musical performance in Santería are defined within the text itself. Only those not defined there appear here.

Agan (Yoruba) Ancestral spirit of tremendous power and authority. This spirit does not manifest itself publicly in cloth. It arrives at night, unseen and voiced. Genealogically this power was transmitted by Oya. (See "Genealogy of a Mystery" p. 144.)

àjẹ́ (Yoruba) An occult power that enables its human vehicle (who is likely to be a woman) to perform effective magic. It is a power that may be used for good or evil purposes. The usual English translation of the word is "witchcraft." Its sense is popularly pejorative, esoterically neutral.

àkàrà (Yoruba. Brazilian: *acará*) A spicy bean cake made with palm oil. One of Oya's favorite foods. Also, Oya's sacred fire in edible form. Akara can be presented ritually as cotton bits soaked in palm oil or even kerosene.

akòko (Yoruba) A tree: *Newboldia laevis* (Bigoniaceae). The leaves are put on the head of a newly installed chief. Branches cut from the tree are used as sacred ancestral staves. Oya is known as Alákòko, meaning "Owner of Akoko." The tree has reddish-purple or pink and white flowers and phallic-shaped pods, narrow, twelve inches long, and spotted.

Akpón Lead-singer (Lucumi). Literally "tte-who-praises."

Alagba (Yoruba: "Owner of the Elder") Senior titleholder in Egungun ancestral cult.

Alapinni (Yoruba) In principle, the most senior titleholder in Egungun. Once there was only one such person, who sat on the king's council in Oyo City. This is no longer the case. In Oyo today the Alapinni, a barrister, does sit on the king's council. His family owns the masquerade called Jenju. There is an Alapinni in Lagos, in Brazil, and perhaps elsewhere as well.

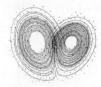

Amuisan (Yoruba) "Wielder of the whip," also an Egungun (ancestral) spirit, one of the original triplets (Oya's "grandchildren"). The whip itself, *ìṣọ́ń*, is made of a flexible stick of the àtòrì shrub: *Glyphaea lateriflora* (Tiliaceae). During Egungun ceremonies and demonstrations, these incised sticks keep the spectators away from the sacred masquerades.

Àràbà (Yoruba) Literally, a great white silk cotton tree: *Ceiba pentandra* (Bombaceae). As a title, the Araba is the most senior priest of Ifa in any community. The Araba of Lagos mentioned in the text is the late lamented Chief Fagbemi Ajanaku, a man of unstinting personal generosity, a teacher who believed in spreading and clarifying knowledge of Yoruba religion, who envisaged an international Orisha community.

àṣẹ (Yoruba) Literally, "So be it." This is a sacred power, an active essence, which flows in varying intensities through plants (as a healing or, it may be, a venomous agency), through animals, people, and the Orisha. Sap and blood carry this numinous energy, as does the uttered word. Those who are committed to the service of the spirits receive *àṣẹ* from them in various ways—especially through the implanting of sacred substances at the time of initiation. A person with strong *àṣẹ* has authority inspiring word and deed. Consecrated icons of divinities also contain heightened *àṣẹ*.

ato A female title in Egungun.

axêxê (Brazilian) Funeral rite of separation and atonement, periodically repeated. The Yoruba word for this event is *ètùtù*.

Babalúaiyé Orisha of epidemics, particularly those affecting the skin, constellated as smallpox at a certain point in human history, now as AIDS. Certain forms of madness also fall within Babaluaiye's province. This divinity is a paradigm of suffering. Known by many names, which are euphemisms (so great is the terror he inspires), Babaluaiye (Honored-father-of-the-world) is naturally associated with powerful medicines and dark sorcery.

barracão (Brazilian) The room in which ceremonies are held.

bàtá A type of drum: conical, held around the drummer's neck by a strap in a horizontal position, with two heads, one of which in Nigeria is whipped with a thong rather than slapped directly with the hand. This drum comes in three sizes. In Nigeria it is used to play rhythms for Shango, Oya, and Egungun. In the Santería tradition of the Yoruba religion, Bata is played for all the Orisha. In Brazilian Candomblé a set of standing single-headed drums is played for ceremonies.

Bayanni A legendary queen, mythologically the sister of Shango, apotheosized as Shango's crown.

Bembé (also *Tambor*, more technically: *Güemilere*) a ceremony with music and dance as offering to the Orisha.

calabash English word for a large, circular, hollowed-out gourd (which grows on a tree) used as a ritual container. Covered with a beaded net, the calabash becomes a musical instrument, notably played by women. In Yoruba this calabash drum is called *ṣẹ̀kẹ̀rẹ̀*. Cut into two large halves, which are then perfectly fitted together, the calabash symbolizes cosmos—earth and covering sky. It is also an icon of secrecy, of the primal egg.

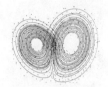

Candomblé (Brazilian) Yoruba-derived cultus. Originally the word referred to a dance of African provenance.

contragun (Afro-Brazilian) A braided fiber amulet worn to protect the wearer from invasion by spirits of the dead.

Dada Divinity (Orisha) of babies. As a legendary figure, he is supposed to have abdicated in favor of his brother Shango. As a cowrie-shell casque Dada is traditionally owned by those who come into the world with curly hair, prognosticating future riches, or by those born with a caul, portending devotion to the ancestral spirits.

deka (Afro-Brazilian) The possible origin of the word is Yoruba: Adé-ká, meaning "The crown as capacity." The deka is a basket-of-authorization given to a senior priestess or priest of Candomblé upon the completion of the "seventh-year obligation." Its contents include substances and utensils with which to initiate others.

donsonton (Bambara) Hunters' fraternity.

Egbomi (Brazilian) Title given to someone who has completed the "seventh-year obligation" and received the deka. In Yoruba the word *Ègbònmi* refers to "My senior kinswoman (or kinsman)."

Egungun Ancestral spirits who appear in masquerade form. More generally, spirits of the dead. Oya's progeny.

Elegba Eshu-Elegba is the Orisha of thresholds and crossroads, the intermediary, the messenger, the trickster, associated with the obligatory sacrifice and also with regressive behavior. Indispensable and primary presence to be invoked and placated before ritual occurrence or crucial personal decision making.

Faro (Bambara) The cosmic principle of water, usually imagined as an androgynous divinity. The upper Niger River, which flows north by northeast, maps Faro's body. Faro is associated with the word: speech and song as cooling containers of impulse.

firma (Brazilian) A large bead on a sacred necklace in which is concentrated the power deriving from the Orisha to which the necklace is consecrated. The firmas "close" the necklaces, making them magic circles through which sacred energy (àṣẹ) continuously flows.

Fon or Fongbe The language spoken by neighbors and cultural affines of the Yoruba who live in what is now the Republic of Benin, formerly Dahomey.

fundamento Broadly: truly liturgical songs; also used to refer to batá drums, which are sacralized by the implantation of Aña (from the Yoruban *Ayan*), the sacred essence of the god of the drum.

Harrakoi Dikko The mother-of-the-waters of the middle Niger, along whose banks Sonrai is spoken. In the Sonrai-Zarma pantheon, Harrakoi Dikko is the mother of the Toru, all of whom are associated with the waters of the river as well as with other atmospheric conditions and elemental substances. Harrakoi's is milk. A white cow is sacrificed to her.

Ifá The regulating system of the Yoruba cosmos available to human beings through divination. Orunmila is the Orisha of divination and monitor of Ifa, whose priests are known as Babaláwo, "Fathers of the Secret." The 256 octograms (odù) of Ifa are the repositories of a wealth of oral traditions regarding the Orisha.

Ifa also provides a taxonomy of herbal remedies, each of which is affiliated with certain Orisha. Among the Ifa combinations through which Oya speaks are Òdí Ọ̀bàrà, Ọ̀bàrà Ọ̀sá, Ọ̀sá Ògúndá, Ìrẹtẹ̀ Ògúndá, Òtúrá Ogbè, and Òfún Ọ̀sá.

igbàlẹ̀ The sacred forest or, in an urban setting, the sacred shed where Egungun materialize, where the carrier of the ancestral mask is magically doctored and robed.

ìrọn vision, theatrical performance, generation.

Iyá Agán The highest-ranking female title in Egungun.

Iyalode Head of the market women—an elective chieftaincy.

mariwo A palm fringe that screens the sacred from profane view and at the same time calls attention to its presence. This minimal masquerade covering is one of Oya's sacred symbols, one of her praise-names. As a group of people, Mariwo are initiated members of Egungun, the cult of the ancestors, who protect the secret.

Nana Buruku An ancient feminine Orisha, mother of Babaluaiye. Her provenance is the Dassa-Zoume region of the Republic of Benin, where the Mahi people live, but it is possible that in ancient times she migrated there from much farther west.

Nupe The language spoken by a cultural group (called Takpa by the Yoruba) whose southern boundary is the Niger River. Oya is considered by the Yoruba to be of Nupe origin. The closest thing to Oya in Nupe culture is the Ndako Gboya masquerade and ritual cleansing.

Nyalé (Bambara) Goddess of fire-and-wind in the upper Niger, Malinké culture area. A rebellious feminine principle, Nyalé was demoted by the powers of reason and balance to the status of a "little old woman with white hair."

Ọbà The name of a river, one of the wives of Shango. In Cuban myth and folklore she is syncretized with Bayanni, Shango's sister.

ọba The generic Yoruba word for king or chief, depending upon the extent and importance of the area ruled over. An oba who is "áladé" has the right to wear a beaded crown with a fringed veil. Such kings, of historically important Yoruba towns, derive their authority from the youngest son of the Creator. These crowned kings have special titles. Mentioned in the text are the Timi of Ede and the Alafin of Oyo.

Ọbàtálá The "king of the white cloth," is the creating Orisha (as opposed to the ultimate principle of creation). Patience, good character, and coolness are virtues associated with this divinity. Substances associated with Obatala include kaolin (white chalk), cocoa butter, cotton, and the moisture of snails.

Odù Generically, a container. The word is applied to the octograms of Ifa, each of which is an odu. But Odu is also *the* sacred container of Ifa itself. As such, she is an Orisha in her own right, primal mother, who led a rather hectic career until "encouraged" by the patriarchal Orunmila to seat herself. It is in this state of numinous retirement that she contains the four primal cosmic substances from which the divinitory odu are derived. Alternatively, she is imagined in myth as Obatala's original consort, whose container contains *àjẹ́* in the form of a bird.

Ogbin An Egungun (or "Nupe") lineage of traditional entertainers.

Ògún Orisha of iron, of war, and of hunting. Ogun is the one who goes before—trailblazer, toolmaker. Oya's consort.

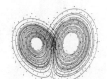

Ọlokun "Owner of the Ocean," the Orisha of the sea, mythologically Yemoja's father.

Onirá Oya's highest-ranking cult officer, who is the guardian of Egungun-Oya in Oyo city. The present Onira is Joseph Ologbin.

òrìṣà The generic Yoruba word for a god (in the text Anglicized as orisha). The Orisha are legion. Some are regional, others are worshiped throughout the traditional Yoruba world. Across the Atlantic they have been linked to certain saints, whose images disguised their African reality from slave owners and governing authorities. The Orisha rule the heads of their worshipers. A head in this sense is not the one that you see, but rather a personal essence or self, prenatally chosen. Choice of head implies choice of and by Orisha, those grander Selves that in turn contain vast cosmic energies.

Ọrúnmìlà Ifa divination when personified as an orisha.

Ọ̀sanyìn Orisha (or some say "spirit") of herbalism. He does not possess his votaries. He is a sprite with only one arm and one leg who may be represented as a puppet operated by a ventriloquist. (Osain in Cuba.)

Oṣùn A river goddess mythologically a wife of Shango. Orisha Oshun is beautiful. Her waters heal barrenness. Diviners usually marry daughters of Oshun, proverbial experts in cowrie-shell divination and privy to magical practices alleviating female complaints.

Oxóssi Brazilian spelling of the Yoruba Ọ̀ṣọ́ọ̀sì, Anglicized in the text as Oshossi. Orisha of hunting, a master of archery. Mythologically, a brother of Ogun, whose temperament is very different. Oxossi is tremendously popular is Brazil, where he forms a bridge into the Indian world of forest, feathers, and bows and arrows.

pade (Brazilian; Yoruba: pàdé, "an encounter") There are several types of pade. The one referred to in the text is a preliminary rite for Eshu-Elegba, in the course of which he is offered corn meal, cachaça, and palm oil. The officiant dances these offerings to the door and places them outside the barracão so that Eshu will not disturb the ceremony to follow.

runjebe (Fon) In Brazil this necklace is a manifestation of Oya. In ancient Dahomey it was a royal necklace. Claude Lepine says it is worn by devotees of Bade, the Fon thunder god.

Sanene-Kontron Bambara hunting divinity, a mysterious couple, variously considered to be mother-son or inseparable though chaste lovers or lovers whose relationship remains ideal because of its separation from ordinary social life.

Ṣàngó Orisha of thunder and of kingship. He is said to have been fourth king of Oyo, the only Yoruba city effectively to have become an empire. This Shango attempted suicide but instead became an Orisha. His wives are river goddesses: Oya, Oshun, and Oba. His salute is "Kàbìèsi!" The Shango personality evinces great charm, ebullience, and at times a ferocious temper.

Santería (Spanish) This version of the Yoruba religion originated in Cuba. The name suggests "worship of saints." Santeros, as those who practice the religion are called, speak of initiation as "making saint." Literally, santeros are carvers of wooden images of the saints. Among Santeros, Yoruba in the form of "Lucumi" survives as a liturgical language.

Sopera (Spanish) Tureen with a lid. A sacred container of the orisha's ashe (àṣẹ) in Santería context.

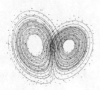

terreiro (Brazilian) The geographical site or sacred compound where the Orisha are housed and worshiped in Brazil.

tratão or *tratado* (Spanish) In common parlance this word often refers to song-sequences for the orisha. There are some who think the word should be limited to songs expressing "treaties" between Orisha and that *sequencias* should be used to denote song-chains.

Yansan A name of Oya. *Mẹsan* means "nine" in Yoruba. Nine is her sacred number. *Yansan* means "mother of nine." She is enshrined as Abesan or Avesan the town of Porto Novo, Republic of Benin (formerly Dahomey). These names refer to "nine heads" at the mouth of the Niger River.

Yemoja "Mother of fishes," known as mother of all the Orisha. She is a river goddess of overflowing breasts who is directly related to the sea. In Africa her father is considered to be Olokun, god of the sea, but in Brazil she is herself a sea goddess, patron of fishermen. Her name is spelled *Iemanja* in Brazilian Portuguese and *Yemaya* in Spanish.

Bibliography

Amira, John, and Steven Cornelius, *The Music of Santéria, Traditional Rhythms at—Bata drums*, Crownpoint Indiana: White Cliffs, 1992.

Barnes, Sandra T., ed. *Africa's Ogun, Old World and New*. Bloomington: Indiana Univ. Press, 1989.

Bastide, Roger. *The African Religions of Brazil: Toward a Sociology of the Interpenetration of Civilizations*. Translated by Helen Sebba. Baltimore: Johns Hopkins Univ. Press, 1978.

Brown, David Hilary. *Garden in the Machine: Afro-Cuban Sacred Art and Performance*. A dissertation presented to the Faculty of the graduate school of Yale University, 2 vols, 1989.

Brown, Karen McCarthy. *Mama Lola: A Vodou Priestess in Brooklyn*. Berkeley and Los Angeles: Univ. of California Press, 1991.

Cabrera, Lydia. *Yemaya y Ochun: Kariocha, Iyalorichas y Olorichas*. Miami and Madrid: Collección del Chicheruku en el exilio, 1974.

D'Aguili, Eugene G., et al. *The Spectrum of Ritual, A Biogenetic Structural Analysis*. New York: Columbia Univ. Press, 1979.

Fadipe, N. A. *The Sociology of the Yoruba*. Ibadan: Ibadan Univ. Press, 1970.

Griffin, Susan. *Woman and Nature: The Roaring Inside Her*. New York: Harper & Row, 1978.

Hillman, James. *Re-Visioning Psychology*. New York: Harper Colophon, 1975.

Idowu, E. Bọlaji. *Olódùmarè: God in Yoruba Belief*. New York: Frederick A. Praeger, 1963.

Mason, John. *Four New World Yoruba Rituals*. Brooklyn: Yoruba Theological Archministry, 1985.

Mookerjee, Ajit. *Kali, the Feminine Force*. New York: Destiny Books, Thames & Hudson, 1988.

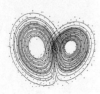

Sanday, Peggy Reeves. *Female Power and Male Dominance: On the Origins of Sexual Inequality.* Cambridge: Cambridge Univ. Press, 1981.

Sandoval, Mercedes Cros. *La Religión Afrocubana.* Madrid: Playor, 1975.

Shiligi, Jerry et al. *Orisha-Rumba Sing Anthology,* P.O. Box 2083 Baly City, CA 94015

Thompson, Robert Farris. *Flash of the Spirit: African and Afro-American Art and Philosophy.* New York: Random House, 1983.

Valdes-Garriz, Yrmino. *Ceremonias funebres de la Santería Afrocubana.* San Juan, P.R.: Sociedad de Autores Libres, 1991.

Verger, Pierre. *Notes sur la culture des orisa et vodun.* Dakar: IFAN, 1957. *Orixás; Deuses Iorubás na África e no Novo Mundo;* Salvador, Brazil: Corupio, 1981.